□

To
Charles R. Wright
and
Joel M. Cantor

☐ Foreword

This book profiles some of the most powerful but least known
men in television—men responsible for choosing the film
entertainment appearing on living-room screens in the United
States and in many countries around the world. The actors who
star on television, their directors, the writers and even some
of the costumers are more often known to the television audience
than those who choose, hire and guide all of them in piecing
together the program or the series to which they contribute
their talents. The television film producer is unlike the producer
in the theater and motion pictures. From a creative and executive
standpoint he is the most powerful force in television.

It is not accidental that he is little known. He prefers to
turn the publicity spotlight away from himself so that it may
shine fully on the program or the series he produces. He welcomes
a secondary role and would embrace even anonymity if that
would help his program achieve a higher Nielsen rating.

His satisfaction comes from a position of power. Because
only three networks offer a market for his product, he must learn
to manipulate network timidity and insecurity so that he can
produce programs the way he wants them produced. As a result,
once a series is bought by a network and scheduled for broadcast,
the television film producer becomes the principal gatekeeper
for most of the entertainment provided for as many as six
hours a day to television sets.

This is an awesome responsibility, and it is fortunate that
an attempt has now been made to profile and evaluate the men

□

shouldering that responsibility. Their potential influence on all of us demands answers to important questions: Who are they? What is their background? What is their goal? What motivates them? What influences them? How do they function? What are their problems and how do they solve them? How do they look upon the audience to whom they direct their creative efforts?

Perhaps the difficulty of seeking answers to these questions has tended to discourage such studies in the past. Also, the television film producer by the nature of his occupation makes such a project difficult because he is wary of both reporters and researchers. I know this from experience gained during a period of nearly ten years as a story editor, associate producer, and producer on several television series.

As a television producer turned professor, I hope this book will be read by those who want a better understanding of the men who shape the intellectual and emotional impact of television, exerting a powerful influence on our national life and destiny.

Frank La Tourette

Department of Theater Arts
University of California at Los Angeles

March 1, 1971.

☐ Preface

This book is about working (on-the-line) television producers. The filmed shows that they produce, the weekly dramatic series, are shown at prime viewing time (7:30 P.M. to 11:00 P.M.) and reach the largest audiences of any of the regularly scheduled shows on the air both in the United States and abroad. *The Hollywood TV Producer* is primarily concerned with how these producers select the content of their shows, how they perceive this selection as controlled and constrained by the various features of the television industry and film production, and how their personal values and reference groups relate to the selection of content. The study is based mainly on tape-recorded interviews with fifty-nine television producers, examination of a variety of public and private documents (scripts, hearings, and reports), and field observations in the studios.

I have included in this book some information that was reported to the National Institute of Mental Health, Television and Social Behavior Program. The report for NIMH was an attempt to find out how twenty-four producers of commercial television series (filmed for young audiences, two to eleven years of age) select content for their shows. These shows are designed for Saturday-morning viewing, which is considered prime time for children.

Through a conversation with Robert Faulkner, I became interested in a study of television producers. He and I were students together at the University of California in Los Angeles

□

where he was also interested in studying the movie industry. While at the university, I was greatly helped by Professors John Horton, Raymond Murphy, Richard Morris, Leo Kuper, Peter Orleans, Jack Lyle, Frank La Tourette, John Brewer, and others.

My greatest debt is due unquestionably to Charles R. Wright, who has been my friend and helpful adviser throughout the time that I have been working on what is now this book. It is with great pleasure that I dedicate it to him, along with my husband, to express my gratitude and appreciation.

I also received assistance and encouragement from Herbert J. Gans, Joan Moore, and Jacques Choron. I benefited from the advice of Jack Lyle and Douglas Fuchs while studying the children's producers. I also wish to thank both the National Institute of General Medical Science and the National Institute of Mental Health, for support while I collected the data that are included in the book.

In today's society, it is impossible for a woman with a family to write a book without the understanding of her husband and children. Murray, Jane, and Jim (my children) always encouraged me, showing interest in my work. They and Joel, my husband, assumed the roles of wife and mother so that I might have time for the studio and typewriter. Joel, in addition to his household help, provided editorial assistance, intellectual stimulation, and good technical advice. My dedication, only in part, expresses my love and gratitude for his continuous encouragement.

Unfortunately, the cooperation of many in the television industry cannot be openly acknowledged. I wish that those who permitted interviews, those who invited me to showings and dubbing sessions, and those who allowed me to visit sets to watch actual production could be publicly thanked. It was my good fortune to have known Irving Elman and William Finnegan of the television industry several years before I commenced work on this book. Irv Elman read the manuscript for technical and

☐

factual errors and he was my sophisticated guide through what might have been an impossible thicket of executive and creative aspects of production. Bill Finnegan was an informative instructor on the craft aspects of production. The eighty television producers who willingly tolerated my intrusion made this book a reality.

Muriel G. Cantor

Bethesda, Maryland
June 1971

☐ Contents

Introduction to the Transaction Edition: The Hollywood TV Producer Twenty Years Later

Not many researchers are given the opportunity to evaluate and extend their dissertations after twenty years. Historically, events of twenty years ago perhaps would be considered rather recent, but in the short history of television, those same events would now be considered ancient. Although television was invented in the 1920s, it did not become a mass medium until the early 1950s when, after World War II, the networks began to invest heavily in expanding commercial television broadcasting. Advances in technology, such as coaxial cable and microwave relay stations, also enabled the networks for the first time to become "national" because the East was linked to the West coast for simultaneous viewing. Advertisers could then be offered a truly national viewing audience.

The occupational category, "Hollywood television producer," had been in existence for less than twenty years when I began studies for this book in the late 1960s[1] and creative and production personnel were still shifting from film-making to television production. Hollywood as a center for television production and worldwide distribution was just beginning. However, the book should be read for more than just "historical" interest. The structure and patterns of production established in that early period still determine the forms that modern television entertainment take. Knowing how the process got started, one can better understand why and how television evolved as it did and remains the way it is. More important, it helps clarify the forces within and outside the production and broadcasting industries that together shape the medium as both commerce and popular culture.

When *The Hollywood TV Producer: His Work and His Audience* was first published, it was ostensibly an occupational study about producers. However, my underlying interest was to determine the role producers played in the tight-knit, small community of decision makers involved in selecting the television dramatic programs to be produced and in the process by which they were created and later distributed to viewers in the United States. Thus, my purpose then and still is two fold: to examine the autonomy producers have to determine the content of the television entertainment programs they make and to learn how they adapt to the economic and political contexts of their work to succeed; and secondly, to describe what I have called elsewhere the "negotiated struggle," the process that producers and writers go through to get "their" content on the air.[2]

This process is fundamental to the production of all mass media, although for media such as magazines, newspapers and local radio, it is more often covert and hidden. However, the struggle in primetime (7 p.m. to 11 p.m.) television has been so overt that it is well documented in memoirs, the media and sometimes public hearings, both Congressional and those of the Federal Communications Commission (FCC). It has even been the subject for satire and commentary on dramatic television shows, movies and documentaries.[3]

Over the years since the book was issued I continued to study the freedom workers have in creative industries, and how those freedoms change as the industries themselves change. I have also come to realize that to gain full understanding about how these workers create and distribute their products, it is necessary to study the workers within the industrial contexts in which they work.

There is no question that the American television industry has changed structurally and occupationally since the study was first done. However, in terms of fundamentals, the industry remains similar in three important aspects: most of the entertainment television produced in Hollywood is still made by comparatively few major movie studios and independent production companies; although they no longer monopolize distribution, the three networks, ABC, CBS and NBC, are still the major buyers of first-run shows for distribution through their network-owned or affiliated television stations; and the production process itself and especially the role of the producer have changed very little. One can read chapters three, four, five and most of six with assurance that most of what was written twenty years ago still holds as a good description of the work of on-line producers. Equally accurate are the accounts of how they are socialized, how they relate to writers, directors and actors, and how the overall process of control in the industry works.

This introduction is divided into two parts. The first elaborates changes in the industry, especially the changes in network television that have occurred since 1971. The second part considers in depth the question of whether entertainment television simply and merely reflects the values of its producers or whether outside economic, political and cultural forces are as or more influential. When this book was written, for the most part, the three television networks exercised absolute control over the production process. As the only market for sales, they could, in effect, set prices and standards as a cartel. In the mid 1980s, they still are powerful as major purchasers but they have lost absolute power and the control they had to determine the formats and content of television entertainment to be made for U.S. audiences. That power diminished in the face of competition that started from other sales outlets available to production companies such as cable systems, video distributors, foreign markets and independent stations.

However, the production companies for which the producers work know that the networks still provide the bulk of work and that cooperating with them can lead to assured program sales. Thus, the networks have retained their power to intimidate the production companies and influence what most American audiences will eventually see.

The beginning of this introduction will focus on the changes that have occurred in the television entertainment industry and how these changes have affected the work producers do. I conclude with a discussion about how the organization and politics of artistic work affect the creative process (the work producers do). As the discussion proceeds, it will become clear which parts of the book remain essentially historical and which describe the present as well as the past.

Who Produces Television

There has been a far-reaching occupational change in Hollywood which must be noted immediately—the increasing role and influence of women. In fact, the title of the book is no longer accurate, and is, if anything, inappropriate. At the time I was gathering material for the book during the 1967 to 1968 production season, not a single female was in charge of production, and there were very few women writers or head writers, even on the children's programs then in production. However, in the past twenty years, a few women have succeeded in gaining recognition as on-line producers and head writers although they have not yet achieved equity with men.

Consequently, a mini-revolution has occurred for women in

television production since the Fall of 1967. I did not seek out women to interview at the time because it was apparent that none were working as on-line producers. However, I recently verified that assumption by re-checking the edition of *Daily Variety* (Western Edition) I had used to gather the original sample. Although a few women were named as casting directors, one woman, Bonita Granville-Wrather, was listed as an associate producer for the *Lassie Show*. Granville-Wrather, a former child movie star, was married to Jack Wrather of the Wrather Corporation, the production company for *Lassie*. Five years later in 1972, some producers remained on the list, some had dropped off and new ones were added but there was still just one female, Granville-Wrather, who had been promoted (or had promoted herself) to full status as a producer. However, by the mid 1980s, women began to show up in the lists with some frequency. Thirty-seven women were listed as executive producers, supervising producers, or producers for the 1986 to 1987 season and some had even become "stars," as well-known for writing and producing as their male counterparts. In some cases, like Esther Shapiro of *Dynasty*, Terry Louise Fisher of *L. A. Law*, and Georgia Jeffries of *Cagney and Lacey*, they were even more successful than many of the men because some shows they produced were among the top twenty in the weekly Nielsen ratings.[4]

Although women are still more likely to find work as producers and writers on domestic and situation comedies with female stars, as producers they are beginning to work in other genres. For example, *Cagney and Lacy*, although it won acclaim for its feminist orientation, is a detective series in the general distribution category known as "action-adventure." Created by two women, Barbara Avedon and Barbara Corday (formerly vice-president of ABC in charge of comedy development), it lists two women among its four producers: Shelley List and Georgia Jeffries. The co-producer of a hit show of the 1986–1987 season, a dramatic series, *L. A. Law*, is also a woman (Terry Louise Fisher).

In chapter four, I developed a typology of producers, showing how producers can be grouped by their backgrounds, education and training, as well as by their aspirations and career motives. Although the typology still has merit, it describes just part of the new reality. Most of the old-line producers I interviewed or could have interviewed at the time have either retired on their savings and investments, or are dead. Several, however, survived the changes in the industry and still work as producers or elsewhere in the industry, enjoying television's fast pace and its financial rewards. The women and younger men who took their place have much in common as members of the "baby boom" or "yuppy" generation. From 1967 through 1968, most were undergraduates or still in graduate school and many, like their predecessors, had started out in journalism or as freelance fiction writers. What distinguishes them is that the generation of producers twenty years earlier had grown up on film as their principal entertainment medium. This new, younger generation has had their concept of entertainment shaped by reruns of *I Love Lucy* and membership in the Mickey Mouse Club. Consequently, they were drawn to television-making, not film-making, and in their view, no medium could surpass television as a career. Whereas, some in the original sample were making a transition (some reluctantly) from films to television, the sole ambition of this newer generation was to start with the industry, remain with it and grow with it.

Therefore, in terms of my original typology, while many current producers still fit into the "Writer-Producer" category, a few fit into none of the categories as described. These few are not "embarrassed" by working in television and have no conflicts about just being television producers. They do not feel guilt that they have not written, directed or produced "the great American film" or play. They do not feel committed to a craft or profession in the traditional sense—they just want to work as producers of television, be it commercials, entertainment, action-adventure or dramatic series. They will take assignments and work as it comes along as long as they can work. Consequently, they avoid conflicts with the production companies hiring them and certainly would have no problem accepting the constraints of the networks. To include them in the typology, another category has to be developed which I label the Drones: the workers who carry out orders. They are accustomed to compliance. Before they became producers, as writers, they worked on assignment and rarely were called on to create original ideas or concepts for series or programs. They also differ from the Film Makers who seek work in television through apprenticeship leading to film making.

The Writer-Producer as originally defined, still exists and makes up a large proportion of television producers. In fact, most of the women and several of men new to the field, and some older ones still producing, can still best be described in that category. As writers, they often create the series they then produce and may write-produce specific episodes within the series. Having learned how the system works and how to work the system, they use their insights to adapt to changing markets and network requirements. The networks also are more likely to respect their talent and experience when a new concept in entertainment is suggested. For example, network officials took a chance on *All in the Family* which portrayed a bigot because among other reasons it was proposed by a successful producer, Norman Lear, who got his idea from British television.

Thus, because of their shared interest patterns and the fundamental structure of the industry, the women and men producing series, miniseries and made-for-television movies in the mid 1980s, in most respects resemble those who performed the same jobs in the late 1960s. When the Lichters and Rothman studied 104 television elites in 1983, they included producers and writers as well as network executives, and found they were white (99%), male (98%), from metropolitan areas (83%) and mostly raised as Jewish (59%).[5] When these findings are compared to the social backgrounds of those interviewed for the book, the differences are slight. However, the fact that they found so few women was specifically due to faulty sampling. To find "elites", the researchers used sources who recommended that just those associated with more than one show be included. In 1982, women were still to break the barriers of production and those with just one show, no matter how successful the ratings, were excluded from their sample.

Whether in the field for twenty years or more or whether newcomers, all those now producing work in an environment which has changed in several aspects from what it was when this book was written. As will be detailed below, those changes include changes in both the audiences and the networks, which in turn have altered the ways producers organize their work and the ways in which their creativity is controlled and enhanced.

What Happened to the Mass Audience

If this study were being published in 1987, it would have to be retitled: *Hollywood TV Producers: Their Work and Their Audiences*. Note that not only would it be necessary to make the word "producer" plural and sex-neutral but one would have to change "audience" to "audiences". Almost everyone who wrote about television in the 1960s and 1970s considered the audience a unified or homogeneous "mass." For example, Herbert Gans in 1966 and again in 1974 claimed that the audience for TV was the most "massified" of all media, but for other public media, the audiences are segmented.[6] Gans and others recognize that by 1974 television was changing and catering to subgroups in the total audience. More recent analysis shows that different taste segments watch different kinds of programs. This fact is obvious—women as a group are more likely to watch situation comedies, men action-adventure shows and sport programs, and blacks shows with black stars or characters. Just a few shows on network television (*Cosby, Family Ties,* and when it was on network, *M*A*S*H*) generate the appeal to attract aggregates of audience segments that could be called a "mass," audiences made up of all genders, social classes and age groups.

Most network television did (and still do) target middle and especially the lower-middle economic strata in society (presumably those likely to use the everyday products such as the drugs, beauty aids, food and household items advertised), and there is no doubt that this large group is made up of most of the heavy viewers of primetime shows. However, within this larger group, there are different taste segments which prefer different kinds of shows. This change in viewing patterns is obvious when one compares ratings over the years. While some programs still command the attention of 50 percent of the audience (the *Cosby Show* and *Family Ties* are examples), the remaining (and shrinking) audience is divided among the two other networks, independent stations, cable, and public television. Moreover, those who tape earlier programs for later viewing or who use their sets for video games and rented video-movies cannot be measured by the usual means.

Along with the new technologies that have provided more choices for audiences, there are demographic and economic changes that contribute to the new diversity. Although it is easier to explain changes in the daytime soap operas through an analysis of how the daytime audience has changed with more women entering the labor force, the shows in primetime (for example, *Miami Vice* and *Moonlighting*) tend to reflect more directly the tastes and lifestyles of the various subgroups among the baby-boom generation. Consequently, the newcomers to production have less trouble finding an audience because for the first time the network executives and a large segment of the audience are of the same age group. Because the producers and the audience grew up watching the same programs on television, they as a generation share certain expectations and preferences for television entertainment that pre-shape content. However, television entertainment is not produced just for those segments. Advertisers and broadcasters also recognize that the yuppie generation will soon be middle-aged and that today's elderly are more affluent than the elderly of the past. Consequently, in addition to network programming (*Golden Girls* for example), these segments can also have their tastes satisfied by the advances in video technology which cater to their taste preferences.

Interest Groups as Audience

The civil rights movement and the racial violence of the 1960s, and the reawakening of the women's movement during the same period, changed the relationship of the audience to the creative process. A landmark court decision in 1969 gave public interest groups the right to participate directly in FCC policymaking.[7] For the first time since commercial broadcasting began in the 1920s, societal supports (both legal and informal) developed in the 1960s which encouraged less powerful and disadvantaged groups in society, particularly minorities and women, to lobby actively on their own behalf to change media content. Although some interest groups were involved with television before the 1964 decision, interest or advocacy groups did not become a problem for producers and networks until the late 1960s and early 1970s. When the interviews for this study were undertaken, there were just a few interest groups of any consequence, which included the United States government, itself concerned with the influence of television violence on social behavior. At the time the book was published, a number of groups using similar techniques to try to influence producers and networks had sprung up. The goals and motivations of these groups are diverse and far-ranging, reflecting the social, economic, cultural and religious pluralism of American society. Among the groups prominent as television activists are antidefamation leagues, trade associations, unions, feminist organizations, gay rights groups, those interested in environmental and other social issues. Especially active were the National Congress of Parents and Teachers, the Moral Majority, and Fortune 500 corporations such as Mobil Oil. In addition, many other groups at times try to influence the FCC, the networks and production companies on adhoc issues, such as depiction of smoking and drinking on camera, and nuclear arms. Still others are less organized but equally vocal as pressure groups.

The extent to which any of these groups can directly influence content is still debated. However, there is no question that when there is more activity from various elements in the audience, the environment in which producers work does change. Although it is conceptually difficult to separate the audience into these interest groups, their impact is obvious when the schedule is examined. Not only are more women and minorities seen in a greater variety of roles than in 1967, but the topics being discussed in primetime differ as well. Although there is a debate, elaborated in the second half of this introduction, about whether the content is too liberal or too conservative, there is no question that it is different from what it was. Topics such as nuclear war, homosexuality, black history, and the like once considered taboo, are now discussed on television, perhaps because of pressure from their interest groups. However, the direct or indirect influence of such interests groups in forcing the change has still to be acknowledged or documented. Whether potent or not, some producers have learned to use interest groups to keep shows on the air. The most famous example is *Cagney and Lacey,* first cancelled and then revived when the National Organization for Women (NOW) initiated a letter-writing campaign to save it.

Network Control and Changing Regulation

Network television was at a pinnacle in 1968. More than 80 percent of the audience were turning on at least one of the three networks each night and they shared a virtual monopoly of the primetime schedule in 1971. There were no videotape recorders nor pay TV cable channels to allow audiences to play theater movies through television sets. Cable television systems were still used to bring just network programs to isolated communities, and public television as an alternative to commercial television was just five years old. Few independent stations were to be found, even in the largest market areas. The early 1970s also represented a turning point for the industry because the FCC was changing its regulations to accommodate the new technologies which were then getting started. There is no question that the power of the networks to control the industry has waned since this book was written. The remarks of CBS president, Lawrence A. Tisch, in addressing the National Association of Broadcasters convention sound like an epitaph:

A once unified and coherent industry seems to be splitting down further and further into separate components as though some unstoppable biological process were at work. In a real sense, the networks helped create [their] own competition.[8]

One would think that with the weakening of network power, production companies would have declared their independence and increased their power to decide content. In reality, however, little has changed. The networks, although still going through changes as I write, remain the single most important institution in determining what kinds of television entertainment will be made available for audiences in the United States and throughout much of the world.

The reasons for the networks continuing dominance can be found in the politics and especially the economics of the broadcast industry. The on-line producers depend on production companies for work which in turn depend on outside companies for both financing and distributing their products. Although other financial sources can be sought out, the networks still remain the best and easiest source because unlike investment banks for example, they readily understand the risks of the business and compete to fund new productions to avoid future low Nielsen ratings. Programs sold to a network, if renewed and given long runs, also make sales to foreign markets and other secondary markets such as cable systems and independent stations easier. Continuing profits to be earned from reruns are a major concern of production companies because their costs of production typically exceed the investments they can get from the networks.

In brief, the networks are the only buyers able to provide a large, continuing audience for the Hollywood production companies but also have the capital to support new, untried productions. Logically it would seem that the television networks need the production companies to stay on the air and prosper more than the production companies need the networks, but that is not the case. For a production company to survive and prosper, it must have at least one hit show on a network each season. Thus, regardless of the number of other possible sources for funding and outlets for sales, the Hollywood production companies first seek financial support for their projects from the networks because it also increases the possibility they will have national audiences. Consequently the networks, and especially their buyers, remain the primary reference group that producers have in mind when developing new shows.

The television industry and American television was also changed substantially by FCC rulings.[9] The major change in regulation actually occurred while the studies for this book were being conducted. In 1970, the FCC which regulates broadcasting in the United States adopted the Financial Interest and Syndication Rules.[10] Until 1970, the networks had been free to hold financial interests in the programs they aired, allowing them two major profit opportunities: first, through the sale of commercial time during a show's initial network run, and then later when the show was syndicated and sold locally on a station-by-station basis. The networks could also, as their own syndicators, limit their competition by controlling not only which shows would be put into rerun sales but also which independent stations would have the rights.

The FCC held that the economic and creative control of networks over primetime had increased steadily from the mid 1950s through the 1960s. The share of all network evening program hours either produced or directly controlled by the networks rose from 67 to 97 percent between 1957 and 1968. For entertainment shows, the percentages were 64 to 96 percent.

The FCC concluded that a direct relationship could be established between new programs bought for primetime schedules and the networks acquiring the right to syndicate them. According to their report of the five-year period studied, the networks had virtually accepted no entertainment programs for network exhibition unless they were given a financial interest. The producers either had to play by the networks rules or leave the industry. Consequently, the FCC had to conclude that their formidable hold on national television broadcasting had created unfair marketplace conditions for production companies.

The Financial Interest and Syndication Rules essentially separated production from distribution. The networks were left with the right to license shows for a set number of showings, usually two, while the rights to syndicate them for future showings remained with the production companies.

A number of other changes in regulation since this book was written have involved issues such as the conflict between the networks and their affiliates over network access to primetime viewing hours for their programs. However, none are as important to the economics of the industry and production as the Financial Interest and Syndication Rules. This change shifted the relationship of the production companies to the networks from what it was when I first interviewed the producers—from coercion to voluntary compliance. Consequently, the change was not as drastic as many would have expected when the FCC issued its ruling, and to a large extent, network control over production remains essentially the same although their approach may differ. Now, however, the producers profit from syndicated sales, and the greatest profits are earned from shows that have been successful on the networks.

Because the networks still finance the pilot projects and select the programming to fill air time, their ability to influence and dominate the producers remains a reality. The revolving door that has developed between the networks and production companies also facilitates the influence. For example, Grant Tinker, the head of MTM productions during the 1970s, became head of NBC television in the 1980s and then returned to production. Fred Silverman, the man he replaced at NBC, went from that job to a producer's job at MGM/UA. There is also the "golden handshake." When network executives leave (or are fired) they may be promised places on primetime schedules which they can use to establish their own independent production companies.

The networks get their power from the hit shows they manage to buy and put on the air. The biggest hit since M*A*S*H has been the *Cosby Show* on NBC. The time slots following its broadcast on Thursday evening have also become the most valuable on primetime television because of the advertising rates that can be charged. Conversely, over the last few years, the time slots opposite and following *Cosby* on ABC and CBS have been the kiss of death. As long as networks favor and reward producers for high-rated programs, on-line producers will give the networks what they want.

The changes in the industry also shifted power into the hands of the production companies which, in some cases, encouraged autonomy. When they have hit shows on the air for several seasons, the profits from syndication can be used for self-financing. This change has allowed several of the larger production companies the freedom to develop and fund projects that might not receive support from one of the networks. There are also at least two other outlets for original productions that did not exist when this book was written: pay TV cable companies willing to contract for TV specials and made-for-TV movies, and most importantly, the large and highly profitable domestic and foreign markets for first-run syndicated programs and series. Even network owned-and-operated stations and affiliates are buying their programs as alternatives to network-supplied shows less popular with local audiences.

While such structural changes in the economy of the industry have enabled the production companies to increase their autonomy and freedom from network control, they have not resulted in similar freedoms being given the on-line producers working for them. As employees, they still must work in formal organizations, some of which more organized than others.

Another major structural change has occurred which will probably have consequences for their work environment. Some of the larger production companies as well as larger movie studios have been acquired by conglomerates. For example, Norman Lear sold his production company, Embassy, to Coca-Cola which had earlier acquired Columbia Pictures. Gulf–Western has acquired Paramount Studios which produces the hit series *Family Ties*. MGM/UA has also changed hands several times in the last few years. Along with other industries in the United States, the movie and television industries have been subject to takeover and mergers. In one recent conversation, a producer–executive at one of the companies taken over reported feeling more constrained by the "bottom-line" mentality of the top executives who seemed less interested in producing the full range of entertainment he had formerly been allowed, including comedies, dramatic shows and movies-made-for television—the freedom he had had with the colleague-employers for whom he had previously worked. Also, as a precondition for some sales, some producers and others had been guaranteed their jobs for one year, but in an industry in which employment is always precarious and with a high-cost life style, many of those interviewed were scared employees. What became clear to them was that to keep their jobs, they had to please the top executives of the corporations. Their new and principal responsibility was to make programs primarily for network sales. Some of the parent corporations also reorganized their internal structure to increase production efficiency and output, and thereby capture more of the marketplace: for example, as of the end of 1986, Coca-Cola Telecommunications, a syndication company, and Columbia/Embassy Television, a production company, with Columbia Television responsible for the whole range of dramatic productions such as TV movies and dramatic series and serials, and Embassy Television now responsible just for comedies, including those formerly produced at Columbia Pictures.

These changes in the work setting do have an impact on the way producers and writers create stories, but they have had little effect on the process itself. As stated on page 53, all major and minor film-production companies devote some time and effort to the development of new ideas, and what has not changed is that the prevalent route into producing is still through writing. However, it is still not clear how often writers with original or good ideas get heard. As in 1971, most of the story ideas for the pilots and movies adopted result from "committees," which might at times include network representatives. The networks still contract with production companies and producers to provide pilots for series the networks will consider for the new season, and the more successful independent producers can often demand guaranteed places on the primetime evening schedules. Also, in the rapid pace of preparing for new seasons, it is sometimes difficult to determine the origin of new ideas for programs. Usually they come from the production companies themselves, rather than the networks or outside sources, and as more made-for-TV movies, miniseries and docudramas on social issues are being made, most of the production companies have hired readers and clippers of newspapers and periodicals whose job it is to find stories that could be adapted to programs. Thus, still another layer of formal organization or bureaucracy has been developed in the industry.

Also, as emphasized earlier, with turnover in the industry and network executives becoming producers and producers becoming network executives with relative ease, and small independent producers and large studios bought and sold in the marketplace with frequency, it has become impossible to keep track of "who's the boss" and where the ideas come from. In addition, as certain shows or formats change in their popularity or become trendy, network executives quickly let the industry know when they are in the market for the next clone of *Cosby, Hill Street Blues* or *Miami Vice.*

However, once a decision has been made on the idea for a series for primetime viewing and its cast, the on-line producer for most shows has the authority to take over and make all day-to-day decisions, working with the writers, directors and editors, selecting locations, picking actors as supporting cast members and for guest appearances, and so forth. Thus, when it comes to the actual production process, on-line producers are allowed full and independent creative control although the business organization for whom all members of the production crew work remains omnipresent in their thinking. In addition, because a major responsibility of the producer is story development, he or she holds power over the assignment and choice of scripts. The producer hires the writers to do one or more scripts (if it is a series) and often works with the writers to direct their tone and outcome. Freelance writers still aspire to become on-line producers because of the relative power and autonomy vested in that role.

As a salaried employee working for a production company (program supplier), the producer of course, does not have complete control and is caught in the middle between those in the networks, owner–corporations and production companies and those they supervise in the production process. The executive producer might have relative job security if a series is a success, but the on-line producers are often not as fortunate. Numerous examples could be cited where series in production for several years hire and fire, or lose their on-line producers. In some cases, the producers themselves become disenchanted with the series and are given the opportunity to change, leave, or more often they are replaced when conflicts develop with the star actors or others in the organization. However, there is incentive to cooperate because on-line producers do have more opportunity to be promoted up the ranks to executive producer and be put in charge of successful series. On-line producers are frequently recruited from the pool of writers working for a series with access to the gatekeepers in the production companies and studios, and because the executive producers and independent producers are then typically recruited from the ranks of on-line producers, those who end up in charge are basically writers and creators of stories.

My interviews showed that producers have several modes of adapting to the basic problem of network and company control. Most get along by "going along," conforming to network policy and standards. Some deny conflict because they already share the values and orientation of those in charge of story selection. Those who do not conform adapt by seeking ways to contest or deviate from known policy whenever possible. However, even these producers know when to accommodate in order to remain on the job. The system allows some degree of originality because without definitive information about audience taste preferences, and where the primary goal is to attract a large enough audience to keep the advertisers happy, network officials and production executives must allow producers room for experimentation. As Todd Gitlin has pointed out, there are no established rules to guarantee success.

Therefore, when the struggle over creative control breaks out between the networks and the producers, the negotiated outcome cannot be predetermined. Sometimes producers win because they can convince the network officials that an idea is good or that it is less offensive than an alternative idea. Producers can also lose when their initial idea is so transformed in story conferences that by the time it reaches the screen, nobody knows who or what organization is responsible for it.

As network power erodes, the production companies, whether large or small, have more power over the creative process. Producers working for the large studios, such as MCA/Universal, Paramount, and Columbia must satisfy their superiors before they are ever censored by the networks. What has evolved is an interlocking system of production companies owned by large conglomerates selling products (television programs) to television networks also either owned by a conglomerate, such as General Electric (NBC) and Capital Cities (ABC), or in the case of CBS Inc., a large conglomerate in its own right. The production companies and the networks both work for a profit, trying to outguess what the audiences will view and what they will reject.

What Content And Whose Values?

In 1967 when I began to study TV producers, I was most impressed by two articles and one book. The articles by Herbert Gans and John and Matilda Riley asked questions about the conditions under which people create content, that is, who determines the nature of content, for what reasons and in what social contexts.[11] The book, an analysis of the power structure of the movie industry, was *The Dream Factory* by Hortense Powdermaker, an anthropologist who started with the premise that Hollywood's social system influenced the nature of the movies it produced.[12]

In his article, Herbert Gans claimed that the differences in motives, methods and roles between elite and popular artists are fewer than had been previously believed by critics. Also false, according to the article, is the image people have of popular artists: that they suppress their own values to cater to audiences. That contention aroused my curiosity. As noted briefly in the original introduction, when I started this research I was acquainted with several producers, actors and other creators in the television industry. One was an assistant director who later became the on-line producer (in Hawaii) of *Hawaii Five-O*. Another had been an executive on-line producer for a number of series during the 1960s including *Dr. Kildare, The Eleventh Hour* and *Bonanza*, and later with his wife worked one year as head writer for the daytime soap opera *General Hospital*. These and others I met and liked had high regard for the art of serious film making, were intelligent, sensitive, literate and had high personal standards for conducting their lives and personal relationships. Consequently, I found it difficult to understand how they could produce programs with low-brow content while expressing high-brow artistic and literary values and preferences in their private lives.

Throughout the book (especially in chapters 3 and 5) I emphasize that the production of television entertainment can be divided analytically into two functions: those concerned with business details and those concerned with the craft aspects of production; or as put by Powdermaker, "the conflict between business and art" (p. 29). Television dramatic entertainment is both an art or cultural form, and an economic commodity. This dual nature of television creates the underlying paradox that has perplexed a number of analysts who have tried to understand why the messages communicated through the medium take the forms they do.

The question of how much the changes in the regulations and the work settings, and adoption of new technologies affect the work of creative people, and more importantly, the content of American television has not been fully investigated. Rather a debate has been on-going about the content itself, particularly, whether television is capable of harming its audience. The debate has also not been one-sided. Conservatives such as Reverend Jerry Falwell, founder of the Moral Majority, as well as liberals believe that television can harm society. The conservatives worry that the influence of "secular humanists" through television is eroding basic family values, while liberals, for example, argue that the ways women and minorities are depicted on television maintain and even foster gender and racial stereotyping. Some argue that women and minorities who internalize the negative images adopt attitudes and beliefs that limit their own behavior. Liberal groups have also been concerned about how violence is portrayed because research findings suggest a direct relationship between children viewing violence on television and later aggressive behavior.

Conservatives also argue that television presents misleading and false pictures of American capitalism and family values. They object to its sexual content but not usually violence as such, unless big business, of course, is depicted as instigating or condoning violent acts. Ben Stein claims that television creators are overtly biased, showing antipathy toward big business and sympathy toward minorities and the poor.[13] In 1983, Mobil sent a brochure to communication scholars, quoting Stein and others who contend that content analyses of television programs confirm that businessmen are portrayed as foolish, greedy and as criminals; that almost half of business activities are depicted as illegal; and that rarely is business portrayed as socially useful or as an activity that benefits society. In 1986, Mobil underwrote a program called *Hollywood's Favorite Heavy: Businessmen on Prime Time TV* featuring interviews with Stein and some producers on the subject which was aired on some PBS stations. As in his book, Stein attributed such portrayals to the personal proclivities of television writers and producers. However Todd Gitlin, on the basis of several hundred interviews with writers, producers, and executives in the industry, takes issue with Stein's conclusion because he ignores the fact that writers and producers do not work in a vacuum—they work under contract to networks, a big business, which buy the programs as they are.[14] I agree with Gitlin that Stein succeeded in writing a book about television content and production without accepting the fact that networks are less concerned with content than with accumulating large viewing audiences "whose attention they sell to advertisers" (p. 267). Several of the producers in the documentary make the same point. For example, the creator of *Falcon Crest*, Earl Hamner, Jr. (who also created *The Waltons*, a popular family series set in the 1930s) recalled a meeting with network executives about his conception of *Falcon Crest*. Because of his success with *The Waltons*, Hamner had conceived of another family show to be aired at 8:00 p.m. However, the network needed a show to schedule at 10:00 p.m. after *Dallas*. Hamner and Michael Filerman, his co-executive producer, were instructed to change the concept for the new series from that of an urban family moving to a country setting to one more "spirited," such as *Dallas*, in which some of the main characters are deceitful and nasty. Both producers and others who appeared in the documentary were in agreement about network power. All said, in one way or another, that a show could not appear on the networks unless it adhered to the standards set by network programmers. What was obvious to me and even apparent to critics such as Stein was that there are few basic disagreements among network officials and program suppliers.

The debate and its issues are complicated by a lack of clear-cut definitions about values and where the responsibility for teaching them rests in modern society. For example, I and others argue that to keep and communicate to its audience, most of the values on primetime television are necessarily middle-class and mainstream. It assumes that the viewing audience has the power to reject objectionable content both vocally through protests and via ratings feedback to the networks and program producers.

On rereading chapter 6, I noted how up-to-date it still is. However, missing from the chapter is the point made earlier in this introduction—that network officials and producers are exchanging places with such frequency that whatever boundary there was between them is close to disappearing. Consequently, it should come as no surprise that the producers and those working as decision makers in the networks hold similar values about what should appear on television. Although conflicts still occur, those who succeed as producers end up conforming to network directives or are adept at convincing network representatives that the show will neither offend pressure groups nor the larger target audience. In the final determination, however, business interests will always take precedence over political orientation. Furthermore, in the world of television the business decision makers do not object to being portrayed as the "bad guys" if those images help increase the profit margin.

As noted earlier, the data in this book are similar to the findings of Lichters and Rothman in 1983. They found, as did the producers interviewed in this book, that their sample espoused liberal values about social relationships but not about the economic system. It is also difficult to disagree with critics about the portrayals of sex and violence on television. Casual observation will show that more sex is being portrayed on television than in 1971, and it has become more explicit.[15] Some businessmen are still presented as greedy, slick, without morals or compassion, and often as killers. At times, blacks and women are still stereotyped. In fact, it is difficult to find much to like about primetime television, especially if you are an "academic liberal." However, it is also difficult to make the connections that the Lichters/Rothman and Stein claim between the political process and television content. There is little if any evidence that any of the values carried on television have influenced voters' choices. For example, if critics such as Stein are to be believed, that the liberalization of social values in television during the 1970s made voters more liberal, then the shift to the right with the election of Ronald Reagan is difficult to explain. In my opinion, television reflects values. However, as in the past, it continues to reflect the core culture and value-system inherent in Western society and the capitalist tradition, as well as sex and violence. Among the values are freedom, friendliness, individualism, competition, achievement and taking risks.[16] To be put on the air, programs must tap into the beliefs which the creators and audience share or be rejected out of hand.

The only book written about producers since this was published, *The Producer's Medium*, by Horace Newcomb and Robert Alley also takes the position that television reflects the values and norms of the creators.[17] However, Newcomb and Alley do not claim that a direct relationship exists between the political values of creators and their content. Rather their theory can be called an "auteur" approach because they see television as primarily a producer's medium and, as such, producers are "cultural carriers." They also bear the responsibility for the programs and the messages they give.

Newcomb and Alley bring up a topic missing from the book as it is, the subject of the creativity of the producers themselves. However, in doing so, they depict the producers as though they can operate outside of the institutional and social context in which they work. Thus, as critics, Newcomb and Alley are free to focus on psychological traits and motives as their unit of study but, as a sociologist, I reach conclusions based on studies of social structure and organization. If people working in the industry are not given autonomy (power), they cannot create without being subject to varying degrees of control from clients, organizations, other occupational groups, members of the audience, pressure groups and public agencies. Thus, the degree of autonomy producers experience in their work activities is modified or regulated by social controls. As a sociologist, my concern is with the conditions under which the creativity can flourish. The sociological question is not who or why someone is creative, but rather when creativity is allowed? One concern is psychological, the other socio-political. To be able to create for television, one must not only be creative but also attain a certain position of power. How is this power obtained, enhanced or limited in the political and economic milieu in which creators must work?

In this book, and in my subsequent work, I argue that the influence of societal factors such as market conditions, government involvement or noninvolvement and working conditions are far more powerful than the influence of individual values, talent or even creativity itself on the final forms "artistic" products take. I base this conclusion both on observations made while doing research for this book and on subsequent work over the years that followed. Since starting my research, I have had the opportunity to meet all types of producers, and in some cases, even interview them. The range of their work and their ability to remain in the industry attest to their ability to adapt to changing work circumstances. They also share a characteristic which might have helped, one rarely mentioned in writings about either film or television creative people. They are for the most part apolitical, either lacking interest or avoiding positions on political or social issues. Of course, there have been notable exceptions. Jack Webb, for example, the creator and producer of *Dragnet*, was a professed conservative, and Norman Lear is a professed liberal. Like journalists who attempt fairness and objectivity in spite of personal views, most of the producers that prevailed see themselves just as storytellers or entertainers and, as such, are not required to expound any view or be consistent in their political beliefs. Consequently, it is rare to have prevailing public values disputed in primetime television. The disagreements between liberals and conservatives that have become public debates mostly concern violence and sex. Probably the most important insight I gained from conducting this research is that television entertainment is created by "committees" of people so closely interrelated that it is unclear who actually generate the ideas and who actually create the television productions that finally appear on the air. It should also be noted that production through consensus not only distributes praise when programs are successful but also protects its participants by diluting blame for failure. Consequently, any extremes in political points of view will usually be moderated by the negotiations that go on. The interviews also alerted me to the reality of the power game, how power is negotiated and how it plays out in the struggles that go on daily. These struggles take place in the marketplace, the Federal Commission, in congressional committees, the boardrooms of networks, conglomerates and production companies, as well as in story conferences and on the sets. Except for Gitlin, most analysts have ignored how creativity is managed and controlled and over the past decade, scholarly analysis and criticism of television content has dealt primarily with textual analysis and ignored the role of work relations (and struggles) in influencing its programs. Few also have been interested in how producers perceive their audiences. The singular contribution of our studies has been to show how the autonomy and freedom of creative workers connect to the larger social structure and to organizational controls.

I also learned a great deal about the day-to-day work life of producers as they perceived it, their "social" construction of reality. Producers reported (and I verified it through observation) that the setting in which on-line producers operate is peculiarly complex and hazardous. Not only must producers organize the teams of writers, actors and directors they need, they must contend with unions and cost over-runs while continually juggling scripts and concepts to gain the approval of the executive producers they report to and the networks for both the scripts and production budgets. Because the networks in effect subsidize the productions, they will not release the funds needed to start until they have been submitted and approved—a reality as true in 1987 as in 1967.

The unanswered questions continue to puzzle me: How is content chosen, by whom and under what social and political conditions? These are complex questions which cannot be answered by just examining a single occupational group, no matter how important and central it is to the process. In addition to the producers who are obviously very important, further investigation will have to include at least four other major and continuing players in the struggle to shape the content of television drama in the United States:

1. The three competing networks along with their local affiliates and advertising sponsors.
2. The major production companies and independent producers who supply the networks with programs from Hollywood, and the on-line producers, writers, actors and craft personnel they employ;
3. The government agencies and organized pressure groups or social critics who attempt to influence production companies through government agencies or the networks; and,
4. The actual viewing audiences.

These interdependent interests, institutions and agencies group and regroup at different times for different purposes on different issues to negotiate the compromises which may lead to changes in the content broadcast.

On reading Newcomb and Alley, one could be left with the impression that talent and creativity are sufficient to have successful careers in television. It is true that actors, directors and producers who are tenacious and work at increasing their skills, can with good luck have successful careers. However, for most who try, failure is inevitable. Some also believe that the truly creative and talented writers in the industry will eventually be recognized and find fame and fortune. However, for every writer able to have one of their scripts produced, hundreds fail. Both objective data and subjective impressions suggest that in Los Angeles and New York, many who try, fail to be recognized. For example, of the 5,000 members of the Writers' Guild of America (West), only 1,500 find full-time work as television or screen writers. (This figure also includes those working full time on production teams as sitcom writers and writer–producers.) In addition to the Guild members and throughout the Los Angeles area, there is an unknown but large number of women and men who register each year for degrees in screenwriting or in individual writing courses, hoping to break in. Given the few scripts actually needed for production compared to the number of screenwriters who are already members of the Guild or who are trying to get started, it is difficult, if not impossible, to believe that even the talented, creative writers among them will find sufficient work to earn livelihoods just from writing. In a systematic analysis of musicians working for Hollywood studios, Robert Faulkner demonstrated that musicians also have little opportunity to gain entry to the film industry.[18] The world for employment in the industry is as closed for them as it is for writers and producers.

It is possible that the myth that talent will be recognized persists because the social scientists, journalists and critics who look for writers to interview, end up interviewing just those who are successful. If "success" at writing is used as the sole criterion for "talent", we face a tautology which is illogical and, worse, can lead to bad methodology. Consequently, better definitions for the terms, talent, creativity and control, must be found so that researchers will agree on the methodology they use and make their results more meaningful.

Even those who sell a script or produce a show cannot be assured of continuing employment, and there is no evidence to show that those who make it are more talented or creative than those who fail. Season after season, most producers have runs of failures as well as successes, and very few producers, especially those able to keep pace with changes in audiences' tastes, succeed in gaining greater control over their work and the creative process. Even that level of achievement cannot assure that success will continue. For example, some of the producers that Newcomb/Alley and Stein interviewed for their books had already passed their prime as "stars." (Several had been part of my original sample.) Most were no longer producing because their shows had been replaced by ones written and produced by men and women newer to the industry. As "stars," they have had power and control, and autonomy. However, even their star-status and outstanding records did not guarantee that they would continue to find work in the industry as producers.

In conclusion, this study and subsequent work show that most on-line producers and freelance writers have little control over their work in the larger sense although at times they are given or "loaned" power to decide what scripts to write or approve for filming, who to cast, and how to edit the shows once they have been filmed. The reality they live with is that outside forces such as networks and other financial sources, other mass media and, often, transient events determine what will be chosen as subjects to be used for television drama. Only rarely do the writers and producer have sufficient courage or power to oppose such forces, or for that matter, bother. This does not mean that the industry transforms its workers as C. Wright Mills and others have suggested it could (see p. 26); rather, most workers already hold beliefs and values congruent to those held throughout the industry and probably congruent to those held by most of the audience. The industry does not set the producer's course, but each worker decides for herself or himself whether to become part of the industry (if they were lucky enough to be hired). Then, once hired, freedom and autonomy are by definition still delimited.

The Hollywood TV Producer examines the work of one occupational group in depth. It shows how creativity is managed by the structure of the industry and conditions under which producers and their co-creators (especially actors, writers, and directors) must work. This introduction has briefly considered the changes in the industry and how these changes have affected the relationships between the producers, the networks and their audiences. In the conclusion of this book, I point out that communications industries are changing constantly. When I wrote those words, I did not realize how true they would remain. The pattern of network buying and Hollywood television production is the same today as it was when this book was written. However, I will predict that twenty years from now the patterns will not be as recognizable. To save costs, production companies have begun to film in locations outside of Hollywood. Because of takeovers in the industry and mergers, levels of bureaucratic organization and control will increase in the studios and production companies. Also, with the decline in earnings and market shares for networks, production companies will have to develop other sources of outside funding to continue operations. In addition, despite showing that it would be in their interest to attract and satisfy the entertainment needs of audience segments rather than a "mass" audience, the networks will still try to attract the largest possible, broadly-defined audience rather than smaller audiences with more differentiated tastes.

Changes in laws and regulations, the ways in which production companies come to be organized, and the ways in which the networks and other program distributors have to operate under changing market conditions will probably continue to influence program content and the "politics of broadcasting" in the United States more than the job producers do or the values they bring to work. The power of business interests will still prevail in the struggle over television content. As described by David Jacobs, creator of *Dallas*, in *Hollywood's Favorite Heavy*, talking about himself and his co-producer, Michael Filerman: "I want to produce art and Filerman wants to create trash, and together we make television."

A Methodological Note

The research I conducted for this book started me on a course of inquiry that still continues. The data in the book were gathered systematically, as noted in some detail on pages 16–17. However, the new material for this introduction, although more comprehensive and more up-to-date in the conclusions drawn than in the original text, was also gathered from observations and interviews albeit less systematically. *The Hollywood TV Producer* was based on my dissertation and work at U.C.L.A. and by the time it was finished for publication, I had become a faculty member of The American University in Washington, D.C. Fortunately for my interests and research, I am still a faculty member, because being in Washington has given me ready access to the FCC and other government resources and lobbying groups. However, over the years, I also assiduously maintained my Hollywood contacts so that I could return regularly to interview and in some cases, re-interview industry workers (actors, international salespeople, and some producers, several part of the original sample).

My purpose in continuing this line of inquiry has been to try to connect the work people do for the industry with the content they create. *The Hollywood TV Producer* was, and still is, an occupational study. However with this new introduction I tried to expand my original orientation to include not only the reference groups as they are perceived by the producers (which I still consider very important), but also the political and economic changes over the years that intervened to affect the ways in which the producers had to work. An industry as dynamic as television, undergoing changes as rapidly as it has, required that I study trends by making observations and conducting interviews over time.

A number of other people have also examined popular culture since this book was written, several of whom are mentioned in this new introduction. One book not mentioned is Howard S. Becker's *Art Worlds* (1984).[19] Although he focuses more on cooperation and assistance and I on struggles and compromises, both of us agree that the production of culture (art) is a collective activity. Producing a scholarly work is also a collective activity—my original dedication remains as true today as it did in 1971. I continue to be grateful to the advice and support I receive from my mentor, Charles R. Wright, and my husband and colleague, Joel M. Cantor. In addition, I would like to express my gratitude to Anne K. Peters who died in February 1987. Over the years, she and I examined the work of actors and how they are controlled by the social milieu in which they work. Those inquiries helped me better understand how the social organization of production, the interlocking networks of people and institutions, define both the work creative people do and the culture they create.

Notes

1. See Muriel G. Cantor, "Television Producers: A Sociological Analysis." Ph.D. Dissertation, University of California, Los Angeles, 1969 and Muriel G. Cantor "The Role of the Producer in Choosing Children's Television Content," Vol. I in *Television and Social Behavior: A Report to the Surgeon General's Scientific Advisory Committee*. (Washington, D.C: U.S. Government Printing Office, 1972.)
2. I develop this idea in three places: Muriel G. Cantor, *Prime-Time Television: Content and Control* (Thousand Oaks, California, Sage Publications, 1980) and Muriel G. Cantor, "The Politics of Popular

Drama." *Communication Research* 6 (1979): 387–406; and Muriel G. Cantor, "The Organization and Production of Prime Time Television" in *Television and Behavior: Ten Years of Scientific Progress and Implications for the Eighties*. Vol. 2: Technical Reviews. Edited by D. Pearl, L. Bouthilet, J. Lazar (Rockville, Maryland: U.S. Department of Health and Human Services, 1982.)

3. For example the movie *Network*, the documentary shown on Public Broadcasting, *Hollywood's Favorite Heavy* in 1986 and the 1977 made-for-television movie, *The Story Teller*.

4. In addition to the 14 July 1967 *Daily Variety*, I have used the *Daily Variety*, "T.V. Shows in Production" 13 October 1972 and *Weekly Variety* 26 September 1986 for the information contained in this paragraph and the one which follows.

5. Linda S. Lichter, S. Robert Lichter and Stanley Rothman "Hollywood and America: The Odd Couple" *Public Opinion* 6 (December/January 1983): 54–58.

6. Herbert J. Gans, "Popular Culture in America: Social Problem in a Mass Society or Social Asset in a Pluralist Society?" in *Social Problems; A Modern Approach*. H. S. Becker Ed. (New York: John Wiley and Sons, Inc., 1966.) Pp. 549–620. Herbert J. Gans, *Popular Culture and High Culture*. (New York: Basic Books, 1974.)

7. U.S. Court of Appeals, *Office of communication v. F. C. C.* 425 F 2d 543.

8. Martin Tolchin, "CBS's Tisch Addresses Broadcasters," *The New York Times*, 1 April 1987, p. C27.

9. The changes in FCC regulations since this book was written have been extensive. [See Muriel G. Cantor and Joel M. Cantor, "The De-Regulation of the United States Entertainment Industry—Political and Policy Issues" in *Comparative Perspectives on New Communication Technologies*. M. Ferguson Ed. (London and Thousand Oaks, California: Sage, 1986.)] Here just the changes in Financial Interest are being emphasized because of their direct effect on producers' work.

10. Federal Communications Commission *Report and Order of The Commission on Network Television Broadcasting*. Second Series, Vol. 23, May 29, 1970–July 17, 1970. (Washington, D. C.: U.S. Government Printing Office, 1971.) These rules are now codified in the FCC rules under the title "Network Affiliation," paragraph §73.658, section (j), "Network syndication and program practices." (see *Broadcasting Cablecasting Yearbook*. Washington, D. C.: Broadcasting Publications, Inc., 1987, p. A–22.

11. The Gans article was written in 1966. See Note 6 above. John Riley and Matilda Riley, "Mass Communication and the Social System." In *Sociology Today*. R. Merton Ed., L. Broom, and L. S. Cottrell, Jr. (New York: Basic Books, 1959.) Pp. 537–78.

12. Hortense Powdermaker. *Hollywood: The Dream Factory*. (Boston: Little Brown, 1971.)

13. Ben Stein. *The View From Sunset Strip*. (New York: Basic Books, 1979.)
14. Todd Gitlin. *Inside Prime-Time*. (New York: Pantheon, 1983.)
15. Stephen Farber, "Sex on TV Becoming More Explicit," *New York Times*. 4 April 1987, p. 50.
16. For a good survey and presentation, see Edward C. Stewart. *American Cultural Patterns: A Cross-Cultural Persepctive*. (LaGrange Park, Ill.: Intercultural Network, Inc., 1972.)
17. Horace Newcomb and Robert S. Alley. *The Producer's Medium: Conversations with Creators of American TV*. (New York: Oxford University Press, 1983.)
18. Robert R. Faulkner. *Music on Demand: Composers and Careers in the Hollywood Film Industry*. (New Brunswick, New Jersey: Transaction Books, 1983.)
19. Howard S. Becker. *Art Worlds*. (Berkeley, California: 1984).

The
Hollywood
TV
Producer

Introduction

During the years I lived in Los Angeles, I met several people connected with film making who eventually became my friends. These people did not fit the stereotype that I and possibly others had of "Hollywood." Most were screen writers or producers though there was an actor or two among them. Regardless of their occupations, none lived in the high style usually associated with Hollywood; instead they were raising children in the suburbs of Los Angeles with values little different from their professional and business neighbors. Their life style seemed almost antithetical to what the Hollywood columnists reported: no fancy costume parties or night clubbing and little drinking. Their parties resembled others in the hills of Los Angeles. When the sexes were separated women talked about children and clothes and men about business and politics. When the sexes were mixed, there was little flirtation.

All this made me wonder not only whether the Hollywood of the past still existed, but if it ever had. More importantly, I was impressed with the intelligence of the people that I met and with their knowledge of film making. It seemed strange that these same people were criticized so extensively for their lack of artistic integrity and for their low opinion of public taste. My observations were, of course, impressionistic and my sample small, but from this experience came the first glimmer of this project.

Also during this time I began to visit sets and watch film

production for television series. I realized that this was a complicated, careful process involving many people who made decisions working together. When finished, the films themselves often appeared overly simplistic, sometimes violent, and stereotypic; by high-brow critical standards they certainly were not works of "art." In fact, an often repeated criticism is that these weekly series seem to be manufactured rather than created. A second question related to my first one then occurred to me. How could people seemingly so knowledgeable and so capable of verbalizing high standards produce films so different from what one naturally expected from them?

From these questions developed the research project itself. The more I studied the literature on mass communications and the sociology of work and occupations, it became obvious to me that not only had there been no studies of Hollywood since Hortense Powdermaker's now outdated study,[1] but there were few efforts to relate the content presented through any of mass media—newspapers, certain magazines, television, radio, or the movies—to the men who decided what the audience reads, views, or hears.

Mass-media research has been and still is focused on the effects of media content on the audience. Yet those researchers who have been most concerned with the effects of mass communication on American life, culture, and personality have repeatedly suggested that research focus on the "communicator," the decision-maker, and the structure of the entertainment industry. According to them, a "proper study of media effects would have to include research on the media, how and why they create the content they do, who determines the nature of the content, for what reasons and with what kind of direct contacts with the audience."[2]

Study of those who create and determine the content of American television has been especially neglected. On the other hand, much public attention has been given to the supposed

□

or actual effects of television. Congress, the press, and various presidential commissions have explored the relationship of television to violence in recent years.[3] Related to the violence issue is the question whether television and the other media spread conflicts in the cities and on the campuses. Still another major area of public concern is whether television has the ability to "sell" candidates possessing certain characteristics that may be irrelevant to actual qualifications for officeholding.[4] Critics of television maintain that personal attractiveness, rather than integrity or ability, has become the most important characteristic of a candidate for public office. Great power is attributed to the medium: the ability to spread conflicts, to turn otherwise peaceful youngsters into violent creatures, and to dupe the voting public.

Social scientists who have been seriously studying television's impact on audiences for several decades disagree with this position, arguing that what appears on television usually reflects commonly held values and that television's power to influence is highly overestimated. Critics are quick to place the blame for television's ill effects on those presenting the content, the network officials, the newscasters, or the production people, they view the audience as easily duped and unselective in their viewing habits, with little control over what goes on the air. Social scientists, on the other hand, usually view the content as given and thereby neglect the officials, performers, and production people; they see the audience as selective both in what they perceive and also in what they choose. It should be noted that both the critics and social scientists view the audience as essentially irrational; however, the social scientist connects this irrationality with certain general social and psychological characteristics of man. A few decades ago some social scientists saw the mass media as having a direct effect on the audience, but more recently many sociologists view the audience as being part of a social milieu; the effects of mass media are tempered by a number of factors, such as the context in which people

□

receive the communication, the levels of communication, the social characteristics of the viewer, and the viewer's values, beliefs, and attitudes. This literature is extensive, and I don't have the space here to delve into the fine details of the arguments, but, essentially, most researchers, when they consider media content and its effects, may see the audiences in social context but ignore the communicators and the social context in which they work.[5]

If the numerous critics are right about the effects of television, then how and by whom the content for televiewing is chosen becomes an essential area for exploration. It also is clear that people, selective or not, cannot be affected however slightly by content that is not available. The communicator and the social context in which he operates are important elements of the communication process. If we are to understand the communication process, it is necessary to explore the social context in which content is selected and the people who are selecting or creating the content.

This realization is not unique to me. Since 1967 there has been an increasing interest in those who create for the various mass media. Newsmen have for several decades been the most constantly studied of all communicators,[6] but until recently those creating and communicating for films and television and those telecasting the news and producing political broadcasts have been largely ignored.[7] Almost simultaneously several studies were initiated in Hollywood of people working in the film industry. Because at this time Hollywood films are being made for television, these studies are concerned essentially with decision-making and creating the programs to be viewed on television, even though the actual medium is the film. Joan Moore, Robert Faulkner, Anne Peters, and myself have been conducting studies on those involved in various aspects of film making for television.[8]

Although these studies differ in focus and methods of gathering data, each does emphasize the relationship of an

□

occupational milieu and a professional group to the content produced. For example, Herbert Gans found that newsmen determine what to broadcast as news principally from media considerations, professional judgments, personal and professional values, and audience reactions.[9] In a study of television news producers in Britain, Jay Blumler found the output to be determined by varying and competing pressures arising from several sources: organization rules and policies, perceptions of the audience, professional standards, and the producer's own attitudes.[10] Primarily, this book considers the same factors and their importance to producers of film dramatic series made for televiewing.

The Working Producer

Why were producers chosen for study rather than directors or free-lance writers? That question has been asked of me several times by both sociologists and others who are unfamiliar with how the dramatic series are made. Those knowledgeable about American film making are aware that the Hollywood producer, unlike his European counterpart, has always been influential in selecting stories, casts, and directors. In series production the producer has become even more important than he is in feature film making.

Thus, the working producer of filmed dramatic television was chosen for study because of his key role and relative power in the industry. He has both executive and creative authority. The producer is in charge of hiring the cast, the directors, and writers for his show; he serves as coordinator between the network for whom the show is produced and/or the parent film company; and he has the final responsibility for cutting and editing the filmed product. This combination of tasks and associated power

□

is common in the role of television producer but is not necessarily associated with the title producer in other media. Indeed, the title has a variety of meanings in the entertainment fields. Often a producer is the man (or men) who raises the money for theatrical productions or feature-film production. Even in television, where most of the production is financed by the major networks or the advertisers, the title may be assigned to someone whose sole responsibility is to see that production costs do not exceed the allotted budget. However, in this study the title refers to those producers who are "on the line" and who are responsible for the day-to-day decisions of film production.[11]

The producer has many of the tasks that in the motion-picture industry are assigned to the film director. When a feature-film director is hired to do a picture, he is given a story to develop and, along with the film editor, cuts the picture.[12] In television-series drama story development is a major function of the producer. Because of time limitation or shooting schedules, the director, although he may be entitled to the same privileges as his counterpart in feature films, rarely has time to remain with the film long enough to cut it. It is often said by people associated with the television and movie industry that the feature film is a director's medium while television is a producer's medium. Three of the major creative parts of television-series production—story, casting, and editing—are under the producer's control.[13] Although casting is a joint effort of the producer and director, the producer has final authority. The director shoots the picture and on the set he is in control, but since he is hired by the producer, he turns to him for final decisions when problems arise on the set.

In addition, because the producer's major responsibility is story development, he holds a position of power over the script writers. The producer hires the writers to do one or more scripts during a season and often works with them, directing the tone and content of the script.

However, because the producer is part of a large, complex

□

bureaucratic organization, he does not have complete control. He is a working producer—a man in the middle between those above him in the networks and production companies and those he supervises in the production crew. As a representative of management, he must fulfill the goals of the organization. Ideally, the producer has responsibility for the creative aspects of the show, but this is always delegated authority because even when a man owns, creates, and produces his own show, the network retains the right to *final* approval of scripts, casts, and other creative and administrative matters.

Most of the producers interviewed reported that their main duty was to hire writers and develop stories with them to make certain that the story idea is carried through to the final product. In reality, some producers did have the authority for entire films while others did not. Some shows have two producers; one handles the stories, the other handles other aspects of production such as sets, casts, and the administration of funds. If a show is unusually long, over one hour, and on each week, there will be several producers. Each producer will be working on an entirely different episode of the show so that the production schedule can be maintained.

More than simply structural differences in organization, there were also differences in the actual degrees of authority that was delegated to various producers from show to show and from studio to studio. In order to give a better idea of how the producer functions and how he perceives his role, ten producers were chosen at random from the sample to tell in their own words what they do.

Producer No. 1, an executive producer for one show and a working producer for another, had produced many different shows through the years and had created several successful series.

I both develop and create ideas for production. Now basically, there is a difference between develop and create. My main function has always been to create. But there are times when I developed ideas without creating them. (He named one of his

□

two shows on the air.) I developed and created that one. The other show no one created. The network created and I developed. Now I am exec producer of that. Here we get into another gray area. At the major studios they have an executive producer who is over four or five shows. His job is really to worry about costs. I don't know if I would call that producing. *To me the greatest thrill I get from producing is the relationship you build up with the writer, the thought processes you go through to develop an idea and story line. Working up a first draft, the writing. The final polish and then the cast. Finally the editing and dubbing. This is producing. This is the job of the working producer.*

Producer No. 2 works as an on-the-line producer for a large studio operating in the Los Angeles area. He was definitely a salaried employee under contract.

First, I have everything to do with scripts. In order to tell you what the duties of a producer are, it is necessary to tell you that I have been a writer, a film writer, in radio and screen for probably eighteen years. Today in television if a producer is not a writer or an ex-writer, he is in a lot of trouble. You have to be a hyphenate in television.

I open the doors wide and announce to any and all that this is what we are going to do. Come to see me. Writers come. I know about 80 percent of the writers in the business. They see the pilot film, come in with ideas. . . . So we meet with the writers, my associate producer with me, and the story editor too. I work with the writers. *After the stories I personally see the production to the finish.*

Producer No. 3 produces a show with one of the longest records of continuous production. He was not the original producer of the show but has been with it for ten years, which was a record.

We don't have a story editor even though the story editor is an important part of any production. When we changed our format several years ago, we decided that the story editor might give us an excuse for the new format working or not. If we were going to go down, I wanted to be sure that I was responsible for going down. So we eliminated the story editor. So far as the producer's function on this show, it is primarily the supervising of the story material. We have a very fine production manager who is immediately responsible for actual production (sets, etc.). But *the producer is still in the capacity of supervising any particular decisions that have to be made during production.* After that there is the editing. I think most producers think of themselves as capable film editors.

Producer No. 4 was producing a successful comedy series when his name was put on the list, but by the time he was interviewed he had changed jobs.

I was producer of the ———————— show but I bowed out. I bowed out after the tenth show. I'm still on the show as script consultant. Script consultant strictly concerns himself with the script and stories. *The producer has to take care of everything, all details; the casting, directors, as well as the script. Every phase of the operation has to be controlled by the producer.* The script consultant just has one area to worry about, that's the script. So for personal reasons, I decided to bow out of producing.

Producer No. 5 is a very young man in comparison to most of the others and is employed by a large studio that moves their on-the-line producers from show to show. At the time of the interview he was one of four producers on a ninety-minute western. He had been with three different shows in the 1967–1968 season.

My job as producer is that I initially work with the writer. I sit down with the writer and develop from a springboard, from a thought, or from a character a story. I am not a producer who says, "Let's do a story about an Indian Stokely Carmichael and go from there." *Writers come in and we start from the very germ of an idea and work from that point to the final completed film. That is my job.* We see to every aspect of making a television film. Developing of the script is one of the most important functions of the producer. From that point the job is to see that things are handled according to the original concept. In the case of a series, being true to the format, being true to the

□

series. Your responsibility ends when you walk over to technicolor and look over the answer print.

Producer No. 6 has created several series that enjoyed long runs on television. This year for the first time he produced a series that failed. At the time of the interview he was no longer producing, but he was still working in the industry. His office was at a large studio where he was developing a motion picture.

To understand producing you have to understand the whole process of making a film. The producer will generally start with the writer. If you are an hyphenate, you are giving away the story to the writer. You say to the writer, why don't you do a story about —— and then you come up with the idea. You'll have to do a lot of guiding and give away a lot of ideas. You'll have to use a pencil and change lines and write and rewrite scenes. You hire the director and have a lot to do with hiring actors. You tell the director how you want the show. You are responsible for budget, of course. You work with the set designer—you work with the wardrobe man. I can't think of all the things you have to do. You read, cut, see the dailies. You talk to the man about the music. *From the beginning to the end you are the one factor that stays with the product.*

Producer No. 7 quoted below works for a small company. The show he was producing was on the air for three years and although he didn't develop the pilot, he was the producer of the series from its inception.

The producer of any series is the man responsible for the entire production; this means from the story line right through the finished product. Casting, dubbing, writing, and directing are all the responsibility of the producer. *This does not mean I do everything, but all these elements reflect my taste.* All these elements have a style to each and this style must utilize the producer's ideas. It shows what you request of your directors and your writers. Your main function is to keep the series consistent.

The next three producers differ from the ones quoted above. One is an independent producer who creates, produces, and develops series. The other two worked during the season under

□

discussion in roles that were not usual for them: one was in charge of production only, with no script control; the other had script control but little to do with other aspects of production.

Producer No. 8 describes what he does as an independent producer. His series, which was on the air a short time during the season, was not renewed.

A producer is a combination business and artistic chemist, a guy who brings all the elements together. Sometimes he can get a project together because he can assemble a star and/or a writer or a director who at the moment is bankable. That is not the way I function. I have always been involved with the project right from its inception. Created it. Brought all the elements together. Taken it to several places until I could find a place that believed in it commercially because that is what it is, a commercial venture. I put the enterprise together.

Producer No. 9 was in charge of production only. He had produced other series completely, but since this particular series operated differently from the others on the air, the working arrangements were different. For instance, this series had three contract writers who were solely responsible for the stories. In addition, there were two full-time directors who had more authority than the director usually does in a television show. Many of the functions of the working producer were delegated to the director and writers on this show.

This particular job is not as fully gratifying as others I have had because the show is so big that the producer's job is split down the middle. I am in charge of all the production and the executive producer and the writers are in charge of the story. The story is ground out like sausage, and we grind out the film. My staff of associate producers, directors, and film editors take care of this side of the film making. It is full time since I supervise them, but it is not as creative as other things I have worked at.

Producer No. 10 was no longer working on the show when the interview took place. The show was in its first season, and although it finished the season, it was in serious trouble according

□

to gossip columnists and others, including the interviewee. His title was supervising producer. No one else interviewed had such a title.

> I developed the pilot script and the network wanted me to stay with the show. I have never produced before. I am a writer, not a hyphenate. Since the show was ninety minutes long, the networks thought a number of people were needed. I was directly under the executive producer. There were two working producers under both of us. Supervising producer was a manufactured title. Don't take it seriously. It is meaningless really because they had to give me some title. On paper it was my obligation to develop the stories, but what they let you do are two different things. The network had an idea of what the series should be, and I'll admit they told me very early. Their idea was that you never do anything that hasn't been done successfully before. I ignored that completely.

The above accounts indicate some variation in the actual duties and functions of a working producer, but it is also evident that an "ideal" occupational role does exist in the minds of those interviewed. The ideal producer would have control of story selection, both theme and content, would be in charge of all other aspects of production, including casting and cutting, and would perform these duties without constraint from the networks and the production company who hires him.

This book in part describes how close reality is to the ideal, but my main interest is how the producer perceives the process of selecting content. My major question is: who is more important to the producer when he chooses a story theme or when he makes related decisions—the network, the audience, or his own craft group?

How Producers Were Studied

The main part of this book deals with producers of live-action filmed drama; in addition, there is some material on producers of children's shows, both live-action and animated. Semi-structured interviews with producers of both types of shows were the main method used to obtain data and information. From September 1967 to January 1968, I interviewed producers who had shows in production during the 1967–1968 season. In January 1970 I interviewed the producers of shows made especially for children.

The interview schedule (see Appendix A) was essentially the same for both groups. However, the samples are not mutually exclusive because some producers of children's programs were included in the first set of interviews. Those producers who were making shows that were shown on prime time, 7:30 P.M. to 10:30 P.M., whether the target audience was families or adults, were included in the first interview round. The second time my research question was essentially the same, but the major focus was on those who were directing their shows to children or children and their parents. There were three producers, therefore, who were interviewed twice, and these data, while limited, will be presented as evidence of certain changes in network policy.

The same questions were asked of each respondent. Occasionally, an additional question or probe was made to a particular respondent when it seemed necessary to clarify a statement or comment. For instance, several respondents mentioned that "good taste" was a necessary quality for a successful producer. When such a response was made, the producer was asked to clarify the meaning of the term. Except for the above deviation, the answers obtained were comparable so that internal analysis can be made between different groups of producers.

The Sample

The original list of producers with shows in production for the first set of interviews was obtained from the Friday, July 14, 1967, issue of *Daily Variety* (Western edition). Each Friday

□

both *Hollywood Reporter* and *Daily Variety* list both the movies and television films that are being made in the Los Angeles area. Because some television series are in production for only four weeks and other shows are added during the production period (approximately June to the end of February in most cases), the Friday *Variety* was checked each week until October to note any production changes, additions, or substitutions of shows. With a new show (one that has not appeared on network television in a previous year) it is unusual for the network to purchase more than thirteen episodes. In some cases the network originally purchases as few as four, six, or seven episodes (usually thirteen) with an option for more shows to be bought if the show has high ratings. Shows that stay on for the season contain between twenty-four to thirty episodes.[14] By checking *Daily Variety* each Friday, I was able to discover the changes and make the necessary modifications in the list.

When I first conceptualized the study, I hoped to interview every producer of every television series in production in the Los Angeles area. At the beginning of the season *Daily Variety* listed eighty *film* shows in production.[15] Of the eighty, only fifty-three fit the definition of a film series; the others were documentaries, movies, specials, or cartoon series. Three of the fifty-three listed were being filmed in another section of the United States or out of the country (one in Africa, the other in India), and therefore the producers were unavailable. As several newer shows went into production, several more names were added to the list. Finally, in all, the list of producers drawn up in this way numbered sixty-four. Three producers refused requests to be interviewed; two producers were only in charge of production and not story development and therefore were eliminated from this study, bringing the final number of producers interviewed down to fifty-nine. This includes four producers who did not have shows in production at the time of the interviews: two who had had producing assignments at the beginning of the season, but whose shows were no longer in production by the time the interviews took place, and two who were still with the shows but in another capacity.[16]

Six others in the industry were interviewed as part of a pretest before the actual sample was selected; these six were all closely connected with production, and three had produced shows in the past. By present occupation they were: a free-lance writer, an independent producer of two documentaries (the only woman interviewed in this set), a publicist and former producer of a series, a production manager and former assistant director on a number of series, a series director, and a producer of animated television commercials. These interviews were most helpful and were used to develop the interview guide. The publicist and production manager together gave me ten hours of time and were able to point out areas that I was unfamiliar with or had not considered important.

The method of obtaining the interviews accounts for the presence of the producers no longer producing. Letters were sent to the producers of the shows rather than to the show itself. When an individual who was no longer producing a show received a letter requesting an interview, he often granted the interview although his connection with the show had been severed. However, several people who were no longer connected with the various shows never received their letters. These letters were intercepted by the present producer, who then responded favorably to a request for an interview.[17]

Other methods could have been used to select the sample but did not seem as appropriate for finding information about the areas selected for study. If the primary purposes of the study were to examine career and occupational mobility in the industry, it might have been more appropriate to select the sample from those who had produced in other years as well as the present one. This, too, might be an appropriate way to select producers if the main emphasis was on success or failure in producing.

□

Because the main purpose was neither, this, after some consideration, was dropped in favor of the method used. The majority of those interviewed have a long history of work in various entertainment media; two were producing for the first time; several were producing for the second or third year. The sample covers men with a variety of backgrounds, ages, and also degrees of success and failure in the industry.

Some might consider the Producers Guild of America a presumably more formalized universe for the selection of a sample. This Guild was not considered because many television producers were not members at the time the interviews took place. The Producers Guild was not a collective-bargaining organization as are the other guilds, and it was not necessary to be a member in order to produce a television series. As it turned out, only eleven of fifty-nine men interviewed were members of the Producers Guild; most belonged to the Writers Guild of America. In fact, all eleven who were members of the Producers Guild were members of the Writers Guild as well. Since then the Producers Guild has won recognition from the Motion Picture and Television Producers Association and now has union status. Presently all producers must join the Guild if they wish to produce.[18]

Both my colleagues and some in the industry suggested that the "best" way to obtain the desired interviews would be through personal contact. Although I did have several sources available to me, I decided not to gain entry through personal sources unless all else failed. First, I thought that a personal source might possibly be a hindrance rather than a help because the interpersonal relationships between the men were unknown and might be antagonistic or competitive. Second, by using the same method to gain all the interviews, the standards could be considered universal. Third, this limited the interviews to only those presently on the line. If I interviewed friends and associates of producers, it would have been difficult to ignore writers and assistant staff people among others.

□

The first interview of the original set took place on September 9, 1967; the last one on January 18, 1968. Because production continued through the entire fall and winter season for those shows that were in production for the fall season, it was possible to continue the interviewing without a break for the Christmas and New Year holidays.

Before starting the interviews, I spent several months reading books and documents and informally conversing with people in other aspects of production, trying to become familiar with the language and operations in the industry. The cooperation from the respondents and many others in the industry was exemplary. I personally conducted all interviews. Most respondents allowed me to tape-record their responses. The two that did not wish to be recorded did allow notes to be taken during the interview. One producer who would not be interviewed invited me to sit in on a production conference, which was informative and helpful. I was invited by many of the producers to watch production and sit through dubbing sessions and the showings of the finished film. I spent much time at the various studios.

The second set of interviews was gathered in essentially the same way as the first. In 1969 the National Institute of Mental Health was examining television and social behavior. My original study had come to their attention and when they learned that I was returning to Los Angeles for a long winter holiday, they suggested that I interview producers of children's filmed programming. I sought these interviews by first writing a formal letter to those producers whose shows were listed as in production in the *Daily Variety* (Western Edition) published on December 5, 1969.[19] Again, the response to the request for interviews was excellent with all but one person granting interviews. The one producer who refused an interview had no shows actually in production and had been listed because he had just finished an animated special. He did not intend to make more shows for children and therefore thought he could contribute little to the study.

□

Several people who were interviewed suggested others not listed in *Daily Variety* who were preparing new shows for the following season (1970–1971). In this way I finally interviewed twenty producers and four writers of children's shows; these shows include animated cartoon series with continuing characters and with each episode a complete story in itself, usually appearing on a weekly basis; animated cartoons specials; film specials; and film series using live actors. While the work situation and the selection of content are different for the producers of Saturday-morning shows and the producers of prime-time evening shows, there are similarities as well. Because of this, some of the material gathered the second time around is invaluable both as comparative data and as a source specifying certain changes in the industry itself. Those who are producing live-action films for children rather than animated cartoons are the same occupationally as the producers in the first set of interviews. As mentioned earlier, three producers of children's shows were interviewed both times. They were included in the first set because their shows were on prime time and in the second set because their shows were directed to children.

Most of the material reported is from the first set of interviews, which does represent most of the men who were producing during the 1967–1968 season. The material from the second set of interviews is offered as additional information on specific points and, of course, will be clearly designated. The major problem examined is how producers select content in relation to their three major audiences or reference groups: those who control the occupational and organization setting (because they determine what will be shown on the air); the craft groups involved in production—free-lance writers, actors, and directors—primarily because they are equal or possibly superior in status or knowledge; and the viewing audience because they ultimately decide the success or failure of a show.

□

Plan of the Book

Chapter 2 surveys the sociological and communication theories that are relevant to the questions asked in the study. Chapter 3 describes the pre-production process, detailing the role of the network, the advertiser, the ratings, and pretesting. Chapter 4 describes the "professionalization" of producers and develops a typology of producers from an analysis of the interviews, finding three major types—the film makers, the writer-producer, and the old-line producer. Chapter 5 analyzes the relationship of the working producer with others who are also working in the craft aspects of production—the writers, the directors, and the actors. Chapter 6 analyzes the relationship of the producer with the business organization, the network, which ultimately controls the final product. Chapter 7 reports producers' reaction to the change of network policy on violent content since the death of Robert Kennedy; it also discusses the producers' own view of the effects of this content on children. Chapter 8 studies the producers' perception of the viewing audience and how this perception can influence content selection; it also examines audience control over the selection process and the producers' own viewing habits and tastes are considered. Chapter 9 summarizes the material presented throughout according to the typology of producers, describing each type and comparing them to one another.

NOTES

1 Hortense Powdermaker, *Hollywood: The Dream Factory* (Boston: Little, Brown and Co., 1950).
2 Herbert Gans, "The Shaping of Mass Media Content: A Study of the

News" (paper presented at the 1966 meeting of the American Sociological Association, Miami Beach, Florida).

3   For instance, see *Federal Communications Commission Policy Matters and Television Programing*, Hearings before the Subcommittee on Communications of the Committee on Commerce, 91st Congress, 1st sess. (Washington, D.C.: U.S. Government Printing Office, 1969) pt. 1 and 2; Otto N. Larsen, ed., *Violence and the Mass Media* (New York: Harper & Row, 1968), esp. pt. 5, "Regulation and Control: Public Participation," pt. 6, "Regulation and Control: Governmental Participation," and pt. 7, "Epilogue"; and David L. Lange, Robert K. Baker, and Sandra J. Ball, eds., *Mass Media and Violence: A Report to the National Commission on the Causes and Prevention of Violence* (Washington, D.C.: U.S. Government Printing Office, 1969).

4   See, for instance, Joe McGinniss, *The Selling of the President*: 1968 (New York: Simon & Schuster, Pocket Books, 1970). Also Kurt Lang and Gladys Engel Lang, *Politics and Television* (Chicago: Quadrangle Books, 1968).

5   The literature on the mass media and mass communications is extensive. Much of it will be cited throughout the book and in the references. If interested in an overview, see Otto Larsen, "Social Effects of Mass Communications," in Robert E. L. Faris, ed., *Handbook of Modern Sociology* (Chicago: Rand McNally, 1964), pp. 349–381; Denis McQuail, *Towards a Sociology of Mass Communications* (London: Collier-Macmillan Ltd., 1969); and Roger L. Brown, "Approaches to the Historical Development of Mass Media Studies," in Jeremy Tunstall, ed., *Media Sociology: A Reader* (Urbana, Ill.: University of Illinois Press, 1970), pp. 41–57.

6   There have been numerous studies of newsmen. For instance, see Warren Breed, "The Newspaperman, News and Society" (Ph.D. diss., Columbia University, 1952); Walter Gieber, "Across the Desk: A Study of 16 Telegraph Editors," *Journalism Quarterly* 33 (1956): 423–432; and Walter Gieber, "News Is What Newspapermen Make It," in Lewis A. Dexter and David Manning White, eds., *People, Society, and Mass Communications* (New York: Free Press, 1964), pp. 173–182.

7   Herbert J. Gans, "How Well Does TV Present the News?" in *New York Times Magazine*, January 11, 1970, pp. 30–35, 38; and Jay B. Blumler, "Producers' Attitudes Toward Television Coverage of an Election Campaign: A Case Study," in the *Sociological Review Monograph: Sociology of Mass Communicators* 13 (1969): 85–115.

8   Joan Moore, "The Hollywood Writer," unpublished manuscript draft; Robert R. Faulkner, "Hollywood Studio Musicians: Theor Work and Contingencies in the Film Industry" (Ph.D. diss., University of California, Los Angeles 1968), also, *Hollywood Studio Musicians: Their*

□

Work and Careers in the Recording Industry (Chicago: Aldine, Atherton 1971); Anne Peters, "Acting and Aspiring Actresses in Hollywood: A Sociological Analysis," (Ph.D diss., University of California, Los Angeles 1971).

9 Gans, "How Well Does TV Present the News."

10 Blumler, *op. cit.*

11 U.S. Department of Labor, Bureau of Employment Security, *Dictionary of Occupational Titles* (Washington: U.S. Government Printing Office, 1965), p. 534, lists several kinds of producers and defines a motion-picture producer and radio and TV broadcasting producer's as follows:

Producer (Motion Pictures) 187.168 Production Supervisor Coordinates activities of personnel engaged in writing, directing, editing and producing motion pictures. Reviews synopses and scripts and directs adaption of screen plays. Determines treatment and scope of proposed productions and establishes department operating budget. Selects principal members of cast and key production staff members. Reviews filmed scenes of each day's shooting, orders retakes, and approves final filmed productions. Conducts meetings with Director, Scenario writer, and other staff members to discuss progress and results.
Producer (Radio and T.V. Broadcasting) I 159.118 Plans and coordinates various aspects of radio and television programs. Interviews and selects Script Writers and cast principals from staff members or outside talent. Obtains costumes, props, music, and other equipment or personnel to complete production. Outlines program to be produced to script writers and evaluates finished script. Suggests changes in script to meet management or other requirements. Coordinates audio work, scenes, music, timing, camera work and script. Gives instructions to Director (motion picture; radio and T.V. broadcasting) to schedule and conduct rehearsals and develop and coordinate details to obtain desired production. Reviews production to insure objectives are attained. May direct programs in small stations or in a limited area in large stations and be designated as Producer-Director; Radio Producer; T.V. Producer.

12 A feature-film director comes in after the screenplay is written (or at least the first draft) and then works with the writer or writers on revisions. The television-film director usually has little or nothing to do with script revisions. In addition, the film director has the first cut on a picture, but unless he is important enough to win this contractually, he does not have the final say in editing the film. The producer of the film and/or the studio retains this right. However, the director of a feature film usually has more power than does the director of a television film.

13 The word "creative" is used here and throughout the book in a very specific and somewhat traditional way. Mass-communication researchers define communicators as "nonclerical workers within communications organizations—people who work on the selecting, shaping and packaging

of programs—communicator's work is "creative," requires "flair" and "personal contacts" (Tunstall, "Introduction," *op. cit.*, p. 15). In other words, doing creative work means that a producer's tasks are not routine; he shapes and selects programs. It will be emphasized throughout that I am aware that most decisions are made in committee or by brainstorming. This contradiction is an essential part of the problematic nature of work in mass-communication industries.

14 Information obtained through the interviews. At one time thirty-nine episodes were made each season, but rising costs and special productions account for the fewer series episodes being made at the present time. During the year the interviews took place, the average number of episodes for most shows was twenty-six; in 1968–1969 it dropped again to twenty-four.

15 See *Daily Variety*, Western Edition, July 14, 1967, p. 4.

16 One was a script consultant, one became an executive producer, another left for free-lance writing, and the fourth became a movie writer-producer.

17 The body of the letter read as follows:

At the present I am working on a doctoral dissertation under the direction of Professor Raymond Murphy of the Department of Sociology on the subject of television as a creative art form. One fundamental question of the project is how content is created and selected. In order to find out, it is necessary to interview knowledgeable people such as you in the industry.

Within the next week, I will telephone you to see if such an interview is possible. At that time I will be glad to answer any questions you might have to clarify the objective of the study. Your consideration of this request is much appreciated.

18 This information was provided by a personal communication from an informant working in Hollywood as a producer.

19 The letter sent to producers of children's programs was essentially the same as the first one. To fit this project the first sentence was changed and read as follows:

I will be in the Los Angeles area for a few weeks as a Consultant for the National Institute of Mental Health, which is conducting a study on the subject of television and social behavior. . . .

Social Criticism and Sociological Theory

The popular arts (motion pictures, jazz, magazine stories, radio and television plays, and variety shows), presented to their audience through the mass media of communication,[1] have been criticized so extensively and so frequently that it is unnecessary to repeat the entire discussion here. According to Herbert Gans, one reason its critics consider popular culture undesirable is that, unlike "high culture," it is mass produced by profit-minded entrepreneurs solely for the gratification of the paying audience. He further breaks this down into three specific charges:

1   Mass culture is an industry organized for profits.
2   In order for this industry to be profitable, it must create a homogeneous audience and a standardized product that appeals to this mass audience.
3   This requires a process in which the industry transforms the creator (communicator) into a worker on a mass assembly line; he must give up the expression of his own skills and values.[2]

Scholars in many fields, including sociologists and social psychologists, have made similar criticisms. For instance, C. Wright Mills has said, "between the intellectual and his potential public stand technical, economic and social structures which are owned and operated by others . . . if the intellectual becomes the hired man of an information industry, his general aims must of course be set by the decisions of others rather than his own integrity."[3]

While the critics disagree about whether the standardized product is imposed from above by those in control of the medium or is the expression of the masses' will,[4] they agree that the creator or communicator has become a tool of the economic system. They maintain that the system generates a low-level standardized product; the men who are working as creators in the media industries are manipulated by the system. Many books and articles about the television industry, in particular, express similar criticisms of both the medium content and the people responsible for this content. This criticism's main theme is "that while television is supposed to be 'free,' it has in fact become the creature, the servant, and indeed the prostitute of merchandising."[5] The commercial system, because it must appeal to mass tastes, limits the freedom of the technicians and artists producing for television to innovate and express themselves; in addition, the commercial system attracts persons of questionable skills and integrity, who use the medium for personal gain at the expense of the public.[6]

While discussion of the structure of commercial television and of the controls and limitations it imposes on the creative people in the industry (writers, directors, musicians, and producers) has mainly been limited to popular magazines and some scholarly publications, the questions raised are essentially sociological. The problem of the effects of social structures on various kinds of workers has been an ongoing concern since Marx.[7] Much recent research has focused on the intellectual, the scientist, and the professional, who have been employed in increasing numbers by organizations and bureaucracies. One main line of inquiry has emphasized the clash between the organization's goals, which are perceived as mere self-interest, and the interests of the professional, scientist, or intellectual, which are perceived as service toward his client or his discipline.

□

Robert Merton, William Kornhauser, Harold Wilensky, Theodore Caplow and R. J. McGee, Peter Blau and W. Richard Scott, and Alvin Gouldner are only a few who have considered the problems of the professional, the scientist, and the intellectual who have to satisfy the clients, the organizations, the publics of the organizations, and the intellectual disciplines.[8] In the case of the scientist, for instance, it is often suggested that the internalized goals of his discipline are in direct conflict with the objects of the work organization. Several studies have examined the career patterns of groups of scientists who work for either industrial organizations or governmental research agencies. It has been suggested that the scientist's orientation determines the amount and kind of conflict. If a scientist is "cosmopolitan" (more strongly oriented to the discipline's outside reference groups and with a relatively high commitment to skills), he is more apt to be in conflict with the goals of the organization, while a "local" is more loyal to the organization.[9]

In some ways the television producer might be compared to the scientist, professional, or intellectual working in an organization.[10] A career in television, as with a science, might mean different things to different individuals depending on their reference-group orientation. However, the model suggested by the above studies may be inadequate to describe the relationship of the producer to both his career and his industry, since it suggests that there are two conflicting positions, each with clearly defined goals. If the journalistic accounts of the television industry are correct, the goals of the networks (the organization) are far from clearly defined. While it is true that the main goal is to make a profit, and thus they are always striving to sell more advertising space, few standards or norms seem to be in operation from year to year; commercial television seems to change its requirements from season to season.

The basic philosophy expressed by those in the industry is giving the public what it wants; if one particular type of show seems to be popular one season, that type of programming will

□

be in demand the next season. However, as one critic, Neil Compton, noted, while television as a popular art form is "in some respects extremely conservative—Westerns, quiz-shows, and situation comedies we shall surely have always with us—it is in other respects amazingly oversensitive to minor shifts in intellectual and social climate."[11] Compton enumerates the changes in themes and content over the last three years, noting that:

> Since I began, less than three years ago, to keep an eye on what the major American networks were up to, I have seen nearly all hawkish TV newsmen turn into at least off-white doves. The Saturday-morning children's cartoons, which used to be oases of wit and sophistication in a desert of mediocrity, have given way to crudely drawn and morally repellent pseudoscientific space fantasies. . . . Teen-age rock shows, camp and Batman have fallen from favor; and drama has returned to the schedules after years of near-exile from prime time. . . . Protean television has suddenly begun to produce programs which assume the absurdity of existence and dedicate themselves to mocking it.[12]

The "public" is so large and seemingly so undifferentiated that it is difficult to determine by methods presently used what will appeal to the largest audience from year to year. The networks seem to have no basic programming philosophy other than trying to capture this large audience.[13] Thus, what will appeal to the networks is not determined by a basic artistic or ideological position, and the producer may not know what is expected of him from year to year because the organization itself does not know. The producer may be artistically and ideologically committed to a particular viewpoint on content and style that may conflict with the organization's goals one year but not the next, depending on what seems to be popular with the audience or what the network officials and advertising agencies think will be popular with the audience.

Like some scientists in organizations, some producers seem to have no or few conflicts with any part of the system. These

□

producers may work to achieve the highest rating (reach the largest audience) forfeiting or not forfeiting any of their artistic integrity, while others may feel stifled by the system in a number of ways. Those who are not in conflict with the system may desire to please the mass tastes of the necessary audience: they may wish only to gain material success and are willing to follow the required formula to do so; or they may consider producing an executive job, rather than a creative one, and thus be concerned only with turning out a technically good product. Others may be in conflict with the system and are only doing the work in order to gain a reputation so that they may someday be in a freer position creatively. Still others may be in conflict with the system only when they are required to produce stories that are artistically or ideologically unacceptable to them.

An examination of how the producer sees his position, to which reference groups he orients himself, and how he was recruited for his position may help either to dispel or to verify the myths and common assumptions that are made in the popular and elite press.

Network as Audience

Another main area of inquiry, which is very much related to the above, is whether the producers are more influenced by what they think the network and studios expect of them or what they think the viewing audience wants. What is known about decision-making in commercial television comes primarily from reports of those who have worked in the industry and are usually not only critical of but very dissatisfied with the system.[14] These reports suggest creators make decisions based both on what the network officials want and on their own intuitive judgment of what the audience wants. Conflicts seem to arise because the officials' judgment of what the audience wants is either ideologically unacceptable to the creator or questions his artistic judgment. There are few reports in print of the absence of conflict between the standards of the producers (and other creators) and the networks, although this may be the situation in the majority of the cases.

Some mass-communication researchers assume that the nature and significance of communications are determined in large part by the expectations of the communicator and the audience, which tend to be reciprocally related. It is suggested that "writers, broadcasters, and political speakers all select what they are going to say in terms of their beliefs about the audience."[15] Ithiel de Sola Pool and Irwin Shulman claim that "the audience, or at least those audiences about *whom the communicator thinks,* thus play more than a passive role in communication."[16] Raymond Bauer goes even one step further, claiming that the audience has much control over what is communicated, since it is the audience that selects what to read, listen to, or watch. However, he does qualify this to conform with his statements on the interrelationship of the communicator and the audience: "Communicators committed strongly to the subject matter may 'distort' their image of the prospective audience to bring it more in line with either their own values or the content of the incoming information and thereby reduce the 'audience effect.' "[17] Essentially, Bauer views communications as a transactional process in which both audience and communicator take important initiatives.[18]

Another group of studies gives a less important place to the audience. A series of studies has emphasized the criteria that media "gatekeepers" have used in deciding what to include or exclude from the press. Walter Gieber made a number of case studies on how editors select what to print from the items that come over the wire services.[19] There were no major differences in what was selected, only in the way the editors

□

explained and rationalized their behavior. Gieber also notes that the "pressures exerted by the reality of the newsroom bureaucratic structure" were common to all. These gatekeeper studies suggest that "news is what the newsmen make it,"[20] and, while readers are relatively unimportant in determining content, other reference groups (secondary audiences), such as other newsmen and the bureaucracy, are very important.

Similarly, Warren Breed points out that newsmen write primarily for their peers and superiors and not for their reader. The "newsman's source of rewards is located not among the readers who are manifestly his clients but among his colleagues and superiors. Instead of adhering to societal and professional ideals he redefines his values to the more pragmatic level of the news-room group."[21]

Breed did not consider what "image" the newsmen have of their audience or readers, since he was trying to find out whether the journalistic ideals to which the newsmen were socialized, their work setting, or the policies of the publishers were the most important in determining how newsmen focused their stories.[22] While Breed and Bauer seem to have arrived at quite different conclusions, both see the communicator operating in a social setting; both consider the communicator as part of a larger pattern; both present the communicator as sending his messages in accordance with the expectations and action of others in the same system.[23]

Thus, some television producers may be communicating to the secondary audiences (reference groups)—those in control of the medium, the network executives and advertising agencies—rather than directly to the primary viewing audience. Each network does maintain script control and has an office that censors scripts. A producer may learn policy and what is expected of him and select stories accordingly after a number of his scripts have been changed by the censor's office.

It is also possible that television producers make decisions

□

with only their own aesthetic standards as reference points. If a producer is successful it may be that his choices are in agreement with a number of subgroups and publics who make up the audience. If the producer is unable to communicate to a large enough segment of the audience, his series is dropped.

The Viewing Audience

There has been a good deal of discussion about feedback from the audience to the communicator. While this study was not primarily interested in how the audience communicates with producers, the problem must be considered. Communicators do not consider those who express approval or disapproval directly, through letter writing or face-to-face contact, as representative of the large audience that television series command. Indirect measures, such as marketing research and rating services, are methodologically inadequate.[24] The Nielsen system, which the networks consider the most revealing index of audience preference, even if it is statistically representative and it may not be, tells nothing about audience reaction to a show; it only tells how many sets were in use and to what channel they were tuned.[25]

The networks compete with each other for audience approval: "specials" and movies are scheduled in opposition to popular series in an attempt to draw a portion of the audience for one week. It is hoped that the next week this audience may return to watch the series. Since film makers, making an episode, often do not know when it will be shown, they find it difficult to imagine who might be part of their audience in advance. Only after they see the postprogram surveys conducted by the advertising agencies, do they have any empirical evidence of what kind of people were watching the show.

□

Most producers interviewed did know, for instance, something about the demographic characteristics of their audience because the main area on which marketing research has focused is audience composition. Logically, this makes sense for the advertiser, who is trying to reach specific groups who would be in the market for his product. Whether or not the producer keeps in mind the advertiser and the audience who might buy the product is an empirical question. It is not a simple one since few programs are sponsored by a single advertiser, and since sponsors may or may not remain on a program for the entire season.

Otto Larsen points out that decisions of what to print, show, and so forth, and the symbols that emerge are more than a product governed by artistic and professional considerations. These decisions are also molded by social, economic, and political norms that develop within an organization or penetrate it from outside.[26]

Denis McQuail makes a similar statement: "There is a need for both a systematic exploration of the effects of variations in structural context on the work of communicators and also for studies of the external political, economic and social pressures in the mass communication organization."[27]

Clearly, the large-scale production of mass-media messages entails a complex organization that operates in a broad social context of positive and negative pressures, which push and pull the mass communicator in various directions with respect to performance.

Therefore, a study of the communicator, if it is to be complete, would have to be a study of the entire communicating organization and the social context in which it operates. This, of course, was not possible. However, it was possible to study one occupational group of communicators, television producers, and to find out how much social constraint, social conflict, and social support the producer thinks comes from the organization, from the audience, and from other groups (either outside

33   Social Criticism and Sociological Theory

□

pressure groups or reference groups that represent the producer's artistic and professional interests) when decisions about content are being made.

Reference Groups

Reference groups are taken as a frame of reference for self-evaluation and attitude formation. According to Robert Merton, reference groups are any of the groups of which one is a member (these are comparatively few), as well as groups of which one is not a member (these are, of course, legion), all of which can become points of reference for shaping one's attitudes, evaluations, and behavior.[28]

Merton's definition must be further clarified to fit the present problem. Merton explains that men, in shaping their behavior and evaluations, frequently orient themselves to groups other than their own. He thinks this fact of orientation to nonmembership groups constitutes the distinctive concern of reference-group theory. Social scientists and laymen alike generally assume that the attitudes and behavior of an individual are greatly influenced by the groups to which he belongs. In a complex heterogeneous society it is also generally conceded that the different groups to which one person belongs may subscribe to different norms and beliefs. How an individual resolves the conflict between the orientations of these various groups is another major problem of reference-group theory.

In this study the identification of reference groups for the producers was obtained by direct questioning. Those reference groups to which the producer orients himself when he makes decisions about the content are of the most interest. The producer may be oriented to a number of groups that in no way influence his decisions in this area or he may be oriented to groups and individuals that the methods of this study are unable to discern. The groups of the most interest when the study was designed were (1) those in control of the medium: studio and network executives, sponsors and their representatives, the advertising agencies; (2) those groups that might represent artistic excellence or achievement; and (3) the viewing audience whom the producer may be trying to reach.

To work in the mass medium of television, a producer, unless he is very well known or very successful, must conform to the norms and policies of the industry. In some cases limitations and restrictions are placed on the producer that conflict with ethical or artistic norms to which he subscribed when he was in a different role in his other activities. Certain subjects are considered taboo in television, which are well accepted in other media. Stories on political or sexual themes and on other subjects that can be considered controversial are often out of the range for selection. It has been suggested that the thematic treatment should not alienate any interest group in the potential audience. However, in some years, in order to placate critics of the media, certain controversial subjects, such as race relations, communism, the selective-service regulations, can be considered fit subjects if they are handled in ways specified by the policy-makers. In other words, pressures from outside the industry may be so great that a controversial subject is considered a possible topic if the policy-makers are willing to antagonize one group in order to gain approval from another.

It is well known that television is constantly vulnerable to attack from censors and pressure groups. The producers, the writers, the directors (all of the people involved in selection of content), as well as the policy-makers, must be constantly on the alert to this reality, and decisions must be compromised in order to placate various groups. Certain rules are known and almost always adhered to by those in production. For instance, names of persons and places should not resemble any that might associate the characters with real people, living or dead, or real places. There should be no unsolicited commercial messages that suggest a payoff between the creator and a commercial enterprise. Street signs advertising products, for instance, must be avoided in outdoor scenes. This is relatively simple to learn but sometimes difficult to adhere to, and such rules can become a source of annoyance to the producer. Shows where much of the action takes place on the streets have to be particularly careful about these rulings. When an advertising sign does appear accidentally in a scene, the scene must be either cut out or redone, which can upset costs and time schedules.

Other things are not as easy to learn because they are less clearly defined. Certain sexual references are permitted or prohibited, depending on the show and the policy of the network. Sexual taboos are probably still the most numerous, and more producers are willing to fight for certain sexual references than for presentation of political or religious references. It is difficult to list the controls invoked by the censor offices since this is always in a state of flux.[29]

The policy of the networks fluctuates from more leniency to greater control. As the analysis of the data will point out, there is a constant struggle between those in control and the producers over such controversies, and the difficulty of predicting the outcome of such controversies is demonstrable. All producers conform to policies most of the time and most producers conform to known policy (either before the story is written or after the policy is defined) all of the time; but, unlike the newsmen of Breed's study,[30] only a few of the producers do so without complaint and without knowledge that they are doing so in conflict with norms that apply in the other media (for producers particularly the theater, network radio of the past which is often idealized, movies, novels, and short stories).

There are definitely conflicting group allegiances, and these various groups are identified and specified in the study. The reason producers give for orienting themselves to one reference group and not another is a major focus of this study.

Values

A value is a conception of what is believed to be desirable for either the individual or the group.[31] In this study certain values relating to the political beliefs, the artistic orientation, and the aspirations of the producer were explored. A section of the interview schedule is devoted to political activities, voting behavior, and attitudes toward government controls in television;[32] another section is devoted to artistic values.[33] This interest in the producer's values is related to the reference-group orientation of the study, since it is assumed that the reference group to which a producer is oriented also reflects his values. This inquiry sought to determine if the producer's values conflict with the decisions he makes, as much popular criticism suggests. A second reason for including questions concerning values is to see if the producer's values are reflected in his operations. It has been suggested in many studies and essays that success is a basic value in American society.[34] What constitutes success can vary from individual to individual and this is explored. For instance, if the producer will not buck policy in order to gain status achievement, it may be that the value of success is more important than any artistic values he might hold.

The two concepts defined, values and reference-group orientation, are basic to the formulation of the study. Other concepts such as political behavior and commitment, for instance, are defined in the chapters that follow. The purpose of the study was to examine the social ties of the working producer of filmed television series, especially those ties associated with his work

□

environment, to see if he was selecting content (stories and themes) to please himself, the networks (and possibly the production company), or the audience.

Conclusion

Critics have stated that the decisions of producers (and other creators for the mass media) are determined by the aims of others who have positions of authority and control. Because of this, the creators of the mass media have limited freedom to express their own talents and desires. Sociologists similarly have discussed how work structures impose limitations on certain occupations. For instance, scholars have examined the constraints imposed by organizations and bureaucracies on the formerly free professional, scientist, and intellectual. A similar but slightly different line of inquiry has focused on the role of communicators for the other mass media. These studies' findings suggest that communicators consider those in superior positions and their coworkers when they select stories and other materials more than they consider the audience for whom the communication is intended. Social psychologists, while insisting that all communicators must have some audience to whom they direct messages, also have argued that these messages need not be directed to the primary audience (readers, viewers, listeners), but to the secondary audiences (those in control of the medium, fellow communicators, and the like).

When selecting content, producers have to consider the organizations who finance and control the series, the craft groups who work alongside them, as well as the viewing audience. By finding out how much social constraint or conflict producers think comes from these various reference groups, it is hoped that the way they select content can be made more explicit.

□

NOTES

1 Stuart Hall and Paddy Whannel, *The Popular Arts: A Critical Guide to the Mass Media* (Boston: Beacon Press, 1964), esp. pp. 45–65.

2 Herbert J. Gans, "Popular Culture in America: Social Problem in a Mass Society or Social Asset in a Pluralist Society?" in Howard S. Becker, ed., *Social Problems: A Modern Approach* (New York: John Wiley and Sons, Inc., 1966), p. 553.

3 C. Wright Mills, *White Collar* (New York: Oxford University Press, 1953), p. 150.

4 See, for instance, Leo Rosten, "The Intellectual and the Mass Media: Some Rigorously Random Remarks," pp. 71–84, as compared to Ernest van den Haag, "A Dissent from the Consensual Society," pp. 53–62, and Hannah Arendt, "Society and Culture," pp. 43–52, in Norman Jacobs, ed., *Culture for the Millions* (Boston: Beacon Press, 1959).

5 Walter Lippmann, "The Problem of Television," *New York Herald Tribune*, October 27, 1959), reprinted in Harry J. Skornia, ed., *Television and Society: An Inquest and Agenda for Improvement* (New York: McGraw-Hill Book Co., 1965), p. 247.

6 See both Skornia, *op. cit.*, and *Public Television: A Program for Action. The Report of the Carnegie Commission of Educational Television* (New York: Bantam Books, Inc., 1967).

7 This literature is too vast to cite completely; it includes studies on how the factory system alienates workers as well as reports on the effects of bureaucracies on professionals and others. See Theodore Caplow, *The Sociology of Work* (New York: McGraw-Hill Book Co., 1964); Lee Taylor, *Occupational Sociology* (New York: Oxford University Press, 1968); and Richard H. Hall, *Occupations and the Social Structure* (Englewood Cliffs, N.J.: Prentice-Hall, Inc., 1969).

8 Robert K. Merton, *Social Theory and Social Structure*, rev. ed. (Glencoe, Ill.: Free Press, 1957); William Kornhauser (with assistance of Warren O. Hagstrom), *Scientists in Industry: Conflict and Accommodation* (Berkeley: University of California Press, 1962); Harold L. Wilensky, *Intellectuals in Labor Unions* (Glencoe, Ill.: Free Press, 1956); Theodore Caplow and R. J. McGee, *The Academic Marketplace* (New York: Basic Books, Inc., 1958); Peter M. Blau and W. Richard Scott, *Formal Organizations: A Comparative Approach* (San Francisco: Chandler Publishing Co., 1962); Alvin W. Gouldner, "Cosmopolitans and Locals: Toward an Analysis of Latent Social Roles—I," *Administrative Science Quarterly* 2 (1957): 281–306.

9 Gouldner, *op. cit.*, and Taylor, *op. cit.*, p. 283.

10 See Norman Kaplan, "Essay Review: Professional Scientists in Industry," *Social Problems* 13 (1965), pp. 88–97, for a review of the scientist in industry.

11 Neil Compton, "T.V. Specials," *Commentary*, June 1968, p. 69.

12 *Ibid.*, p. 69.

13 See Otto Larsen, "Social Effects of Mass Communications," in Robert E L. Faris, ed., *Handbook of Modern Sociology* (Chicago: Rand McNally, 1964), pp. 371–378. Also Bernard Berelson, "The Great Debate on Cultural Democracy," *Study in Public Communication* 3 (1961): 3–14.

14 For instance, see Fred Friendly, *Due to Circumstances Beyond Our Control* (New York: Random House, 1967); Merle Miller and Rhodes Evans, *Only You Dick Daring!* (New York: William Sloane Associates, 1964).

15 John Riley and Matilda Riley, "Mass Communication and the Social System," in Robert K. Merton, Leonard Broom, and L. S. Cottrell, Jr., eds., *Sociology Today* (New York: Basic Books, 1959), pp. 537–578.

16 Ithiel de Sola Pool and Irwin Shulman, "Newsmen's Fantasies, Audience, and Newswriting," in Lewis A. Dexter and David Manning White, eds., *People, Society, and Mass Communication* (New York: Free Press, 1964), p. 143.

17 Raymond Bauer, "The Communicator and the Audience," *Conflict Resolution* 2 (1958): 66–76.

18 *Ibid.*, p. 74.

19 Walter Gieber, "News Is What Newspapermen Make It," in Dexter and White, *op. cit.*, pp. 173–182.

20 *Ibid.*, p. 178.

21 Warren Breed, "Social Control in the Newsroom: A Functional Analysis," *Social Forces* 33 (1955): 326–335.

22 Warren Breed, in his unpublished dissertation, does discuss reading publics. See Warren Breed, "The Newspaperman, News, and Society" (Ph.D. diss., Columbia University, 1952).

23 Riley and Riley, *op. cit.*, p. 567.

24 See Skornia, *op. cit.*, chap. 6, "Ratings and Mass Values," pp. 120–142.

25 See Appendix C for a full discussion of the Nielsen ratings.

26 Larsen, *op. cit.*, p. 376.

27 Denis McQuail, *Towards a Sociology of Mass Communications* (London: Collier-Macmillan Limited, 1969), p. 67.

28 Robert Merton (with Alice S. Rossi) "Contributions to the Theory of Reference Group Behavior," in Merton, *op. cit.*, pp. 225–275.

□

29 See Appendix B for the code of the National Association of Broadcasters, which is used as a guideline by the three major networks.

30 Warren Breed, "Social Control in the Newsroom," p. 328.

31 Values are defined according to their usual meaning in sociology and anthropology. See Clyde Kluckhohn, "Values and Value-Orientations in the Theory of Action," in Talcott Parsons and Edward A. Shils, eds., *Toward a General Theory of Action* (New York: Harper & Brothers, 1951), p. 395.

32 See Appendix A, Questions 26 through 30.

33 Questions concerning values and beliefs about artistic matters were not as direct. See Appendix A for the entire questionnaire.

34 For instance, Robert Merton, "Social Structure and Anomie," in Merton, *op. cit.*, pp. 121–159.

41   Social Criticism and Sociological Theory

The Work Setting

This chapter explains what a series is and how it differs from other forms of television entertainment and details the preproduction process. Attention is given to development of the series form, the merger of film making and broadcasting, the role of the networks and advertisers in deciding whether a series will go on the air, and some other programming decisions.

The functions involved in the making of a film series can be divided into two major categories: those that are outside the production company—the business-type operations and decisions—and those that are within the production company or crew—the creative functions of actual film making. These are very much interrelated, but it is possible to separate them analytically.[1] This chapter primarily deals with functions that involve the sponsor and with the business or profit-making aspects that are more the concern of those outside the production crew. The dependency of the working producer on the institutions that have developed in the industry's structure is evident throughout this study, but this dependency is nowhere more obvious than in the preproduction selection process.

The Television Series

The television series is a serialized dramatic show, usually one-half hour or one hour long, which appears on a weekly or biweekly basis.[2] The main characters continue from episode to episode; each segment or episode is usually a complete adventure revolving around the main characters. The series itself has a basic story concept that helps determine the content of each segment. This concept is usually relatively simple so that various stories can be told from week to week. Among the most popular themes have been the adventures of a single parent trying to raise a child or children, detective and mystery stories, westerns with sheriffs in frontier towns, and the adventures of people in "glamour occupations" such as law and medicine.[3] A successful series principally requires a story broad enough to allow a number of adventures or incidents that will fit both the main characters and the story concept.[4] It is difficult to categorize the series into various types, since many can be considered mixed, but most reviewers and people in the industry distinguish four major categories: western, detective or mystery, situation comedy, and dramatic series (a catchall category).

The series, along with the variety or comedy show, the quiz show, the dramatic anthology, the feature film and sporting events, make up the entertainment programs that are televised during the prime viewing hours in the evening.

The television series differs from the variety or comedy show in several respects. The series for the most part is filmed, while the variety hours are usually taped. Until recently, there was much more freedom in both camera techniques and editing with film, but now, because of new techniques and equipment, these differences are minimal. However, film is still easier to ship and store than is a taped episode. In addition, a film can be shown both in the movie theaters and on the television screens. The format of a variety show is quite different from a series; in fact, the variety show is much like vaudeville except that it often revolves around one or more star performers. While several variety shows have also used the series idea by showing repeated sketches of fictional characters, this is relatively uncommon.

The dramatic series differs from the dramatic anthology in that the latter does not have continuous characters or a basic

□

story concept. At one time there were a number of such anthologies on the air, but during the season when the first study was conducted (1967–1968) only one such show remained. However, there were several "specials" that could qualify as anthologies. Some of these were adaptations of old movies and plays done on tape. None of the people engaged in such productions were part of the sample; however, many of the producers interviewed had produced and written drama of this type in the past.

The anthology has been replaced partly by the series, but mostly by the feature film. Many of the feature films shown have been rereleased for television after they first appeared as first- or second-run motion pictures in movie theaters. They were made for the large screen without thought of the commercial break. At the present time, because the feature film is very popular with audiences and because it is in short supply, a number of feature films are being made specifically for television; these resemble anthology drama more than series. These feature films are often shown in the movie theaters as well as on television in order to make a profit for the production company involved. These are not usually shown in theaters in the United States, but are distributed in Europe, South America, and Asia. Also, an occasional series story will be made in two parts, each one hour in length; then these two episodes are made into one feature film, which is distributed in foreign markets. One exception was an "U.N.C.L.E." movie, which appeared in the United States in movie theaters as well as on television.[5]

The series episode, the dramatic anthology, and the feature film made for television have certain qualities in common, distinguishing them from other types of dramatic production. All drama made for television has to follow the convention of fifteen-minute segments that was established in radio drama. The series, more than the other kinds of filmed drama mentioned, represents the merger between broadcasting and film making.

Since commercial television was developed and sponsored by the radio networks, it was originally viewed by its developers as "radio with pictures."[6] The arbitrary segments that are multiples of fifteen minutes in length, the commercial and station breaks, and the type of programming predominating in commercial television, all have their precedent in commercial radio. The quiz shows, sports events, political broadcasts, comedy shows, and news broadcasts, as well as the series, all were part of commercial radio programming, but only the series incorporates the rigid time schedules of radio broadcasting with moviemaking techniques. The requirements that commercial breaks must be inserted after twelve minutes of dramatic presentation and that each program must be a multiple of fifteen minutes in length severely limit the writers, directors, and producers.

The other distinguishing characteristics are due mainly to the time limit on production and to the limited funds available for television drama in comparison with films made for the theater. An hour television drama, whether it is series segment or one play of an anthology series, is filmed in a maximum of six days at a cost of approximately $175,000. The feature film made for television is usually two hours in length (actually ninety-six minutes of film is devoted to the story) and may cost as much as $1 million.[7] This is obviously more costly than the series and other drama. However, even such films are considerably less expensive than a class A motion picture, and certainly they are made in a much shorter time.

One of the reasons usually given for the development of the dramatic series on film is that it was necessary to fill the many program hours that stations are on the air. (A few stations in the larger cities are now on for almost twenty-four hours a day, and most stations must fill from ten to sixteen hours.) Originally, most drama on television was "live." The only way live programming could be recorded for more than a single viewing was by filming it. The process of filming live drama, known as kinescope, had several disadvantages. The quality of these films was extremely poor. In addition, union contracts at that time did not allow films to be used more than once within thirty days of the original production; thereafter, it had to be retired or destroyed.[8] (This was before the development of videotape.) Direct film production of a play or story was both better in quality and not as restricted by union agreement as were the kinescopes. Although the unions had agreements (and still do) with the production companies and networks to receive a percentage of the receipts from each showing (known as residuals), it is much more profitable to rerun a film a second or third time than to reproduce drama "live" or to fill an unused hour with other types of new programming. When a series, for instance, is filmed and a large number of episodes made, it is possible to show these series either on prime time on nonnetwork local stations or on the network stations during the day and late night hours as reruns. This is the aim of almost every producer when he originates a series, but in order to qualify as a show that can be rerun, several years' supply of episodes are necessary.

Networks and Hollywood

Most of the filmed dramatic television series are produced and filmed in the Los Angeles area. Network executives in New York actually select programming to fill the network time. The shows and most of the ideas for the shows, as well as the film work, come from the same Hollywood studios that once hummed with feature-film activities before the advent of television.[9] The rise of television has had the greatest impact on the film industry in the United States. After fighting against the new medium, notably by withholding its vast stock of old feature films, Hollywood capitulated within a few years. Stocks of old film were sold to the networks and independent stations. By 1956

□

ABC had bought $3 million worth of film from the J. Arthur Rank Organizations, and all of the new programs that year were made on film. Because the film-production companies in Hollywood were suffering financially (box-office receipts were down), independent agencies were able to rent studio space and develop and package low-budget series, usually thirteen weeks long.[10] However, because such programs must be sold to advertisers who are more concerned with audience appeal than with cost, the larger studios and the networks themselves have been able to once more capture film production. There are only a few independent companies operating profitably in Hollywood at this time. Most of the studios have changed hands since the heyday of Hollywood, and the networks have started to produce film for both dramatic television and theater. CBS, for instance, has taken over the former Republic Studios in the Los Angeles area and is using the space for both series production and feature film making. Universal Studios was bought by the Music Corporation of America agency and is in full operation both as a producer of series and as a maker of feature films for television. The agency started producing series because it had under contract a number of performers who were no longer working when the movie industry went into its decline in the first part of the 1950's.[11]

As stated earlier, the series is a television form that was borrowed from radio. The situation comedies, the western, the detective and family shows, all were presented on radio and were transferred to television. Several former dramatic radio series were translated to television shows directly with little change in format, for example, "Gunsmoke" and "Dragnet." The series are considered the bread and butter of both the networks and the Hollywood studios. However, there is some indication that the series will no longer be the bulk of the prime-time television fare. At its height (1960) there were seventy-six series on the air during the prime viewing hours. This does not include the "daytime serials"[12] but only those that appear from 7:00 P.M. (or

□

7:30 P.M.) to 10:30 P.M. (or 11:00 P.M.). The trend at this time is toward full-length (two-hour) films made especially for television. The reason usually given for this new trend is that the "longform" attracts and keeps the audience of sometimes more than 30 million people in a single night and thus gives much higher Nielsen ratings (see Appendix C) than any of their competition.[13]

During the 1967–1968 season there were only fifty-seven series (in the prime-time hours) on the three networks compared to the seventy-six in 1960. By 1970 the season started with approximately forty-five series. Whether or not this means that the series is a dying form is not yet clear; however, since television entertainment forms seem to run in cycles, the predictions that television is changing at this time can be considered valid.[14]

The feature-length film does have several things in common with the series. Besides the fact that both are made with the commercial breaks in mind, the most important similarity is that all films made for television must be sold to a network (or possibly a syndication firm) before they can be seen. At this time practically no film is being made without some financing from the networks (this will be discussed in more detail in the section to follow on the pilot film). At one time (in the 1950's) it was possible to make a film and sell it without network approval, but because of the rising costs, this is no longer true. Both the series pilot and the television movies are financed by the packaging firm who produced the film and by the network who options for its production.[15]

Pilot Films

In former years most of the series that appeared on the air were presented to the networks for purchase in the form of a pilot film. The pilot film is still used as the primary method of selection of new series, although several series have been bought without it. Fewer pilots are being made than formerly for several reasons. The obvious one is that fewer series are being programmed. The second reason is that the feature-length movie described earlier is often used with a dual purpose. The movie is not only shown as it was intended, but also serves as a pilot film for a new series. *To Catch a Thief*, made in 1967, is an example of a feature film that became a series. Since pilot films are often longer than a series segment and are produced in a more costly manner, it makes sense for the studios to go to the two-hour length for pilots, since they can be shown in film houses if they are not sold as a series. In any case, whether the pilot is made as a feature film or as a pilot only, it is a "showpiece," and both the networks who finance part of the production and the production companies who make the film are aware that the series will be made for less money, in a shorter length of time, and will therefore be less polished. All three major networks finance pilots and, although there is some variety in procedure among the networks, the steps that a producer or writer (or others) with an idea must go through before presenting the finished product to the network that finances the pilot for final approval or disapproval are similar.

The making of pilots has been explored in the popular press and by various people in the industry. The most famous exposé of pilot making by Merle Miller and Rhodes Evans, *Only You Dick Daring!* has been well publicized. To quote Miller:

> *Only You, Dick Daring!* largely deals with the intrigue, insanity black magic involved in the production of *one* pilot for one fifty-two minute television series called *Calhoun*. . . . The script for *Calhoun* was totally rewritten at least nineteen times by me; it was partially rewritten by Evans 782,946.17 times. It was tampered with unnumbered times by people I have never seen and by people I have seen.[16]

In the end the pilot film was made but not purchased as a series. Several producers interviewed for this study suggested that

□

the story presented by Miller and Evans is true. Not all writers and producers, however, go through the horrendous experiences that Miller and Evans describe. From the interviews and from reading the trade journals, it is possible to give direct accounts about the necessary steps from the story idea to the finished product on the air. Following are two separate accounts of the steps an idea must go through. The first is an account of an idea in process when the interview took place; the second is a completed project that did not meet approval.

1. A producer, who worked for a production company that is owned by one of the major networks in partnership with a very successful executive producer, had an idea for a series. Even though the production company was owned in part by one of the major networks this was no guarantee program ideas would eventually be produced.

Ideas for series are closely guarded and although several producers who were interviewed shared some of their ideas for stories, it was with the understanding that such ideas would not appear in printed form. However, this producer's account of the process of getting a series accepted can be repeated without divulging the story line. This particular idea was unusual; the main theme dealt with the political activities of three young people under the guidance of an older man. Before a script can be written, the story idea is presented to one of the network's executives, usually a man in charge of programming. This is done by conversation because under the Guild rules nothing should be presented in written form without a contract. At the time of the interview, the producer had presented his idea through his agent, and the network had contracted first for a story presentation and later for a pilot script. The script was in the process of being written.

Even after a script is written and paid for by the networks, there is no guarantee that the network will finance a pilot film. The story being considered had a much more "liberal" theme

□

than is usually considered safe by the networks, and the producer was not optimistic that he would receive the go-ahead for the pilot. Since he was in constant communication with the network people, he was able to judge their reaction to parts of the script before it was completed. Besides the reservations because of the political theme, he was informed that the network was hesitant to finance the pilot because another well-known producer also had a similar idea that was at the pilot stage at the same time. Both the network and the producer being interviewed were concerned that the other producer might think that his idea was intentionally stolen; therefore, this producer was changing the script so that no one could accuse him of plagiarism, deliberate or otherwise.

When the script is completed, it is the property of the network. They have the option of contracting for rewrites if they are not satisfied, either from the original author or someone else they may bring in. If and when they are satisfied with the script, they decide whether or not a pilot film should be made. If the pilot film is made, it is shown to the various advertisers (actually the advertising agencies representing the sponsors) to see if one or more of them want to buy advertising time spots for that program. If the advertisers buy the idea and the network executives think that the series will appeal to the audience, the network will place an order with the production company or independent producer for a certain number of additional scripts and films to be produced. This order may be for as few as four or six scripts but the usual minimum order is thirteen. It is unusual for the network to order shows for a whole season (twenty-four to thirty scripts).

The arrangements between the production companies and the producers do vary. In the case under discussion, if the network does not like the script when it is completed, the production company has several other options. They can try to get other financing and make the film as a theatrical or feature film to be shown in movie theaters. If the pilot is made but not sold, the two-hour pilot can be shown as a feature film, though usually not for distribution in the United States. All these possibilities did not exist a few years ago when the pilot either sold or it did not. Most pilots do not sell and therefore are rarely seen by any other audience than the businessman interested in programming. One network has for several seasons put the unsold pilots on during the summer months as time fillers. Very rarely does a pilot shown in this manner receive enough direct audience approval to justify making it into a series. The pilot often becomes the property of the network that finances it, and if no additional shows are ordered, it is almost impossible to show it on the other networks. In the case under discussion the final decision was made not to present the series on the air. In fact, the script never was made into a pilot film.

2. The following account is one producer's story of the difficulty of getting a television series on the air, reprinted from *Daily Variety* (Western Edition). It should be noted that, although NBC did order additional scripts to be written, the production company did not make any additional films, and the series at the time of this writing was considered dead.

Lee Rich today detailed his travails in trying to get the illfated "Sheriff Who?" through the bureaucratic web (network) mills last spring and summer. . . . Rich traced the "Who?" story from the time it was first suggested to him by writer Larry Cohen in Hollywood on March 8, 1966. After lining up writers, Rich took a treatment on NBC programming veeppee Mort Werner and Grant Tinker, then in charge of NBC West Coast programming.

They liked it on first sight. Rich lined up actor John Astin with considerable difficulty at $6,000 for the pilot, $3,500 per episode plus residuals. NBC agreed to pay $125,000 toward production of the pilot for which they received 45% ownership and agreed to give Rich a series price of $75,000 per original and $16,500 per repeat. He also hired director Jerry Paris at

□

$7,500 to direct the pilot, plus a bonus of $2,500 if the series sold. Dick Shawn was hired as guest star of the pilot at $7,500 for the eight days' work plus transportation from New York and $50 per diem living expenses.

Things began to get snarled, Rich related, when Tinker was transferred to New York and Herb Schlosser was put in charge of coast programming for NBC. Then Tinker quit NBC entirely.

Rich related the pilot got a good response in a private theater test, and he showed it to NBC execs (who raved) and finally to NBC prexy Don Durgin. "His comments," Rich said, "were guarded."

From there, "Who?" was turned over to the NBC sales and programming departments and Rich found himself out in the cold in a welter of buck-passing. His old agency friends refused to return his phone calls. NBC finally let the series option drop on March 1, 1967, and the next day Rich took it to CBS. "It was the second best pilot we have seen this year," a CBS program exec said, "next to our own *He and She*, but our program schedule is locked." The head of programming at ABC said: "It was a great pilot, but I don't think it could make a series."

NBC ran the pilot as a pre-season special and got a rave review from *Life* magazine. NBC picked up another option and ordered three more scripts.[17]

New Ideas—Where They Come From

While the number of pilot films being made is considerably less than it once was, the pilot film is still the major vehicle for presenting new ideas to the advertisers. All the major and minor film-production companies devote some time and effort to the development of new ideas. Several of the producers interviewed had arrangements with the networks to make several pilots during the year with the guarantee that one would be definitely bought for production for the next season. For instance, one production

□

company had a contract with a major network for four ideas a year (story presentations), plus one hour of guaranteed television time during the year; others interviewed were developing pilots with financial backing from the networks, but in their case there was no guarantee that the pilot would be sold and more films ordered.

Ideas for new series can come from any number of sources, but they are more likely to come from the large production companies and Hollywood studios than elsewhere. Most often writers or producers will present ideas to executive producers or officials of the production companies, who then decide whether the ideas merit further consideration. Practically the entire sample had at one time presented an idea to be considered for a series. Many of them had produced pilot films in the past or were in the process of developing a pilot at the time of the interview that had already been approved and financed for filming. Table 3–1 gives the details on the various producers who were interviewed.

TABLE 3–1   Producers' Ideas—Pilot Films

No ideas	15
One or more ideas (story presentations only)	14
One pilot from his idea	5
More than one pilot	25

Of the thirty producers who were either making a pilot film or had made one, only twelve had had their ideas finally made into a series. However, most ideas for television series are not original ideas from one man. This point should be emphasized because it is very important to understand the decision-making process throughout the industry. Most ideas are born in committees. Most often a number of men together brainstorm new ideas; some of the most successful series on television were the products of such brainstorming. A now prevalent way of developing new series is to turn successful theater films into series. This practice is particularly common in the bigger studios: for instance, in 1968 Paramount had three pilots in production based on former movies—*Barefoot in the Park, House Boat,* and the *Mating Season.* Another successful method of developing new series is to spin-off characters and stories from a successful series. "Gomer Pyle," for instance, was a spin-off from the "Andy Griffith Show." In this way it is possible to by-pass the pilot because an episode from the successful series serves as a pilot for the new series.

When the producers were questioned on new ideas, several of them were hazy on how the series actually was formulated. This was particularly true of producers who had not been with the shows from their inception, but even producers who were very familiar with the show said that it was not always possible to give credit to any one person as the originator. The credit seen by the audience often is given to the man who owns the show or seemed to be the most instrumental in presenting the idea. Ideas go through so many stages and changes before they are finally in the pilot stage and often even afterward that it is rare for a series to be the creative effort of a single man.[18] While the final decisions for the programs rest with the networks, the network officials do not often have ideas for the series.[19] The packaging companies (both independent and the larger studios) are the primary sources of ideas for the evening series.

Saturday-Morning Shows

Shows aimed specifically at children and broadcast on Saturday mornings are selected and produced similarly to those shows broadcast at prime evening hours. The animated cartoon shows

□

that personify animals or animate human subjects differ from those shows that use live actors in technique but are similar in other respects. However, both types differ from the evening shows because the segments are shorter, with stories completed in ten minutes rather than the twenty-four minutes typical of evening shows. Each half-hour program is divided into two ten-minute stories with ten minutes reserved for commercial advertising.

If the Saturday television schedules of cities in the United States that are outlets for all three major network were reviewed, it would be noted that starting as early as 7:30 A.M. or 8:00 A.M., the programming is aimed mainly at the younger audience. A few programs are reruns of series that had been evening shows of former seasons, but most had been made within the last few years specifically to be shown on Saturday mornings. Saturday morning has been devoted to children's programs for some years, but it is only within the last two or three years that that particular time period has become important to both the producers and advertisers. Both the producers of Saturday-morning shows and the networks consider the time period "prime time," comparable to the evening time slots aimed at the general or adult audiences. Early in 1970 special persons were assigned by the networks to be in charge of children's programming, whereas formerly daytime program division had assumed responsibility for such programs.

There are approximately twelve hours of television time available for the children's programs under discussion, four hours on each network. Because the time available is relatively limited and a number of the hours are used for reruns, the actual number of new shows produced is small, although growing. Also, as each network becomes concerned with children's programs, they tend to contract for new films rather than continue to use old adult evening shows and cartoon features originally made for movies.

All three networks operate in a similar manner when

determining the number of segments to be produced for a series. When a series is purchased from a production house or an independent film producer, the producer signs a contract to make seventeen half-hour episodes or thirty-four segments. The network usually guarantees that each of the seventeen episodes will be used six times in two years. Occasionally, a guarantee will be for eight showings in three years, but this is rare. After the initial run of one or two years, an especially popular program might be shown during the second and third years with several new episodes to spice up the offerings.

Although a producer of daytime Saturday-morning shows makes less money per program sold than does a producer of evening film series, he is able to build a larger audience through word of mouth acclaim and good critical reviews. Evening television, while more lucrative, is also more risky. When a production house or a producer sells a show to the network, the contract is usually for eleven or thirteen episodes with an option for the same number to finish a season. There is no guarantee that a series will finish a season and even if it does, no guarantee that it would be renewed for the following year. When a series fails, does not finish the season, or is not renewed for the following year, it is shelved and not used again; thus, there is no chance to build an audience and thereby be revived. Because of the high cost of prime-time series production, such programs are financial failures unless enough episodes are rerun either during the daytime by the networks or in the evenings by local stations who purchase the series from a syndicating company. To be syndicated requires at least two years' supply of films and preferably more because the more episodes made and shown on prime time, the more likely the series would make a profit for the production house that produces it.

Although the profit is smaller for children's programming and the number of hours available for showing is smaller than for evening adult viewing, once a series is sold, the chance for failure is practically zero. Not only may such a series build an audience, but it is also more likely to be syndicated after being used a number of times on Saturday mornings by a network. In addition, some children shows can be revived often because of their timeless character and the ever-changing audience.

Most of the shows appearing on the air on Saturday mornings are also filmed in Los Angeles. However, they are rarely filmed in the large Hollywood studios, but in studios owned or rented by the independent companies that produce the films. Animated shows can be filmed in a small space and, because of this, a new producer can easily find adequate space for the artists and film work for relatively small amounts of money, thereby remaining independent of the larger Hollywood production companies. An ordinary suite of offices could be used as a studio because the equipment used to film animated cartoons can be easily moved. Also when in use, the equipment is stationary; therefore making an animated film does not require the large sound stages that are necessary for live-action filming.

There are three major and several small independent companies that now share the twelve hours of television on Saturday mornings. The three major companies have as their primary function the making of all types of animated films, including not only the cartoon shows, but also animated titles used for live drama, both television and films. A large portion of their operation involves the making of animated commercial advertisements. They make their facilities available on a contract basis to producers of educational films, which are shown on public television or in the schools. At times such films are created in their studio under the direction of those contracting for them in the same way the networks contract for a series.

There are almost no animated films being made to be shown in theaters at this time. The producers of animated films try to sell the major studios ideas that could be made into full-length animated films of the type that the Disney Studio made so

□

successfully in the past, but as an ongoing operation, that source of revenue is closed. In addition, the short films that used to be part of the film packages sold to theater owners in the past are rarely made. Today, the primary buyer for the animated cartoon film is the networks. Once in a while an advertiser will contract directly for a show and syndicate it in various cities throughout the country. One show, refused by the networks, was later syndicated by a leading toy manufacturer and had great success, playing in 103 cities for several years and still being shown in forty-two cities. Such shows are not as profitable for the producer as those purchased by the networks because the syndicating company takes so much of the profit.

How Saturday-Morning Programs Are Selected

There are three major ways in which Saturday-morning shows are created. First, a network creates an idea and the studio develops it; the studio is then responsible for each episode based on the idea purchased, although the original idea comes from the network itself. Second, the studio creates an idea and sells it to the network; development of the segments is handled by the writers and animators with network approval. Third, the studio buys a property from someone outside, which is then developed in-house before presentation to the networks; instances of such ideas could be a well-known book or character.

The spin-off is fairly common in children's programming as well as in evening shows. For instance, a show on the air can provide the means to introduce new characters and plots in a segment that later can become a new series with an identity of its own. Of course, the characters and story line presented in this way must meet with network approval but, if they do not, little has been lost. The production company sold the episode and made a profit. They also do not go through the usual approval procedures for new ideas, which often entails the investment of a great deal of money and time. They can skip the story-board or pilot-film stage because the regular scheduled program provides the means for presenting new material. Once in a while, the networks themselves may pick up a subsidiary character in a regularly scheduled show and contract for a series based on it, but more often the character is introduced in a deliberate attempt by the studio to attract network interest.

According to one respondent, ideas are actually created on both levels, coming from the studios (production houses) or the networks. Between the two the producer hopes to get an agreement on an idea. Thus, a production house might create twenty shows and, if it is fortunate, a network might like one or two. Conceivably, this can sometimes be turned around with the networks saying to a producer: "Why don't you do this kind of show?" However, regardless of where the ideas come from, the network must approve of them or the show is not likely to get on the air.

The studio or production house, therefore, does not necessarily create the shows they produce but just the ideas for the shows, with the actual creativity, that is, the series' concepts, coming from a variety of sources. For example, in the 1970–1971 season one of the three big production houses produced two series for viewing that originated from show ideas given to the company for execution by the network contracting for their production. The production company had submitted about twelve new show ideas, none of which met with network approval, but the network wanted to use the talent and facilities of this production company and gave their own ideas to be developed by the company's staff artists and writers.

One producer noted that although he had staff writers, not one had ever come up with any ideas that were sold to the networks. This particular production house, as is the case with several in the children's programming field, is owned and operated by two men, one of whom has been an animator since the beginning of his career. This particular producer explained that he and his partner either come up with the story ideas themselves or find properties they like and translate them into usable form for animated film series or, at times, specials. The staff writers then do the "actual nuts and bolts working out." On the rare occasion that a famous author's idea is purchased, the author himself may be asked to participate in the translation process from story idea to story board.

In selling animated programs, few pilot films are made. The series are bought by the networks from story-board presentations (a series of cartoon drawings that presents the characters and some dialogue). Voices might also be recorded to give the networks some idea how the characters will sound. Only the lesser known independent houses are ever forced into making an entire film before it is bought.

This sales situation differs from the making of live-action films. As pointed out earlier, unless an idea generates as a "spinoff," the networks usually want a pilot film (often in the form of a full-length movie). The pilot film is often pretested or previewed at one of the theaters operated for this purpose by the networks themselves or by the advertiser. Animated shows are usually previewed by showing a series of drawings to children whose verbal reactions to the characters are recorded.

In order to sell, an idea must go through certain stages, the most important of which is network approval. The networks, to repeat, are the most important buyer of ideas. Advertisers buy and sponsor specials and will at times syndicate series, but they are a small market compared to the networks, although the process of selling to advertisers is similar to that of selling to networks. In the following account a producer describes how he goes about selling ideas each season. Producers interested in making specials go through similar procedures with the advertising agencies for cereal accounts and toy manufacturers, who sponsor the largest number of children's programs.

Early in September we came into the network with twenty-five or thirty ideas. Generally an idea is represented by a page or two of written material and possibly a sketch or two of the characters that will be involved in a potential series. If the networks are interested in what you have to show them, they will enter into a development deal with you. They will put up x number of dollars to develop a story board, have you record voices and characters. The well-established houses do not have to make pilot films. The networks know the quality of their work. They are only interested in content and what the idea is. My partner and I sit around and develop ideas and characters and hand them down to the staff. After the story board and voices are recorded, we go back to the network with the finished product. This is usually about now (January). If they like what we did, we get a purchase order for seventeen episodes. If not, too bad—no sale.

At this stage of the production process, the producers consider only the networks and the advertisers as the audience for whom they develop and create ideas. The kind of programs popular with the networks in a particular year is uppermost in their minds. Although they know that children are the target audience, they also know that it is the networks and particularly the programming men who must be satisfied. Of course, shows that never pass this stage, this audience, never get the chance to be popular with children because obviously the children would never see them.

The only purpose of all programming is to sell products and therefore advertising time. If a production house itself is willing to invest its own money on a show, it can be conceived, developed, and translated to the drawing board and film without considering the advertiser or network. However, few houses are willing or able to do this too often because of the money involved. There is really very little chance that a show made as a "speculation" will ever get on the air. Occasionally, one or two "specials" made this way have been bought either by a network or studio, but they are rare cases. Only very successful producers or those just starting out in independent production, who need to advertise their skills and craftmanship, can risk the expense of producing a whole show without some support from the networks or advertisers.

The Advertiser

At one time the advertisers and the advertising agencies were very powerful in deciding what would go on the air.[20] Although the pilots are shown to the advertiser, and usually those that the advertiser will sponsor are bought, the networks have been known to buy pilots that have only moderate success in selling time with the idea that as audience interest increases, more sponsors will be enticed into partial sponsorship. Advertising agencies no longer finance and develop pilots as they once did. Up until 1967 a few of the more prominent sponsors were still making an occasional pilot, but even though these pilots had a guaranteed sponsor, often they were not bought by the networks. This is viewed by several of the producers interviewed as a mixed blessing. Whereas formerly there were two hundred potential buyers for a series, now there are only three potential buyers for an idea and only one for a pilot, the network who finances the filming. The main reason why sponsors no longer develop series is that the series are rarely sponsored by a single advertiser. The increased cost of both the pilot and the segments have made it financially unfeasible to have a single company produce a show; at the present time the sponsor buys time spots instead. This is called the magazine concept of television advertising because it is similar to buying ads that are interspersed

□

among the stories and articles in a magazine, but it is not a true magazine concept. In England and other countries it is up to the network and not the sponsor to decide where to place the commercial, just as a magazine does.

While the authority of the advertiser is limited, they still have some power. The producers related several incidents where an actual film segment for a series was made but not shown on the air because the advertiser did not approve. This happens rarely, but it is not rare to have the sponsor through his representatives in the advertising agencies disapprove of part of a script prior to filming.

The decision-making process in the television industry has to be understood in the general construct of commercial television. The main function of the entertainment programs generally is to attract large audiences in order to sell products; therefore, if a show does not attract a large enough audience, it often will be dropped. The advertiser wants a certain number of viewers for his money; in fact, the "cost per thousand" viewers often determines whether the advertiser will stay with a show. The number of viewers usually is determined by the Nielsen ratings. In addition, the program has to fit the client. Some sponsors are willing to stay with a show even if the ratings show a smaller number of viewers than is usually considered a good return for the advertising dollar because the particular viewing audience is more likely to buy their products. As an example, a hair-coloring company continues to sponsor a show starring a very attractive young woman, even though the show does have a low Nielsen rating, because the audience is made up of young women, who are potential buyers of their product.

Deciding what shows to sponsor before the season begins is another problem. Here the advertising agencies consider themselves in the business of placing money on an unknown quantity. The agencies have programming men who select what the clients should buy.[21] Decision-making in this area was once the job of intuitive programming men, but now it is gradually being assumed by fact-minded media men who use computers and statistical data as well as pretesting in special theaters before deciding what shows to buy. Even with scientific methods, success at prediction is a fitful thing. One trade journal suggested the "art of placing money in network television programs before the season begins is not much closer to perfection than the art of betting on the horses."[22] Pretesting a show before it goes on the air is very difficult, and it is usually the advertising agencies that use such services. Agencies either have their own marketing-research operations or contract such services from firms specializing in market research.

One such television testing service advertises in its brochure that it evaluates the appeal of program ideas, that is, the basic concept around which a television program is produced. They make several claims: to be able to forecast audience composition by sex and age with reasonable reliability, to have predicted accurately 70 percent of the time in measuring 136 program ideas.[23] This is better predictive ability than it would seem at first glance, since the mortality rate for new shows is very high. In the 1964–1965 season 60.5 percent of all the new shows did not continue into the following season. The next season the success of the new shows was somewhat better; 57.6 percent were not continued. In 1966–1967 the rate of failure again rose to 65.7 percent. Since the risks of a new show failing are so high, most agencies try to spread the risks. While new programs have a high fatality rate, the shows that continue into the second year are more apt to remain on the air a third season or longer. Table 3–2 shows clearly the survival record of shows.[24]

It is much easier, therefore, to obtain sponsorship for shows going into their second and third years.

For the 1967–1968 season (when the study was done), there were only thirty-four new shows (twenty-four series). There was obviously no guarantee that any would last the season.

□

TABLE 3-2   Renewal of Shows on the Air in 1966

Shows:	Renewed for 1967–1968	Rejected[a]
New 1966 (N = 35)	12	23
Carry-overs in 1966 (N = 58)	47	11

[a] "Where Do Shows Come From? Where Do They Go?" *Television* 24 (September 1967): 47.

Neither the stars, nor the time spot (to be discussed later), nor the ideas seemed to be a good enough predictive device of whether a show will get the share of the audience that is almost always necessary for it to remain on the air. Whether or not the Nielsen ratings are an accurate picture of audience approval or disapproval of show has been questioned on statistical grounds and on account of the limited information available from the system. However, since both the advertisers and the networks use the ratings as measures of success and failure, it is considered by almost everyone as an important consideration in production.

Programming and Producing

If a series is bought after the long journey through the network and advertising-agency bureaucracies, a number of decisions still have to be made before and during production that have little to do with the content or the stories but are considered important to the success or failure of a series. Some decisions are administrative ones that remain with the networks; other decisions are artistic or creative, and here again the networks, the production company, and the producer usually consult to reach agreement. Decisions such as the days and times the programs are presented are primarily decided by the networks.

According to the sample, the time slot can make a difference between the series' success or failure.[25] However, there seems to be a great deal of confusion as to the importance of the time slot. Shows in the early evening hours are considered family-type shows that will appeal to the very young viewer as well as to adults in the audience; later shows are often more sophisticated and geared to more adult audiences. When an adventure show, for instance, is slotted for 10:00 P.M., the producer may not be concerned that half of the potential audience is no longer awake and viewing. Shows that follow a known popular show are said to have a better chance of staying on the air. This is explained as audience apathy; once a channel is tuned in, the audience will remain with that channel rather than get up and turn the dial. These things do seem to make some difference to the success of the show, but how much is not clear. From the Nielsen devices that record channel switching, it is obvious that at least those families in the Nielsen sample do switch channels in the middle of a show. It does seem that time slot is more important than the night of the week, but how important is not too clear. Shows that have switched nights have maintained high ratings.

The creative decisions, such as permanent casting, the choice of producer, and location of shooting, are often decided after the pilot has been sold. The networks may like the story idea but not the stars in the cast of the pilot. This decision is made on an executive level between all the parties involved. The choice of producer is also decided by the production company and the network. The man who originates the series often becomes the executive producer,[26] and a working producer is hired to handle the stories and other aspects of production for the series itself. Many times the network will insist that the creator of the series remain as producer. One producer in the sample who had created and produced three successful pilots remained with the series for the first year each was in production. All three stayed on the air several seasons, but the job of producer went to another man.

□

Shows, such as "Gunsmoke" and "Bonanza," which have been on the air for a number of years, have had numerous working producers.

It may seem that once a series is on the air, the control and limitations imposed by those in control of the business decisions are less important than during the preproduction period. This is not entirely the case, because the business organizations remain one of the several significant or important "others" for the production crew to consider while making a film. Whether or not a series goes on the air is almost entirely the networks' decision, although they depend somewhat on the production people and writers for the idea; whether or not a series stays on the air is dependent on the networks and other considerations as well.

NOTES

1 Joan Moore makes the distinction between the functions that belong to the crews and those that belong to the "front office" or sponsor. See her article, "Occupational Anomie and Irresponsibility," *Social Problems* 8 (1961): 293–299.

2 The half-hour series seems to be losing favor with the networks. Most shows except for a few situation comedies are one hour or more in length at this time.

3 Another theme that has been popular in the past concerns one or more persons traveling from place to place in search of adventure or escaping from danger ("Route 66," "Wagon Train," "The Fugitive"). This allows a number of guest stars to be used while maintaining the importance of the continuing characters; the writers also have more leeway with story ideas.

4 Series have been failures, according to those interviewed, because the story line was not right for the serial format. A show that was mentioned several times is a case in point. In the pilot episode an older woman leaves a million dollars to a shop girl who was kind to her. After "Cinderella" had the money, there was no more story.

5 "U.N.C.L.E." is a spy story developed after the James Bond series (originated by Ian Fleming). The series was still in production in 1967–1968, and this information was supplied by the working producer.

6   Arthur Knight, *The Liveliest Art: A Panoramic History of the Movies* (New York: Macmillan & Company, 1957), pp. 274–278.

7   The figures vary depending on whom you read or talk to. These figures were given to me by many of the producers interviewed.

8   This agreement with the unions (guilds) was changed in 1961. Now all drama is eligible for residuals. Filming still has advantages over taping even though taping techniques have been improved over the years.

9   "Hollywood and Television," *Television* 20 (September 1963), entire issue. See also Wilson P. Dizard, *Television: A World View* (Syracuse, N. Y.: Syracuse University Press, 1966), pp. 155–159.

10 Gilbert Seldes, *The Public Arts* (New York: Simon and Schuster, 1964), pp. 181–182.

11 John Deminor, "Universal: The New Hollywood," *Life*, December 20, 1963, pp. 46–50.

12 A series is different from a serial. In a serial the story continues from one show to the next, unlike a series where each story is begun and concluded within the framework of the hour and episodes can subsequently be rerun in any random order.

13 "Where Do Shows Come From? Where Do They Go?" *Television* 24 (September 1967): 46–47.

14 Cole Trapnell, *Teleplay* (San Francisco: Chandler Publishing Co., 1966), p. 48. This is discussed by the respondents as well.

15 This material is based on general reading in *Daily Variety* and *Hollywood Reporter* as well as on the interview material and personal observation.

16 Merle Miller and Rhodes Evans, *Only You, Dick Daring!* (New York: William Sloane Associates, 1964), p. 2.

17 "Who Lowers Boom on Web Nabobs? Lee Rich, That's Who?" *Daily Variety*, October 11, 1967. (Reprinted with permission of Daily Variety)

18 The "created by" credit is determined by the Writers Guild on the basis of who actually created the series format and characters in writing. It is in most cases one person, occasionally two, rarely more.

19 Miller and Evans, *op. cit.*, p. 34, cites an exception. He relates how James Aubrey got the idea for the ill-fated pilot described in the book. Aubrey is quoted as saying, "I see a man in a dusty pickup in the Southwest. The man is wearing a Stetson and Khaki pants. I don't know exactly what he is, but he's not a cop; he doesn't carry a gun. I don't want him to be a policeman or a law enforcement officer." From this skeleton idea a pilot for a series was developed.

20 In radio the advertiser owned and produced most of the shows and therefore the sponsor controlled the content. After the quiz scandals in 1959 control went to the networks.

□

21 "They're Off as Often as Not," *Television* 24 (March 1967): pp. 23–25.

22 *Ibid.*, p. 25.

23 See the brochure from the Home Testing Institute TVG, A *Study of New Programs*, 1965–1966.

24 All figures quoted are from "Where Do Shows Come From? Where Do They Go?".

25 Very popular shows such as "Gunsmoke" have been moved from one night to another (or one time spot to another) and remained high in the ratings. "Gunsmoke," for instance, was moved from Saturday night to Monday in 1967–1968 season with little change in rating.

26 The title "producer" is discussed and defined in Chapter 1. Executive producers are often but not always different from working producers. An executive producer is usually in charge of several shows for the production company. The title may also designate someone who owns the shows. The executive producer may or may not be the working producer, but usually he is not.

The Producer:
His Training
and Commitment

How professional are the men who produce television series? To answer this question it is first necessary to specify the meaning of "professional" and to explain why this is important in a study of producers and their selection of content. The term "professional" has a variety of meanings. An ongoing discussion has maintained that various technical and artistic occupations have become more professionalized; that is, they have increasingly assumed the technological, organizational, and ideological aspects of professionalization. Nelson N. Foote describes the three aspects of professionalization: (1) "a specialized technique supported by a body of theory," (2) "a career supported by an association of colleagues," and (3) "a status supported by community recognition."[1] It could be argued that because occupations in entertainment and communications have creative aspects, they could never meet such requirements. However, a specific educational system develops film makers and writers as well as others in production. Careers are also supported by an association of colleagues (the various guilds), with entrance into these guilds relatively simple. Foote's third point is not relevant to this study, but the popular press and other sources demonstrate that there is community recognition of the occupations connected with film making and television, especially in the Los Angeles area.[2] This is not to say that writers and producers are "professionals" in the classical sociological sense; the usual characteristics of a profession presented in the literature form an "ideal type" rather than a reality.[3]

A case can be made from the above criteria that film makers are generally becoming more professional. However, an important part of communication and organization theory provides characteristics for defining a professionalized occupation that Foote has ignored. Possibly more important than a body of theory, an association of colleagues, and a status supported by community recognition is the quality of commitment to the standards and values that an occupational group has developed for its members. The term "professional" has often been used to mean such commitment. This definition is especially appropriate to the study of occupational groups that have to operate in organizations whose standards of behavior for their members differ from the occupational standards. For instance, Warren Breed considers certain ethical standards of journalists, such as responsibility, impartiality, fair play, and objectivity, as ideals that can be considered professional norms.[4] Jay Blumler suggests that freedom to exercise professional judgment (freedom to make decisions without outside control) should be added to the list.[5] Both he and Breed realize that these professional standards or ideals influence the everyday behavior of newsmen when they must make decisions about story or broadcast content. Herbert J. Gans, dealing directly with the control of television news stories, also points out that while one must consider the medium itself as the most important determinant of content, both professional judgments and the professional values of the television newscasters are also important.[6] These professional values help regulate how the journalist reports events. The newsbroadcasters studied by Gans seem to be committed to the

□

values of fairness and objectivity, though these ideals are not always achieved. Gans also stresses that freedom to make decisions without control from the hiring organization is most highly valued.

Freedom to make decisions without control is the main criterion of professionalism to be used throughout the remainder of this book. It has been found that television producers vary in the amount of their commitment to the value of autonomy in the decision-making process. The differences among producers are related to their history in the industry and to their personal background. In this chapter the training and apprenticeship of producers are explored in relationship to their aspirations; my purpose is to describe the various types of producers and the degree of their commitment to freedom from control by both their colleagues in the craft side of film making and the organizations hiring them. Also investigated is the commitment producers have to their own ideals about television film making and the way they translate this commitment to their everyday activities.

Background

The experiences of people in a rapidly changing social environment such as the communications industry are often dissimilar because of historical circumstances and technological developments. It is obvious that the older men in the industry, who started their work careers in most instances before the advent of commercial filmed television, would have different experiences from those who are younger and had most of their working experience in the electronic media. While age and history are important to consider, the impact of professional training and education is also important. This, too, is related to age and history because communication and film-making schools are relatively recent; therefore, mostly the younger men in the industry would have such training. The older men were trained through various apprenticeship routes, usually the Hollywood movie studios and radio networks, both of which were used in the early days of live television to recruit the neophytes for production in an uncharted communication setting. It seemed logical to analyze the interviews by separating the samples into age groups that coincided with historical periods. Producers were divided into three age groups: those thirty to thirty-six, those thirty-seven to forty-five, and those over forty-five. My rationale was that those between thirty and thirty-six were more likely to have most of their relevant experience in the movie industry after television film making became the mainstay of Hollywood: those between thirty-seven and forty-five had more often worked in both live and filmed television, though several in this category had all their work experience in Hollywood and were connected entirely with films. Those over forty-five had usually been part of either network radio or the movie industry before the advent of television. Unfortunately, this division of the data, while showing differences in education, income, and, of course, recruiting patterns (since this was the characteristic that separated the groups in the first place), did not distinguish between producers in regard to the important consideration for this study: how they select content in relationship to the major reference groups.

The interviews clearly showed that certain producers shared a common view of the audience and a pattern of relating to the networks and their fellow craft workers. An analysis of the material reveals three types of producers. These types are heuristic models, not descriptions of actual producers, although in each group there are typical cases. The first group, the film makers, are usually the younger producers who have little experience in other media. Most of these men considered series film making a training experience that would enable them to

□

make more artistic and personal films in the future. Fame more than money seemed to be the goal, but the two are obviously related. Their training was more likely than the other two groups to be in the formal schools of communication and in film making rather than in writing, the theater, or pretelevision radio and the movies. The next group, the writers-producers, had been free-lance writers before they went into production. Unlike the film makers, their aspirations or ambitions are connected with television rather than with theater films. They would like to make more "meaningful" television films, that is, films with social messages. Therefore, they were more concerned with story content and less interested in technical aspects of film making. The third type, the old-line producers, had worked in several media, but primarily had been in movie production or radio before coming to television. Their main goal seemed to be maintaining financial success in any entertainment field. They are able to move easily from one medium to another, depending on the financial gains and the popularity of the medium with the public.

While the three groups overlap the three age groups discussed earlier, they are not identical. Although most of the film makers are, in fact, young, this is not always the case. The old-line producers are likely to be over forty-five, but again several of the younger men fit this category. The producers of the animated series in the second set of interviews tend especially to be younger men who are more like old-line producers in description. The writers-producers, too, are drawn from all three age groups, but most are at least over thirty-six. Therefore, this typology was not developed on the basis of age, but from two other dimensions: (1) education and apprentice training (which, as stated earlier, is clearly related to age) and (2) more importantly the ambitions and aspirations of the men. This is theoretically justified because these two dimensions represent the producer's occupational orientation.

75   The Producer: His Training and Commitment

□

Entry and Recruitment

Entry to the occupation of producing varied for each group because of the differences in training and apprenticeship. Only a few people ever become producers, and many who do often return to other occupational roles either in or outside of the industry. Producers are therefore an unusual group in an unusual industry. Their career patterns and aspirations are important to consider when examining how content is selected because of their uniqueness and their important position in the production process.

Unlike many other occupations, entry into the occupational role is not necessarily dependent on a specified apprenticeship route.[7] There are, of course, more colleges and universities presently offering courses on film making and television production; in addition, both the American Film Institute and the industry itself recently instituted several apprenticeship programs to train promising candidates on the job. However, it is possible to become a producer without attending such a school, and, of course, the apprenticeship program has not yet trained anyone who is presently producing. Indeed, it is unlikely that most television producers of drama had as their original occupational goal their present occupation. Students of film and television seem to be studying in order to direct, write, or perform.[8] It is from the ranks of other occupational groups in the industry that producers are usually recruited.

The interviews show that most producers, regardless of type or age, had been writers early in their careers. If someone were to ask what would be the best route to becoming a producer, the simplest answer would be that somehow the aspirant producer should try to write a script. The realities of the steps leading to the occupation are more complex than simply trying to write a script and selling it. However, in answer to the question "How did you get started in the industry?" almost all mentioned script writing at some time in their careers. The role of producer is complicated and as such demands individuals who possess a variety of skills and knowledge that are learned by first filling other roles (usually assistant producer or assistant to the producer). Therefore, while it is not a formalized apprenticeship and often not a direct route, a training period is necessary before one can "produce." This chapter explores that training or apprenticeship route for the three types of producers. The focus is on how the men entered the occupation and how they were trained to produce the film series. The training varies from type to type, but there seems to be main routes and entry patterns for each type. There are only a few producers who were deviant cases and fit into none of the three types. Two producers, for instance, came into the industry because they married the boss's daughter, but even these had to have some apprenticeship before they were able to produce films. For all the producers there seems to be a process of "mobility," rather than a step-by-step climb up a career ladder.

The Film Makers

The film maker for the most part had grown up professionally with television films; their work experiences and even their education was connected with communications, often film making. Most of those closely fitting the model had college training in a relevant field, such as theater arts, television communications, journalism, or English with emphasis on writing. Those who had no such training were either business majors or had major work in a preprofessional program. The group had several distinctive characteristics: all had completed two or more years of college; most worked for a large, bureaucratically organized studio that rotated producers from show to show; all had had no experience in live television and

□

began their careers either as a copywriter in advertising or as a contract writer for a studio making movies and television films. Because of this group's homogeneity, it is possible to report verbatim from an interview on the career of one producer and apply it to the entire group. (The following quotation has been altered slightly to protect the anonymity of the respondent.)

The question asked of each respondent was: "How did you get started in the industry?"

I always wanted to be involved in motion pictures—I always wanted to be in some aspect of entertainment would be a better way of putting it. I started working in radio when I was in high school. I dabbled in writing on a newspaper and really didn't have any particular aim other than going into an entertainment field even after junior college. Then I went to a local *Southern California University, noted for its film department. I was going to be a radio major and hopefully make a fair living as a radio director or announcer. While in school I worked as a copywriter.* I got involved in the motion-picture division when they were casting a movie . . . you know those student movies they make. There I met a man named —————— who was an old-timer in the business and is now deceased. He was such an inspiring man. I never met anybody who had more effect on young people. He really wasn't a professor—I don't think he ever completed his education, but he taught in the division. He influenced my getting into the motion-picture division. He influenced my whole life.

After I graduated, I went into the service. When I came back, I went to work at —— as a mailboy just because everyone says that is what you should do. You don't go down to the studios and say I would like to be some kind of writer or something. *I had tried writing while in the service.* A couple of things clicked but nothing was produced. While I was at —————— I got a call from someone here who was the head of the story department. *She had read one of my scripts—a half-hour western that I had written. She asked if I would like to have a job as part of the story-development department writing synopses.* I did that for a couple of years. The job was simple. I wrote a page or more description of every show that was made here.

□

This was for legal and copyright purposes. Also it was done for syndication—they sent them out with the films so people knew what to publicize. The most important thing for me is that it exposed me to an awful lot of scripts and eventually that led into a story-analyst job because I did make contacts here. *Once you are here, you are bound to make contacts. I worked as a story analyst and was moved up to head of the television story department,* which was in the process even then of being absorbed by the motion-picture story department. Before that happened, I went to work as an assistant producer on a show, and from that point on it was a lot of exposure to the total production rather than just the story aspects of it. Three years ago I got my first real producing job and have been with it ever since.

From the above quotation and also other interviews, several points stand out. The respondents in this group, almost without exception, started by writing free-lance scripts or short stories. They spent much of their time in the beginning either working in the mailrooms or for the publicity departments in some clerical capacity before being noticed by someone and moved up the hierarchy. Their spare time was spent writing more scripts, and this writing effort was shown to directors or others in the studio in the hope that their scripts would be produced. Occasionally, this did happen, but it was more likely that, because of their presence on the scene and their ability to write, they were moved up the production ladder within the organization.

How mailboys, messengers, and the like are recruited is not known. It may be necessary to know someone (only several admitted to this), or it may be that recruitment for such highly prized jobs is based on recommendations from the local schools. Most of the film makers were educated in the Los Angeles area. Both the University of California, Los Angeles, and the University of Southern California have excellent departments in film making and electronic communications, and men from the industry teach students and sometimes recruit and sponsor favorites.

79   The Producer: His Training and Commitment

□

The Writers-Producers

Most of the writers-producers had their work experience in
television and related communications, but they differed from
the film makers in several ways. Because many had started their
working careers shortly after World War II, several had had
experience in "live" television and radio before television films
were being produced in Hollywood. Many of them started as
script writers under contract in the studios, which at that time
were concentrating on feature-film production. In addition, their
career patterns varied: they were more apt to have had both
failures and, of course, more successes than the film makers. They
did not show the same occupational stability in either the kinds
of jobs held or the length of time under contract to a particular
studio or to a production. In fact, these men seemed closer to
the prototype of the producer that is generally accepted around
the studios and in the press. They were not only less stable in
jobholding but were often unemployed; thus they often described
their work experience as "feast or famine." Upon questioning,
their "feast-or-famine" declaration seemed to stretch the facts
considerably; when the men in this group were without
producing contracts, they were able to do free-lance writing or
possibly directing and consequently were rarely without income.
This was true in the past, but as film-making opportunities
"dry" up, the writer-producer may be the least likely to survive
the "new Hollywood." Thus, their lives (and incomes) were not
as orderly as the film makers under long-term contracts.
However, one compensation for such job instability was much
higher income when working as producers.

Members of this group were less apt to be trained in
academic programs in the Los Angeles area, although several
were. However, they did have training related to their work, but
this training was more likely to be in advertising, journalism,

or the theater. The schools attended ranged from Ivy League institutions to commuter colleges of large metropolises. It should be stressed that their education usually was not in film, radio, or television. When they did work in communications, they were usually writers in either Hollywood or New York in the early days of television.

Although their career patterns were generally less ordered, sometimes they were considerably more spectacular. One producer, for example, came to California after completing a B.A. degree in advertising; he did not know anyone in the industry and had no employment prospects. While writing scripts, he did what he could to earn a living, such as working as a night watchman or loading freight cars. His first script was purchased for a radio show in 1951. Eventually, he was able to sell enough of what he wrote to stop working at odd jobs. He soon was selling scripts to the movies, and the next stop was a contract with a major studio as a "rewrite" man, a common role for beginning contract writers. His progression from rewriting to series producing closely followed the history of the developing television-film industry. This producer is a success: he claims to have sold everything he has written; he had produced several award-winning series; and at the time of the interview he was moving out of series production into movie production, not because he didn't like television but because he needed more freedom.

Another producer in this group did not have as illustrious a career because he had not produced or created as many successful series. However, similarities could be found in their careers. He also had started as a writer for radio before working in "live" television. However, he wrote for his college newspaper and, on graduation, worked as a reporter on a large metropolitan daily. On returning to the United States after serving with the army during World War II, he went to Los Angeles, also with no connections or friends, and sold scripts to radio and "live" television.

This group of producers were satisfied with television work, although they had the most problems in producing freely and therefore the most role conflict. The reason given most often for continuing to produce series was the financial rewards. Those who were just salaried (all but three, who as independent producers still worked on the line) made extremely high salaries, over $50,000 a year. Besides the financial rewards, they apparently liked the fast-moving pace of television and took pride in their ability to make the decisions that their jobs required of them. Many who had worked on high-budget theatrical films complained of the slow production schedules and the long time necessary to complete such films. Thus, a conflict between what was considered art and the work role itself seemed present; this will be discussed in detail in the remaining chapters of this book. Their definition of art—to make films that are "honest," have a "worthwhile social message," and show tolerance—caused them difficulties with network officials (see Chapter 6). Their skill in writing and dramatic presentation made them valuable as producers to the networks; however, because of their work orientation they were the most troublesome of the three groups.

The Old-line Producers

While the overall work experience of this group differed markedly from the others, most also had been writers at the beginning of or during their careers. Their writing experience had often been in several media and was not part of their immediately previous occupation. Many of them had been in production for a number of years and, although they had once been writers, it was not an occupation with which they usually identified.

Several had started as journalists, a few had been playwrights and worked as screen writers, and a number had written for "live" television in New York. For this group the two main paths into television were from network radio and Hollywood film production; those who had started with radio were more likely to have worked in "live" television, while those who had been with the movies usually went into television when it moved to Hollywood. However, several of the former movie people had experience in "live" television in New York as well in the early 1950's, because they had been unable to find work in Hollywood when movie production was low.

Fewer of this group had some college education; of those who had attended college, most had majored in fields of studies that were unrelated to their occupations or career. Two of these producers were trained in the law, one in engineering, and the others were former teachers or had general business or liberal-arts backgrounds. Of those who were trained in related fields, just one had training in the communication field (radio); the rest were English, advertising, or journalism majors.

Many of this group had colorful careers or job histories. One producer, for example, had been a radio comedy writer for many of the notable comedians in the 1930's. He went from local radio performing to network writing, then to "live" television in New York and to films in Hollywood. At the present time he is the producer of a successful show. He said he was responsible for the first filmed series in the early 1950's.

One producer had been associated with B films in Hollywood and moved into filmed television when production on B films stopped. One had been a rather well-known network announcer for shows that had been on network radio for as long as ten years. (He was also the only one of the sample who had been a director-producer in radio. The director-producer for a radio drama has duties somewhat similar to the television producer.) Several others also had been performers of some note, and one

83   The Producer: His Training and Commitment

□

still performed as well as producing and directing the show that had made him famous. Others had been well-known screen writers. (They either adapted novels and plays for the screen or originated screen plays themselves. Occasionally, the names of a number of these men will be found in the credits of old movies on television.)

Others, of course, did not have as colorful or as successful former careers, but there was no question of current success because all of them had one or more series on the air for more than one season. In addition, this group included the majority of originators of ideas for new series. They were responsible for over twenty series ideas that were made into pilots and sold for series production. An accurate number of pilots made that did not becomes series (that is, were shelved) could not be obtained. However, each producer who sold one or more series did recall making at least one pilot that did not sell. These men frequently worked on the line with the series that they created. Sometimes, however, the production company of the network removed them from producing their own series, but all at the time of inter-viewing had been on the line some of the time during the season.

In this group four granted interviews although they had either returned to a former occupational role (in two cases, writer and story editor) or were no longer with the show. It is of interest that the group also seemed to have more recollections of periods when work was impossible to get. Several recalled the lean days in Hollywood in the early 1950's when movie production was at a low ebb and television was not yet in full swing. At that time several moved to New York to "try their luck" with "live" television. Several also mentioned how difficult it was to find other assignments as producers when a series they had in production was not renewed. During such times they would usually turn to free-lance writing, but several preferred to wait so they would be available for production and story development when a production company wanted their services. One producer was unemployed for a year after producing three series that had remained on the air for a number of years. (The last series with which he had been associated was a critical success but a failure in the ratings, the type of failure, according to him, that makes it difficult to find new assignments.)

The respondents were asked to state their present income and also their highest and lowest incomes for the past five years. This group reported the greatest variation ranging from no income for one year to over $100,000 for one year.

When interviewed, most of the old-line producers considered themselves to be at the height of their careers, the final stage of a long career pattern. Some were looking forward to retirement activities such as travel, golf, and writing. One just wanted to sculpt. Others, however, anticipated returning to feature-film production, a form of semiretirement from the hectic pace of television. Some already had a mixed career because of involvement in series production and in the production of feature-length film for television.

Career Commitment

Much of the mythology of the industry suggests that career patterns are not as linear as in some other high-status and high-income occupations. This can be disputed if the organization of the industry is taken into consideration. The route up in this particular field is rarely with one studio, network, or agency. From the reports of the men themselves and the trade papers, it appears that producers, as well as others in executive positions, move from production company to production company and from network to network. One producer suggested it was like a game of musical chairs. The impression gained from the data, as well as from other documents, is that most men who have "made it" remain relatively high in income, at least throughout most of their working careers. This can be explored by reviewing the careers of those who had produced both successful and unsuccessful series in the past and following their work history.

More important for this inquiry are the educational backgrounds of the producers studied. This group is somewhat better educated than similar groups studied in the past, and, more importantly, their education is in more relevant areas.[9] While no one was educated to be a producer, a large number were educated in fields related to communications, and thus their education should be considered as a possible reference orientation when selecting content.

Joan Moore did an exploratory study of television writers in Chicago and suggested that, because most writers she studied were not educated in relevant fields (she does not consider English majors to have had a relevant background), this contributed to the normlessness of the occupation.[10] She argues: "The lack of standardization of patterns of recruitment training, and admission to professional standing for the two major production occupations (writers and directors) implies that social norms governing the professional conduct of the writer and director are weak."[11] However, it could be that producers who were educated in a discipline that is related to their work and that stresses artistic integrity and craftsmanship have developed norms that conflict with the norms of the industry itself. Joan Moore's justification for calling production occupations normless is that writers and directors turn to each other and to other studio colleagues for norms of professional conduct and for evaluation of their performance. These characteristics in an occupational group would point to more professionalization rather than less. One hallmark of a profession is the inability of the laymen to judge performance; rewards are given by colleagues' recognition.[12]

The profit-minded executive, who is more interested in ratings, advertising space, and audience composition, represents

□

a different ideology than producers, who are trained to do a technically good job either in writing or film making. Throughout the literature on mass culture and the popular arts there is an ongoing discussion about the internal norms in the industry. This is not to suggest that those who are part of the business end of television are without social responsibility, but the philosophy they usually express is to satisfy the largest possible number.[13] What an audience seems to want (which in itself is no simple matter to determine) or what the networks and advertisers think the audience wants may be quite different in both content and technology than what the producer thinks is creative or artistic. As those on the creative or technical ends of television become more educated or more "professionalized," the conflicts with the industry executives could become more pronounced.

Because the executives are committed to making a profit and to serving the largest possible audience, they, from all reports, seem to cater to pressure groups and to advertisers who are afraid of alienating large segments of the buying public. This can determine content in ways that basically have no relationship to the political ideologies of the network executives themselves. The producers, because they are from groups (see Appendix D) that are traditionally more "liberal" in political orientation, may have values that conflict directly with those acceptable to the final arbiters of such matters. Positive reference groups, such as political parties or political factions, may be a source of conflict because the networks maintain script control. This is also explored in the remainder of the study.

Social control in the form of the power to hire and fire also remains with the networks and the production company. The producer is a highly paid person who, in order to retain his position must have successful shows. Thus, the dilemma arises between the artistic, educational, and political values and the salary, position and the style of life that have become highly valued.

The researchers who have studied newsmen (Breed, Gans,

87   The Producer: His Training and Commitment

□

and Blumler) found that professional commitment is an important consideration to them.[14] The problem of the importance of commitment to occupational ideals is not simple, because strategies are influenced by more than just the ideals of one's craft. Newsmen also consider the editor, the reading or viewing public, as well as other colleagues, when selecting stories. There is no doubt that producers also shape their content in terms of their perception of what network officials, the guilds, fellow craftworkers (especially writers, directors, and actors), and studios expect from them. Consequently, the remainder of this work will show how the different types of producers also relate differently to their various reference groups. Their own occupational or role definition of their work is just one important consideration among others in determining how content is selected. Possibly both the stress and gratification from film making arise from the producer's authoritative position in the organization and his professional commitment to his craft.

NOTES

1   Nelson M. Foote, "The Professionalization of Labor in Detroit," *The American Journal of Sociology* 58 (1953): 371–380. Also see Howard Vollmer and Donald Mills, "Industrial Technology," in Vollmer and Mills, eds., *Professionalization* (Englewood Cliffs, N.J.: Prentice-Hall Inc., 1966), p. 21.

2   Another indication of community recognition is that producers now have gained occupational status. The Producers Guild of America is now a collective-bargaining union.

3   For instance, see Bernard Barber, "Some Problems in the Sociology of the Professions," *Daedalus* 92 (1963): 672. Barber says a profession has the following characteristics: (1) exclusive specialized knowledge, (2) community orientation, (3) self-regulation by a code of ethics, and (4) symbolic remuneration for services. While these characteristics do not apply to the producers as a group, producers on a continuum are closer to professionals than are manual laborers, for instance. See T. H.

Marshall, *Class, Citizenship and Social Development* (New York: Doubleday and Co., 1964), pp. 163–164. Also see Lee Taylor, *Occupational Sociology* (New York: Oxford University Press, 1968), pp. 87–133.

4 Warren Breed, "Social Control in the Newsroom: A Functional Analysis," *Social Forces* 33 (1955): 326–335.

5 Jay G. Blumler, "Producers' Attitudes Toward Television Coverage of an Election Campaign: A Case Study," *The Sociological Review Monograph: Sociology of Mass Communicators* 13 (1969): 85–115.

6 Herbert J. Gans, "How Well Does TV Present the News," *New York Times Magazine*, January 11, 1970, pp. 30–35, 38.

7 This is not a socialization study, but rather an "occupational" study in that the major emphasis is on the structure of the occupation and how men act or perform in their occupational role of producers. However, because the socialization patterns are important to understand the occupational role that has developed, it is necessary to describe the pathways into the role. More structured or specified routes into various occupations have been discussed in the sociological literature. These occupations are usually those that are considered trades or professions. See, for instance, Basil J. Sherlock and Richard T. Morris, "The Evolution of a Professional: A Paradigm," *Sociological Inquiry* 37 (1967): 32–37 for a discussion of the socialization of dentists.

8 This is surmised from the interviews as well as from conversations with students studying film at UCLA. Not one producer interviewed started out in the industry with the desire to become a television-series producer. The older men in the sample did not even consider television as a career because it was either nonexistent or remote before World War II.

9 Sidney Willhelm and Gideon Sjoberg, "The Social Characteristics of Entertainers," *Social Forces* 37 (1958): 73. Leo C. Rosten, *Hollywood: The Movie Colony, The Movie Makers* (New York: Harcourt, Brace and Co., 1941). See also Suzanne Keller, *Beyond the Ruling Class—Strategic Elites in Modern Society* (New York: Random House, 1963), p. 304.

10 Joan Moore, "Occupational Anomie and Irresponsibility," *Social Problems* 8 (1961): 293–299.

11 *Ibid.*, p. 294.

12 See Taylor, *op. cit.*, pp. 413–428, for a full discussion on colleague recognition and support.

13 Otto Larsen, "Social Effects of Mass Communications," in Robert E. L. Faris, *Handbook of Modern Sociology* (Chicago: Rand McNally, 1964), p. 373. Also Bernard Berelson, "The Great Debate on Cultural Democracy," *Study in Public Communication* 3 (1961): 3–14; Max Wylie,

89   The Producer: His Training and Commitment

    Clear Channels (New York: Funk and Wagnalls Co., 1955), esp. pp. 219–244, but the theme throughout is a defense of the cultural democratic position.

14 Breed, "Social Control in the Newsroom"; Blumler, *op. cit.*; and Gans, *op. cit.*

The Producer and His Role Partners: Writers, Directors, and Actors

As stated earlier, the production process can be analytically divided into two functions, those concerned with profit and business details and those concerned with artistic functions.[1] This chapter considers the reference groups associated with the craft aspects, rather than the profit aspects, of production. A separate discussion of the two aspects is necessary because the relationships between the producers and other production people are qualitatively different from those between the producers and business people. In reality, this dichotomy is false because the functions are interrelated. However, the profit-making aspects of production are more bureaucratically organized than the production process, which necessarily must be craftlike.[2] "Craftlike" refers to the production process as an organization of groups of "professionalized" or "occupationally skilled" individuals, performing roles for which they are trained by education or long apprenticeship; these craftworkers are represented by craft-type or white-collar unions open only to those occupational groups rather than to all employees of the industry.[3]

□

This chapter will focus on the writer, director, and actor; unfortunately, many of those also important to the technical processing of a television film have to be ignored. From story to the final print, many individuals play important technical and creative roles in film making and contribute to the success or failure of particular episodes. There is no doubt, for example, that an incompetent cameraman can ruin a film; in addition, the work of those concerned with sets, wardrobe, dubbing, and especially editing are of utmost importance to the final product. However, because this study is primarily concerned with story selection and the creative process contributing to the final product, these others are of peripheral interest.[4] The producer has authority over these aspects of production and, with the production company, chooses who will do these technical and housekeeping chores of film making and make up the more or less permanent cadre operating during the season. Although a production crew can have difficulties in the interpersonal as well as creative aspects of production, this is not usually a major worry. Writers and directors are, however, a continuing concern because they usually work on a free-lance basis and, by the nature of their work and position, are the most necessary and also the most independent of all those working on a film. The permanent cast also presents difficulties, because the actors, probably more than any of the others, can be the difference between a producer's success or a failure; therefore, depending on the actor's popularity and other qualities to be described later, he can be a powerful influence in story selection.

The Producer and the Writer

As reported in Chapter 4, most of the producers started their careers as free-lance script writers, contract writers, or story editors. Forty-eight of the fifty-nine first interviewed still con-

□

sidered themselves writers or "hyphenates" (writers-producers), and, as such, were members of the Writers Guild of America West. The most important "other" to the producer probably is the free-lance writer, not only because producers basically identify with writers as an occupational group, but also because the two occupational roles are by necessity mutually dependent.

The producer of a series on the air for a full season needs at least twenty-six scripts from writers unless he or his story editor are themselves able to write a script or two. More than twenty-six scripts are actually needed even if the series is on the air for just twenty-six episodes; several extra scripts are required for emergency contingencies. There have been cases where the network or advertiser who has final script approval would not permit filming of a particular script.

One producer, for instance, gave the following account of how a script was shelved by the network:

> I have just had a show called ———— removed from our schedule. It was the story of a child who was trapped in a well and everybody in town went without sleep for fifty-seven hours and risked their lives in a heroic effort to save the child, and of course, were successful. The network refused to allow this show to go on the air because the child was in jeopardy. I pointed out that we had depicted the most heroic aspects of the human character in the show and that if any child saw the show, rather than having bad dreams of being trapped in a well, it seems to me that he would have an enormous sense of security because he is going to say to himself, if anything happens to me, the entire adult world is going to get together to help me. But they would not listen.

Several cases were also reported of a completed film never being used because of disapproval from a pressure group or advertiser. One often-repeated story concerned a film about an executive who was portrayed as a drunk. The script was approved, but when the advertising and company executives saw the finished film, they refused to permit its release. According to one respondent, they thought it "gave all executives a bad image." While the film was never shown on network television as part of the first-run series, it was sold as part of the series when it was syndicated. It is rare that a completed film is not used, because of the financial loss involved, but everyone in television-series film making is aware this could happen. Several extra scripts must therefore be available as backup in case of such occurrences or in case the network decides late in the season that several additional episodes are needed.

Because so many scripts are needed, most producers were continually concerned with stories, story ideas, and script development for almost the entire season. A few producers were able to line up scripts early and finished that part of the work sooner. One producer did his own writing. However, usually producers were concerned with some stage of script development until the end of the season.

The first problem for a producer of a new series or even a continuing series is to find those writers able to do the exact kind of scripts necessary for that particular series. The scripts have to adhere to the story theme of the series. Obtaining story consistency is a major concern of most on-the-line producers and is considered their primary responsibility. Several producers or production offices give writers descriptive brochures or statements of the series' basic concept and philosophy before they start writing. If the series has been on the air for a few years, the producers may use writers who have already written scripts for the series. However, many times a series changes its basic idea, which presents a new problem. For instance, a show that has been on the air for several years may add a new character or group of characters to give the show a new direction. Several successful series have lost leading characters because of death or other reasons; when these characters are replaced, the basic series idea may be changed as well. A well-known example of a basic change in a series concept is the "Lassie" show. At one time

Lassie was owned by a farm family consisting of a mother, grandfather, and young son; later, the show format was changed completely to a Forest Service background. Writers, according to producers, can become "stale" or become too busy with other assignments and therefore unavailable. Thus, there seems to be a continuing search for writers.

The work arrangements between the producers and the writers follow certain formalized (rational) rules, which are in the contract adopted by the Writers Guild and Motion Picture and Television Producers Association.[5] Although most producers are members of the Writers Guild, while playing the role of producer they represent the Motion Picture and Television Producers Association and therefore must follow their rules. The contract was adopted after a writers' strike in 1960. Presently, the collective-bargaining and negotiation procedures protect the Guild members and established writers. These procedures make it difficult for those trying to get started as writers; thus, finding new writers is not easy under the present legal structure and Guild rules. It is rare indeed at this time for a writer to do a script on speculation and expect to sell it, though this was rather common during the early days of television. The practice is discouraged today, and, if an entire script is submitted for reading without a contract, the writer is asked to sign a waiver in case the same idea is already in production or in a story-presentation stage. It is much more common to have writers near at hand begin to write scripts under the guidance of someone in the studios. This accounts for the "discovery" of writers in mailrooms and publicity departments explained earlier.

The free-lance writer faces the problem of finding a producer interested in him and his ideas. Often, the producer seems to be looking for writers able to express his ideas rather than writers with their own ideas. The writer's reputation is important because most producers give higher priority to those with the most credits.

Free-lance writers can talk over script ideas with a producer, but the rules of the Writers Guild of America restrict the talks to two; after that, the writer must be hired for at least a story presentation. Talks or interchanges between the writer and producer lead to either a contract for a full script or for the story presentation. A few well-known writers opt for the full script and will not go through the intermediate steps. The producer most of the time prefers to have what is known in the industry as a "story cutoff." A typical script (one hour) costs the producer about $4,500 and its story presentation about $650–$700.[6] With a cutoff at the time of a story presentation, the story ideas belong to the producer and under Guild rules someone else can be hired to go ahead with the same story, or the producer can do the rewrite himself. Many producers build up a cadre of writers they hire to do one or more scripts a season, men and women who have worked with the producer previously and whose work is well known to him. Producers, however, constantly seek new writers to add to their cadre because the very few well-established writers are much in demand throughout the industry.

Whether the producer tells the writer that he wants a story about a certain topic or the writer suggests the idea, the producer's office is the place where most stories originate. The story conference seems to be institutionalized in the industry. The producer, the writer, the story editor (if there is one), and an assistant producer meet to discuss the story outline or presentation. After the first draft of the script, therefore, it is rarely the effort of one man; it is usually the work of a "committee." The term "committee" as used in the industry is an euphemism to mean an effort by a group of people, rather than the creative effort of one man. By the time the script is mimeographed and ready for distribution to the network censorship office, the director, and others with a stake in the production, it might no longer resemble the script the writer originally submitted. Rewrites are commonly done by the producer or the story editor (or both) to

□

represent the desires of the producer, of the production company to whom the producer is directly responsible, or of the network.

The following is a direct account from one producer interviewed describing how he selects writers and gets the scripts needed for his show.

You know that we have strict rules—contractual agreement with the Writer's Guild. We have no more than two meetings with the writer. Either it is decided to employ the writer to do the story or not.

At the end of the second meeting there is a cutoff so that if we don't intend to go onto teleplay we can terminate at this point. A writer comes in and generally there is a discussion. He may have five or six ideas, and I pick one that I like. I usually tell him to give some more thought to it, and I will also. We shake hands, and he comes back in a couple of days with more thoughts about it.

At that point you must employ him to develop it further. This is the point where a deal is made. He either has a deal to write a story outline or a teleplay. Each writer has his own idea of what an outline is. If I like the outline, then he goes back and does the teleplay.

Most of the time if I ask for an outline or story treatment, I usually have that writer do the actual teleplay. When I select writers, I usually play it safe. I pick those I know have a track record, who are established and who are respected. I like to make the main stream of my story telling from people who are successful. That way I can be more sure that when a script comes in it will be shootable. At least there is a better chance that it will be. However, generally speaking, it (the script) is being changed right up to camera time.

(Question: Who changes the script?)

I work with the writer to accomplish a final script. I would rather let the writer make the contributions. If he fails, I will employ somebody else to rewrite it. Even though I am a writer-producer, I never rewrite. Many producers do. Not me. I haven't enough time to rewrite.

97   The Producer and His Role Partners

□

Most producers related procedures similar to this one, although a number of them admitted to a considerable amount of rewriting. Several suggested that unless they rewrote the scripts it was impossible to get the story into the form necessary for production for their show.

Many of the producers considered rewriting ability to be their most valuable contribution to film production, but it also caused the most friction between free-lance writers and on-line producers. In fact, several series divided producing functions into two main areas: one concerned primarily with scripts, the other concerned with the other aspects of production. In most cases the second function (production and technology) is delegated to others trained in editing, dubbing, and set management, whether or not the authority remains with the producer; the first function of story production was not delegated as often, although producers did receive assistance from story editors and assistant producers in the selection and rewriting of stories.

The sequence of story selection and production makes it necessary to have films in various stages of production throughout the season. The first order of business is to find scripts; ideally, the producer will start the season with four scripts ready for production. While he searches for more scripts, the "best" of the four is made into the first film to be presented early in the fall. Thus, it is necessary to have filming, script selection, and possibly postproduction procedures all in operation at the same time. While one script is being written, another is being filmed, and a third is being processed until the production season ends in February of the following year. Most producers, of course, would prefer to have the script selection finished long before the last film is ready to be shot, but this is not always possible. First, the production company may have received an order for a minimum of eleven films at the beginning of the season. Whether or not the production company will receive additional

□

orders determines, of course, whether or not more scripts should be written. Second, there may be difficulty in finding suitable scripts, especially for those programs specialized in content and difficult to write.

The interrelationship between the writer and producer is one of mutual dependence and conflict. Producers depend on writers for scripts, and free-lance writers must work well with producers if they wish to sell their scripts. The conflict usually occurs over screen credit, because, according to the contract between the Writers Guild and the Motion Picture and Television Producers Association, whoever receives screen credit as the writer receives residuals or royalties if and when the episode is shown as a rerun or as part of a syndicated series. Producers are salaried employees and while they receive large salaries, they do not receive residuals for the films they make. However, if a producer changes a story to such a degree that he thinks his name should appear in the credits, the matter must be settled by the Writers Guild Arbitration Committee. At the time of this writing, the only ways a producer could receive payment for reruns was to either have partial financial ownership of the series or have his name appear on the credits as a writer (or director) of an episode. The producer is the only one of the four "equals" (the writer, director, producer, and actor) not getting residuals.

Often a writer will file a complaint to the Guild, either because he did not get full screen credit for a story he had written or because he received no credit at all. This does not mean that he was not paid for his efforts; it means that when screen credits appeared on the television screen, he shared credit with either someone on the production team or another free-lance writer, or his name was not shown at all. Most often, according to articles in the trade paper and reports by producers, the writer accuses the producer of rewriting a script just to receive residuals. Most producers hotly denied rewriting unless necessary, claiming that their overall duties are so time-consuming that, if they

99   The Producer and His Role Partners

did not need to change a script, they would not. Some producers stated that they never rewrote. Others thought that, along with selecting writers, it was most important that they not only rewrite when necessary, but that they change every script to fit the series. In fact, several insisted that they rewrote at least 50 percent of all the scripts but took credit just 2 to 4 percent of the time.[7] As one producer noted:

> There are very few scripts that come into a television office that are shootable the way they stand. There are only a handful of writers in this town that deliver scripts which are shootable in the first draft. This is an extremely difficult business, and you have to shoot a show in six days, and on budget. You have forty-eight minutes of film, certainly half a feature and you know how long it takes to shoot the average feature film, and we do it in six days. Obviously, something has to give. You have to be able to tailor scripts to what you can afford, produce, and also you have problems with stars. This show has been going on for ——— years, and the characters of the people are set. New writers coming cannot always catch the flavor and *somebody has to catch that flavor* or the show does not go on and that's my function. Many times when we are shooting on the very next day, I have been up 'til three o'clock in the morning to finish the pages we are going to shoot the following morning.

During the period when the interviews were conducted, a number of writers-producers joined the Producers Guild of America in hopes that this organization would become a collective-bargaining unit for them as the Writers Guild of America is for the writers.[8] Producers who had joined the Producers Guild and were working toward recognition for that organization hoped it would solve the conflicts prevalent between writers and producers. The Producers Guild has been traditionally considered a "social club." Its members were movie producers who were considered to be part of the management in the movie industry, "lesser gods" according to Hortense Powdermaker.[9] But with the advent of television film making, the

□

"employee-producer" discovered that there was no union to represent him. The producers interviewed, except for those with partial ownership of their series, considered themselves workers, not management. Not only were they salaried, but also none had the usual attributes of management. While the producer may be consulted about hiring personnel, the prerogative for such decisions remains with the production company. Because the producer is the only one at his level not getting residuals, he is looking for an organization to represent his interest with the management.

Therefore, the producer (especially the producer-writer) often wavers between retaining his membership in the Writers Guild and joining the Producers Guild. Most of the producers interviewed were members of the Writers Guild (forty-eight out of fifty-nine), while just eleven were members of the Producers Guild.[10] The writers and producers have very similar functions, and the producer can be considered the chief writer of the series. As previously stated, most producers started as writers and their career patterns seemed to go from writer to associate producer to producer. Since the function of associate producer and producer are closely tied to story writing, script selection, and idea formation, most producers continue to function as writers. Because of the job insecurity connected with producing, many producers return to free-lance writing if and when series fail or are not renewed, and they do not get other producing assignments. Very few producers, therefore, sever their connection with the Writers Guild. In addition, the Writers Guild was trying to resolve the conflict that had developed between producers and writers by forming a committee whose main purpose was to keep the producers from breaking away en masse.[11]

Since the producer is a writer but is also responsible for securing scripts that he as a producer would consider "shootable," he is confronted with a serious dilemma. For instance, several producers reported incidents where a writer finished a second

□

draft and still had not done what the producer required to make the script acceptable, therefore, a rewrite was absolutely necessary. If the producer has to rewrite from the beginning, the Writers Guild Arbitration Committee might allow the producer credit after examining both scripts, but most likely the Committee will inform the producer that he should not get credit because it is part of his job to put the scripts into workable form. In the latter case the script would carry the name of the original writer, although he might have had little to do with the final product.[12] The writer-producer frequently complained that he was not given credit when he felt he deserved it, because the Writers Guild considered him a producer when it came to residuals, but considered him a writer when the Guild called a strike or other collective action. If strikes occur, as they have in the past, the producers are expected to "lay down their pencils," along with the free-lance writers, and if they do not, they face expulsion from the Writers Guild. One writer-producer told the following story, which makes the above point clearly:

I was working on a certain show just before the Writers Guild strike. Now I was (and still am) a member of several guilds. I was producer of that particular show and at the time I was also directing the show. A script came in three days before we were about to shoot. The writer had been paid for second draft so he was not entitled to any more work. He hadn't done anything that had been requested in the second draft. It was awful. I sat down and *rewrote the script from page one.* I did not ask for credit on it, but someone in the front office of the production company, seeing the differences in the two scripts, sent the scripts to the Guild for arbitration. The Guild sent a notice back to me, which is how I found out it was sent there in the first place. The note said, *"You were hired as a producer of the show. The producer's job is to do whatever is necessary to make a show shootable. If you feel you want to change a writer's material, well tough luck boy."* So I said to myself, "Fine, I wasn't asking for it, and I understand that is my job. That is what I am being paid for, and it doesn't happen that often.—Dissolve—Five months later there is going to be a writers' strike, and I get a call from the Guild, and they say, "The strike is at midnight tonight so drop your pencil." I asked who I was talking to, and they said that they were from the Writers Guild. Then I asked if it was the same Writers' Guild who five months before said I was being paid to rewrite scripts from page one for no salary, no residuals, no nothing. They said, "You strike or you get thrown out of the Guild." So this is what the fight is about between the writers and the hyphenates.

The problem of the relationship of the producer to the writer is twofold. First, producers would like to be represented by a guild or an organization that would bargain collectively for the rights (especially residuals) that they consider legitimately theirs as producers. Most producers who were members of the Writers Guild thought the Guild useful if they were to write an occasional script or return to writing, but it was not working in their interests as producers. Several said they continued their membership to see the weekly movies shown by the Guild, which they would not otherwise be able to see as early or as conveniently. Second, the producer must depend on writers for scripts that are not always satisfactory and therefore must be rewritten. Dissatisfaction arises when producers, considered management, often do not get credit for their rewrites and the ideas they generate.

This second problem is seen as more serious by the writers-producers than by the film makers or old-line producers, because they consider themselves principally writers by occupation. The film makers and the old-line producers see their roles differently from the writer-producer. Although practically all of the producers started their careers as writers, many of them no longer identify themselves as such. The film makers see their present role as that of apprentice and are more interested in the technology of film making, in directing, and in editing than in script writing. They also are more apt to pick only successful writers who are more likely to provide them with shootable scripts. It has been years since most old-line producers earned their living by writing; many indeed felt incapable of rewriting and depended on a cadre of men whom they have usually known as friends during their careers to provide scripts. In addition, many of the old-line producers are associated with situation comedies, which often hire contract writers to do the scripts or assign ten or more scripts during a season to one free-lance writer. If contract writers are used, there is less chance rewriting will be necessary because the contract writer fulfills one of the producer's functions in that he is able to maintain character continuity and is knowledgeable about the series concept. One person who is a deviant case but in many respects can be considered an old-line producer not only created the series he produced, but also wrote all the scripts himself. The old-line producer was very concerned with the problems of residuals, and most of the eleven producers who had joined the Producers Guild of America fit into this category.

Eventually, in 1969 the Producers Guild did gain recognition as a collective-bargaining agent for producers, and all producers have to join the guild in order to produce series. At this time, however, they have not succeeded in receiving residuals for the series they produce, and the problem remains essentially the same. In order to get residuals a producer must have his name appear in the credits as writer or director. Rewriting in any case appears to be a self-identified problem for producers because no question directly related to this was asked during the interviews, and all but four of the fifty-nine producers interviewed brought up the subject spontaneously. All the writers-producers brought up the subject on their own volition; Table 5–1 provides evidence that the writers-producers are more apt to rewrite than the other two groups.

From the table and the responses, it appears that other

□

TABLE 5–1   Rewriting and Occupational Identity

	Rewriting		
Occupational Identity	50 percent or more of the time	Less than 50 percent of the time	Never
Writer-producer N = 30	10	14	6
Others N = 29	5	9	11
Total[a]	15	23	17

[a] Because this question was not asked directly in the interviews, four producers did not bring up the topic of rewriting; therefore, the number of total responses is less than fifty-nine.

writers are more important as a reference group to some producers than to others. The film makers, who perceive their present role as an apprenticeship for future work as feature-film producers or directors, have different training and background than the writers-producers, who were previously free-lance writers and consider writing their major occupation. The film makers are more apt to be trained in the technical aspects of film making, while the writers-producers are more apt to be trained in fields closely allied with writing, such as journalism, English, advertising, and therefore related to their present occupational identity. The film makers are more oriented to future occupational identity. The old-line producer is oriented to the mass audience (this will be discussed more thoroughly in Chapter 8). Because he is interested in success with audience and does have an image of what this audience wants, he will rewrite occasionally, but unlike the writer-producer he is not committed to writing as an occupation. In all cases the story is very important to the producers, and because of the dependency of the producer on the writer and vice versa, the conflicts that do occur seem inherent in the structure.

□

The Producer and the Director

Because the producer's major function is to control the material going into the series, one would think that his relationship to the director would be as full of conflict as his relationship to the writer. However, this is not the case in television film making. The reasons for this become clear when one studies the way television films are made.

First, because the director cannot change the scripts, he has limited power over the film making. This was one area where there could be conflict, because the producers seem adamant about not allowing a word to be changed. In addition, while producers are not in the least awed by the writer's work because most of them had been writers, most seem awed by the director's work. However, even the few who were producers-directors did not get into the type of structural conflict reported earlier between writer and producer. A director is hired to direct and does so usually with minimal interference. If the producer-director wants to direct an episode (and several did throughout the season), he is the only director and responsible for the entire directing job. There is nothing comparable to rewriting because there is no chance to redirect the film. There could be artistic and personal quarrels over direction, of course, and these possibly did occur, although no such cases were reported. However, directing a television episode is not considered as "artistic" as feature-film directing, and the freedom of the director is limited by the brief time spent in production and the general structure that has developed. A director is usually brought in a week or so before filming begins. Along with the producer, he helps select actors for supporting roles. He has the final scripts to "prepare" for shooting. Sets, costumes, and music must be selected. Subsidiary personnel, who do these jobs week after week, assist the director. The director with the producer has a "say" in such matters, but the producer is the final arbiter. According to some of the subsidiary people around the studios, the producer's tastes are considered first when making certain selections.

In motion-picture film production the director has the right to the first "cut," in accordance with an agreement between the Directors Guild and the Motion Picture and Television Producers Association. The right to edit his film is important to the director because he can choose scenes to keep or cut, a prerogative highly prized because the sequencing and editing of a film constitute much of the creativity of film making. The same contract, of course, holds for television film making, but because of time limits and economic considerations, few directors take advantage of this prerogative.

The directors of series are usually not under contract to the show but work on a free-lance basis. They are hired to do one or more episodes of a series, which are shot in three days (half-hour episode) or in six days (hour episode). When the filming is completed, most directors go immediately to another assignment with a different series and, therefore, are not available to cut the picture when it's ready. In most cases the producer fills this function. The producers who acted as producers-directors of their shows of course did their own editing. Only one producer reported a case where the director of an episode insisted on returning to edit his film. In this instance the director was a well-known actor-director, who, according to the producer interviewed, took such pride in his directing that he insisted on all his rights as director. However, as the producer pointed out, because this actor was not dependent on television directing for his livelihood, he was freer economically to return after the film was processed.

Even though most of the editing was done by the producers or by film editors selected by the producers, there seems to be no institutionalized conflict between directors and producers as

□

between free-lance writers and producers. This possibly can be explained economically because by contract the director does not share credit with anyone else, whether or not he cuts his own film. In all cases he gets residuals for reruns of the film.

The Producer and the Actor

The free-lance writer and the free-lance director reflect the producer's ideas and through them he controls the material presented. Another important element in film making, of course, is the actor, because without appealing actors, a series cannot be a success. The permanent cast has usually been chosen before the working producer enters the scene, and often the choice is made on the popularity of the actor with the general public. Therefore, the producer has less control over the main or starring actors than he has over the others who play an important part in film making.

Many important stars have clauses in their contracts giving them consultation rights over scripts. This does not mean full creative control, but they could refuse to do an episode they consider out of character for them, or in the case of comedy stars, a scene that they do not consider funny. Some stars have the right to refuse to do scenes that make them uncomfortable or that might not show them off "properly." This was not true in the early days of television when many of the performers were relatively unknown and therefore less powerful. Now, because many are well-known personalities, they have much more influence over what goes into the script.

Producer respondents differed somewhat in their assessment of the amount of control that actors had over the completed film series. Several insisted that the main characters would never change a line, that such changes were forbidden. Several others

□

claimed that the actors had either contractual clauses allowing them to refuse to play certain scenes or stories or even that certain stars, especially in very successful series, had usurped control because without them the series would certainly fold. In one presently defunct series, which was highly successful and broadcast for over five years, the star starting as a relatively unknown personality, had become valuable. He reached a point of control where he could refuse to do certain stories not suiting him, and several producers who had worked on the series over the years reported that the actor was in charge of the content. Another actor, who thinks of himself as a Humphrey Bogart type, demands action parts for himself and the producer tries to find stories to satisfy him.

Other actors control scripts in less obvious ways. One well-known actor insists on filming all of his scenes for the season during two weeks in the fall. The remainder of the scenes with the rest of the cast are filmed in the usual way throughout the season. Because of this, the star is seen in scenes just at the beginning of the fifteen-minute segments and often alone rather than in sequences with groups. This, in turn, not only limits the kind of stories that can be done, but also requires the producer to have ready in advance all the scripts needed for the entire season.

The relationship between the actor and producer seems quite different from that between the producer and writer or producer and director. Regardless of the difficulties they have with each other, the producers consider writers and directors as colleagues. Most producers, for instance, named other writers as the close friends they would choose to spend their leisure time with, and they considered directors to be craftsmen and, as such, much admired them. But the actor was considered either a "child" to be humored or a valuable "property" who might halt the series if not treated with kid gloves. This relationship was prevalent in Hollywood in pretelevision days, and as certain Hollywood "superstars" turn to television and build their

□

following, it is recurring. It should be noted, however, that television stars differ from movie stars because there does seem to be evidence that the series makes the star famous rather than the star making the series famous. Few television actors and actresses have been successful in different series, although several have been. It is more likely that the series character becomes the success; that is, it was Richard Chamberlain as Dr. Kildare or Vince Edwards as Ben Casey[13] that audiences seemed to idolize, whereas in the movies the actor himself drew the public's adulation. In actuality, the end result is the same because the person playing the role becomes the important "other" for the producer making decisions.

Besides temperament, the producer must also consider ability to play certain scenes. Some actors and actresses are more gifted than others, of course, but many times the problem of using their ability is more complex than just talent or capacity. According to the producers interviewed, many very talented performers would rather not work on television series because the range of the part is not rewarding enough. The challenge to the producer is to use their talent without sacrificing simplicity and losing an audience, which, many believe, does not want to see arty films or stories with a message. In other words, many producers felt that some of their permanent cast had a great deal of ability that went untapped because the series concept does not allow the plot to be too complex or the acting roles too demanding.

Conclusion

This chapter described the relationship of the television producer to the writer, director, and actor to show that the producer, although he has final decision-making authority, is not always in the position to use that authority to carry out his will. Others of almost equal status and professional ability, supposedly his subordinates, also must be considered when he makes decisions.

The producer and the writer are most closely related in function and possibly background. The dependency of the producer on the writer and the problems that have developed because the producer did not have a guild or organization to represent him have caused the greatest conflicts.[14] It is possible that we will witness the differentiation of one role (that of the writer) into two, and if the role of the producer becomes more institutionalized, the relationship of the two groups will become more clearly defined. This probably means that the role of producer defined in this book will continue as long as there are television series. The series as it has developed needs someone who can write scripts to maintain "quality control" over the film segments. Quality control does not necessarily refer just to artistic aspects of the film but also includes making the series consistent by keeping the stories within the general series concept. Because a series needs a chief writer responsible for the continuing story line, the producer's role developed. Whether the title "producer" should continue to go along with the duties is not the important question, because as long as the duties persist, there will be a necessity for the role. Because the training for such a job can come primarily from apprenticeship rather than from education only, the colleague system seems to operate in the industry.[15] No doubt the route to the job has become somewhat institutionalized, and those trained in other aspects of production probably can be recruited to fill these roles. However, as the role has evolved at present, writing background seems to be the most favorable experience for a series producer.

In the theater the author of the play has been law. Ideally, television producers would like a similar prerogative, but because they must share with others and the field is too new to have traditions, this is rarely the case. The producer must depend on

other writers for initial scripts, which hopefully will reflect
the producer's ideas rather than the writers'. Even if all writers
were "hacks," which, of course, they are not, it is still
difficult for anyone to develop an idea exactly as conceived by
the originator himself. The first compromise, then, occurs in the
script writing. The story conference that brings several subsidiary
personnel into the creative process continues the process of
weakening the producer's authority. For example, when I tried
to trace the origin of certain ideas, such as series concepts or
titles, more often than not the interviewees were confused about
who first proposed what. One producer, telling a story about the
title of a famous series, said, "We were all trying to think of a
good title when the secretary suggested the one we finally used."
Then he pondered for a few minutes and said, "No, it was the
associate producer . . . you know, I am not sure. Really, I can't
remember. But it was a gold mine." This would be an example
of "committee" work.

All these factors, plus the fact that directors and actors
have more status in certain instances than the producer does,
make the producer's authority less than all-embracing. This does
not necessarily mean that all producers are dissatisfied because
their creative authority is being undermined—often, they see their
role as mediator rather than creator—however, many are unhappy.
Of course, styles of work vary and some producers have more
authority than others because they demand it; but, on
the whole, if anyone has central creative control in television,
the producer does.

Television is seen as a producer's medium, as feature films
are a director's medium, because the producer is the final arbiter
of controversies and is the one person responsible for those
decisions about the unexpected that must be made quickly. Since
a television film is limited in both time allowed for production
and the amount of money that can be spent, many decisions
do have to be made quickly, a point that came up throughout the
interviews. A proposed set, for instance, might be too costly and

□

not only must a substitute be found immediately, but the script might have to be changed to fit the new setting. Only the producer has the authority to change the script. Possibly an actor is taken ill during shooting of an episode; the producer has to think of ways to use what has been filmed and finish the film without the actor. In the course of the interviews one actor acquired a black eye after some sequences of the film had been shot. Because the film is not usually shot in the same order it is finally shown, the filming already done was of scenes later in the play than the ones remaining to be filmed. The producer's problem was to account for the actor having a black eye at the beginning of the episode because in the later scenes (already shot) the eye was normal. After some discussion, the producer added new lines and changed one scene in the script in order to extend the time covered in the playlet. This made the black eye seem as though it had been planned, and extending the time period allowed for recovery of the black eye. This aspect of television film making, the necessity to make quick decisions, made television exciting and a desirable career choice for many of the producers. Some considered feature film making to be boring in contrast, because of the time required to shoot, edit, and put together a film for the theater.

The major complaint about producing was the lack of political and artistic freedom; this will be discussed in Chapter 6. However, this was not considered a problem by those "professional" or "creative" people working on the sets because such decisions are made elsewhere. The stars who want script control or the occasional director who demands the right to edit his film understand that there are certain limitations on television films before they accept the assignment. It is the producer who fights, if anyone does, with the network to be able to present certain ideas and views. These controversies are on a different level from the ones presented here, which are primarily craft-type conflicts rather than conflicts of ideas.

NOTES

1 Joan Moore, "Occupational Anomie and Irresponsibility," *Social Problems* 8 (1961): 293.

2 Lee Taylor, *Occupational Sociology* (New York: Oxford University Press, 1968), p. 573, says that the definition of occupational categories is not easy. This lack of precision is due partially to the limited degree to which workers are occupationally organized from within.

3 Arthur L. Stinchcombe, "Bureaucratic and Craft Administration of Production: A Comparative Study," *Administrative Science Quarterly* 4 (1959): 168–187.

4 If interested in film making and the development of the film, see Arthur Knight, *The Liveliest Art: A Panoramic History of the Movies* (New York: Macmillan Company, 1957). See also Kenneth MacGowan, *Behind the Screen: The History and Techniques of the Motion Picture* (New York: Dell Publishing Co., 1967) for a good introduction to the techniques of film making.

5 The Motion Picture and Television Producers Association is an industry-wide association of studio owners and independent producers who represent management.

6 Cole Trapnell, *Teleplay* (San Francisco: Chandler Publishing Co., 1966), p. 140, discusses the payment to free-lance writers. He says that a typical script costs about $4,000 and the outline about $400, but these figures are too low. Since he wrote his book, costs have increased. However, these figures in the text are averages. If a writer is well known, he can command more. The Writers Guild in arbitration with the Motion Picture and Television Producers Association agrees on a minimum amount.

7 "Hyphenates Hop Over to PGA," *Daily Variety*, Western Edition, October 12, 1967.

8 Since the interviews were completed, the Producers Guild of America, which has been in existence since 1932 under several names, won recognition for the first time by the Motion Picture and Television Producers Association as a collective-bargaining agent for producers of telefilms and feature movies. It is now a union, which it was not when the interviews were administered. However, it has not yet won residuals for its members as producers. The same conditions about residuals still held at this writing (1969) as when the producers were interviewed. Therefore, the information presented here is still applicable. There is now a jurisdictional dispute between the Writers Guild of America and the Producers Guild of America over representation of the hyphenates, which may be headed to the courts for resolution.

9 Hortense Powdermaker, *Hollywood: The Dream Factory* (Boston: Little, Brown and Co., 1950), pp. 110–120, describes the role of the film producer in film making in the 1940's. Leo C. Rosten, *Hollywood: The Movie Colony, the Movie Makers* (New York: Harcourt, Brace and Co., 1941), pp. 321–379, presents a more detailed and more objective description of the men who were titled "producer" in Hollywood before the advent of television.

10 Table 5–2 lists the number of producers who belong to the various important guilds. At this time, of course, all producers belong to the Producers Guild as well as other guilds. See note 8.

TABLE 5–2   Guild Membership

Writers Guild	48
Directors Guild	21
Producers Guild	11
Actors Guild	6
Film Editors Guild	2

This adds up to more than fifty-nine because many producers had multiple guild memberships. Several belonged to three guilds, others to only two. For instance, all eleven producers who had joined the Producers Guild at the time were also members of the Writers Guild, and several were members of the Directors Guild as well.

11 *Daily Variety*, October 12, 1967, p. 10.

12 The basis for writing credit now has been changed, so that the credit derives from the size of the contribution, regardless of its source, writer, or producer. In an arbitration writers' names are removed from the versions submitted so no one judging can be prejudiced (private communication from an informant in the industry).

13 This was mentioned by several producers during the interviews, as well as by some of the actors with whom I spoke on the sets.

14 As noted earlier, the Producers Guild still has not obtained residuals for its members. Thus some of the same conflicts still exist over credits; see footnote 8 in this chapter.

15 See Taylor, *op. cit.*, p. 419.

The Producer and the Network: Professional Versus Bureaucracy

As pointed out in Chapter 5, constraint on ideas for television can come from several sources, but final control rests with the networks who "buy" the shows. It is also within the power of the networks to encourage new ideas and creative production. However, because the networks' purpose is to reach the largest possible audience to sell products, they would more likely be a constraining force than a creative one. The basic philosophy of the three commercial networks in the United States, as publicly espoused, is "cultural democracy," which is defined as giving the people what they want.[1] There is a continuing fear that an angered segment of the public might boycott products of those sponsoring the programs. Therefore, the networks' main objective is not to offend the buying public. This, along with continuing fear of governmental control, has made the networks cautious and clearly not too innovative in programming new ideas.

Much space has been given to the subject of network control of the medium by both the popular press and the more

6

scholarly critics of television. American television is principally a commercial enterprise and, because its manifest function is to provide entertainment and information to the general public, it is a prototype for mass media generally.[2] The large bureaucratic organizations that have developed in the industry through which most of the television programs are presented have become so complex in operation and organization that the three major networks not only finance and control most of what the public views but are now producing teleplays on film and feature films as well.[3]

The major inquiry of this chapter is the influence of this complex organization: whether and how the producers of television series comply to the aims, directives, and other controls imposed by the networks; and if the producers are able to make their own creative efforts take precedence over those of the networks. However, to analyze the relationship between the network and the producer, it is first necessary to describe a network's bureaucratic organization. Following that discussion the chapter will then discuss two major topics: the conflicts that arise from the bureaucratic standards imposed on production by the networks and the conflicts that arise from bureaucratic supervision.

Definition of a Television Network

A network is part of a national broadcasting system characterized by (1) competitive free advertising (the networks are dependent on advertisers for economic support); (2) syndication of programs by means of a national network of stations; and (3) government regulation (as a compromise between public and private interests). The network's functions include: (1) *economic function*, the selling of advertising spots and programs to national advertisers, (2) *program distribution*, both origination and transfer of the programs, and (3) *program production* with facilities for production or release of programs produced by others (the series, for instance).[4] A network has also been briefly described as "a group of connected stations broadcasting the same television programs."[5]

Due to the nature of the medium (syndication of program material and a repetitive pattern of broadcasting), the major television stations find it desirable to affiliate with a major network. The network-affiliate relationship is contractual and controlled by government regulations. Networks can also own and operate stations, but they are limited to seven (five if VHF) by the Federal Communications Commission. Such stations provide income as well as a production facility for the network. Most stations, therefore, are affiliated by contract, not by ownership. A station may contract for one or more programs and may be a primary or secondary affiliate (to be a primary affiliate for CBS, a minimum of 40,000 homes must be reached). Thus, not all network shows reach national audiences and the local affiliated station, if it is not network owned, controls what actually appears on the air.[6]

The main office of a network is generally organized as follows: (1) *sales division* with departments for research, advertising, and promotion; (2) *distribution division* with departments of engineering, station relations, and traffic (communications networks); (3) *program division* with departments for production, production services, continuity acceptance, news, public affairs, and general programming; and (4) *business division* with departments for administration, finance and accounting, purchasing, labor relations, personnel, and legal matters. Headquarters for the three major networks are in New York City with each of the networks also maintaining major production centers in the Los Angeles area.[7]

The departments in the program division concerned with production and continuity acceptance are of major interest to

□

this study. All three networks subscribe to the television code
of the National Association of Broadcasters.[8] The code has been
revised several times since adoption, but its essential character
and functions are to keep governmental regulations minimal by
avoiding program practices that would offend pressure groups
and advertisers. Each network program division has a section to
approve or disapprove the content of shows (called "continuity
acceptance" or sometimes "broadcasting standards"). In
addition, the programming division has liaison personnel working
with the producers to suggest changes and approve the film as
it is being finished and before it is shown on the air.

All scripts are censored and approved by "continuity
acceptance" before they are filmed, and, if necessary, the liaison
men can keep the film or part of a film from being shown on
the air. In other words, for the producer the network in its role
as censor and filter for stories is a "secondary audience." When
deciding on material for production, he must keep the
networks in mind.

Network Control

Although much has been written on the limitations and controls
imposed by commercial television on the creative or craft aspects
of the industry, it has been essentially as social criticism, and
not as a topic for study in the sociology of work, occupations, or
communications. This study attempts specifically to determine
how the producer satisfies his several "clients" or "audiences,"
each of whom might have different goals. The differences in
goals among the key professionals working with the producer
were discussed in Chapter 5. The writer, director, and the actor,
regardless of the internal conflicts that arise in series production,
essentially work together to satisfy the two major audiences who

are their clients, the network and the viewing audience. For all the professional people working on a production to be "successful," the show itself must remain on the air and must satisfy both the network and the viewing audience. The viewing audience will be discussed in Chapter 8. It is the producer's conflicts or disputes over the artistic and substantive content of the show that are of concern here. It is quite likely that in order to please the networks the producer must subordinate his own obligation to his artistic discipline, which he might perceive as freedom to produce technically consistent or creative films or to produce controversial stories.

The conflicts that arise resemble those reported between other groups, such as scientists and professionals, and the bureaucracy for which they work. Peter Blau and W. Richard Scott believe that areas of conflict arise because professionals (including all those socialized to a discipline, although there are essential differences between scientists, craftsmen, and service professions) and bureaucracies have different modes of organization.[9] The conflicts that arise when professionals work for bureaucracies are of a special kind. Usually these are: (1) the professionals resist bureaucratic rules; (2) the professionals reject bureaucratic standards; (3) the professionals resist bureaucratic supervision; and (4) the professionals have conditional loyalty to the bureaucracy.[10] These are not the only possible areas of conflict, but they represent major sources of conflict for most groups who, because of training and occupational orientation, have one set of goals and standards, but must function under the standards of another group or organization.

In the communication industries the professionals producing messages or entertainment have a similarly complex relationship to the bureaucracy for which they work. Much of the sociological and communication research on journalists, for instance, focused on differences between the occupational standards of newsmen and the goals of the newspaper. It has also been pointed out

□

that newsmen are more concerned about the reactions of fellow reporters and the publishers than those of the reader.[11] The publishers may be oriented to standards that seem antithetical to the internalized values with which the newsmen are socialized, and freedom of the reporter seems subservient to the goals of the publisher.[12]

Raymond Bauer has suggested that because all communicators must have an audience in mind when writing or speaking, certain reference groups of the communicator become more important than others.[13] These reference groups are audiences to whom the communicator directs his communication. In the case of the producer, as with newsmen, the reference group of first importance is the audience that must approve the communications. For newsmen this is the publisher; for producers it is the network officials and censors. John and Matilda Riley also argue that the recipient of the communication must have a major influence on the communicator, and that major conflict can develop when the goals of the various groups in the social structure interact on the communicator to produce or change the message.[14] The Rileys, Herbert Gans, and Warren Breed have studied the situation where a communicator might be in direct opposition to those who control the medium in which he works, and how such a communicator must accommodate his beliefs to those for whom he works.[15] The producer, in order to remain successful, also must accommodate his beliefs to those of the network, or he must be powerful enough in his own right to be able to change the directives of the network. A major insight that comes from an exploration of the literature is that in the communication industries, as well as in the other work situations, two groups with basically different orientations interact, each influencing the other when decisions are made. The decision-making process is exactly that—a process—and must be considered in its interactional aspects. The major power over the producer does lie with the networks, because the producers are dependent on the economic resources of the networks. However, the networks are also dependent on the production staff for the product and thus must accommodate the producers.

Throughout the interviews it became obvious that network control was a basic problem for the producer. In the questionnaire used, the interviewees were given several opportunities to report on the structural constraints and the rewards they received from their work.[16] From the producers' reports it is evident that the networks use their power in the selection process to support or obstruct decisions made by the producers. As an aside, it should be noted that just a few of those interviewed mentioned the production company or the executive producer directly supervising them as an obstruction when making decisions. In most cases the producers claimed almost complete independence from their production company and their immediate supervisors—the executive producers—but they often declared that other production companies were much more repressive than their own. However, as will be discussed later, the studio structure does operate as a constraint for some producers, but the network is the most important constraint.

The network controls operate in several ways. In the case of new shows a network liaison man often sits in on the story conference where ideas for shows are developed. All scripts (whether the show is new or not) must be submitted to the network censor for approval; in some cases the story idea or story presentation must also be submitted. No show goes on the air without final approval from the network.

The conflict generated from this power of approval is different from the conflict reported between writers and producers. The latter is basically a labor dispute concerning economic rewards (residuals), but conflicts with networks, when they occur, concern artistic values; they are disputes over creative control of ideas. Of course, these conflicts also become economic in their consequences if the network cancels a show or forces the production company not to rehire the producer when the show goes into another season. The producer usually has a one-year contract with a production company (or a seven-year contract with yearly options in favor of the production company). However, it is possible and, indeed, not at all unusual for the network to demand that a producer be replaced even in midseason. Although the producer does not lose his income for the year, he is, of course, a less valuable property to the production company or studio than formerly. Because the actual difficulties that arise from disputes with the censorship office and, more importantly, with the network liaison men rarely concern financial rewards or costs but involve ideas, themes, and scenes, they are considered value disputes for the purpose of this study.

Analytically, the network control over the producer takes two separate forms: one directly from the network and the other from the network through the censor's office. In the first form the producers often resent bureaucratic supervision as such; in the second form the producers react to what seems to be arbitrary bureaucratic standards. Many producers see both types of control as limitations on their creative freedom to express themselves according to their own beliefs and standards.

Network as Censor

The idea of censorship is so negatively loaded that few media censor or monitoring agencies have publicly discussed their activities in detail.[17] However, during the last two years the audience has become more aware of television censorship as a reality because several comedians have discussed on the air the problems they have had with the networks. Occasionally, "talk shows," broadcast late in the evening, have words or statements missing from the sound track because they were blanked out by censors.[18] Such shows are usually taped earlier in the day for presentation at later hours; because they are recorded "live" (without retakes), the cutting or censorship technique is by necessity crude and obvious. Less obvious, of course, and rarely complained about publicly is the censor's control over scripts in film production. The censors use the television code to justify eliminating certain themes or specific phrases from scripts. The categories in the code (as with most codes) are so loose that they can be interpreted in various ways at the discretion and will of the person acting as censor.[19] The first difficulty the producer encounters is the lack of clear-cut objective standards in code interpretation by the censor.

In fact, the censor's objectivity does seem to vary from network to network, although the three networks all use the same code as justification for decisions to delete objectionable material. The producer who is highly committed to a particular idea, theme, or segment soon finds out what the censor for that particular network approves or disapproves. Most of the producers interviewed, especially the older ones, had had a number of years of experience dealing with standards; this experience was incorporated into their decision-making process. The producer quickly learns whether the particular censorship office over him has certain "prejudices" or is more apt to disapprove material in special areas.

A number of producers talked about compromise or fighting strongly and the general constraint they felt in having to consider the network censor. Occasionally, a producer will feel strongly enough about a particular story or idea, considering it worth fighting the censor's office. In most instances, however, the producer already knew exactly what would be approved and disapproved. It was in discussing this area that a number of producers used the term "good taste." By "good taste," most meant excluding overtly lewd, crude language and images

□

referring to bodily functions and certain types of sexual behavior. Because of legal considerations and because certain acts are generally considered antisocial by the majority of the population, such decisions are not troublesome to the producer; in most instances they rarely present a problem, and when in doubt the censor's edict is followed.

However, the major areas of conflict, either overt or covert, are sex, politics, and racial-ethnic matters. Of the three sexual matters are of the most concern to the censor's office. The other two, especially if there is continued pressure by a producer to include such topics week after week, become the concern of the network officials. Occasionally, the censor uses the code to delete controversial content of a political or racial nature, but the producers soon learn what is acceptable to the censors in those areas, or the argument between the producers and the networks moves from the sensor to the network officials concerned with programming.

In an analysis of the number of deletions or comments made by the censor in 1956, Charles Winick listed fourteen categories.[20] Of these (advertising, animism, antisociality, crudity, politics, ethnic matters, etc.), "sex" leads the group with 19.9 percent of the total deletions, compared to 14.3 percent in the "spoofing the serious" category, the next highest. The political and ethnic categories received just 2.4 percent and 8.7 percent, respectively.[21] The data obtained in this study confirm part of this finding: more producers mentioned difficulties with the censor in the area of sex than any other (fifteen out of fifty-nine).

Conflict occurs most often between the producer of comedy shows and the censor's office. The producers of comedy shows more often come from the ranks of performers or comedy writers for the theater and night clubs. As Winick points out, sexual taboos differ considerably from one medium to another, and the movies, for example, since the advent of television, have become much more emancipated and enjoy greater freedom of expression than they once did.[22] Because of this a particular problem has arisen. Many movies that the networks probably would not allow to be filmed especially for television are shown on television during the prime viewing hours. Such movies have caused several producers to protest the "double standard" prevailing. Also, local stations seem to have more freedom in this area, and shows made locally seem to be freer than network-filmed shows.

If a sexual topic is considered to have some educational value, such as the problems of abortion, illegitimate childbirth, or homosexuality, it is not as likely to be censored. However, producers who have been involved with such shows point out that the outcome must meet specified standards. For example, one cannot show a happy homosexual. Some themes, however, border on the unacceptable but are approved on an *ad hoc* basis. The 1968–1969 season had one show on the air with the main character a man posing as a woman.[23] However, the role carefully makes clear that he is not a deviant, a transvestite, but because he is impersonating a woman, there is a possibility for misunderstanding. One pilot that was viewed during the course of the research concerned a man who was a bigamist. As far as this investigator knows, the pilot did not sell, but the fact that it was made and financed shows that network executives thought the subject could come within the code regulations.

The networks' relationship to the producer and the areas of conflict that arise are not limited to the censor's office. Through network directives and constant supervision by the liaison staff, the entire process is influenced. Problems that arise in the political area usually do not concern the censor's office; few producers mentioned this as a topic where the censor presented difficulty. Yet almost all the producers (forty-seven) had some comment about the network censorship from the liaison men or from directives from network officials concerning political and racial themes.

The Network as Supervisor (Creative Decisions)

Shows that have high ratings are usually exempt from network supervision except in unusual cases. (All shows are subject to the censor's standard.) Even when the network owns the show directly, that is, the network is the production company as well as buyer of the show, there seems to be little if any concern for the content of a show that "has made it." Several producers stated that the networks are essentially apolitical and within certain limits are little concerned with the ideology or philosophy of a show if the ratings are high and the advertisers are satisfied.

However, when a show is new there is much concern over all types of content decisions; these could be artistic, technical, or political. Here the presence of the liaison men at the story conferences, through phone calls and personal visits, is a threat to all. This depends, of course, partly on the reputation of the producer and, to some extent, of the executive producer. The more successful producers find that they have less interference, but because most executive producers have histories of successes and failures, the producer's reputation is no guarantee that the network's representative will not be present to watch each step. While the reputation of the men involved is some consideration, the subject matter of the show seems to be more important. It is well known that networks are reluctant to try new ideas and would rather remake series with themes that have been successful, particularly in the recent past. When a show is considered "different," creative, or controversial, the networks take more interest in its production.

For example, one producer envisioned a series with forensic psychiatry as its main theme, but according to him:

I had to change it from a forensic psychiatric series to a general psychiatric series. *Network X had bought it, and they told me in no uncertain terms that I change it into a general kind of psychiatry with general kinds of stories.* They said that no one had ever heard of forensic psychiatry, but I thought the combination of courtroom drama with psychiatric themes would be interesting and different.

The same producer had recently left another show because of network interference. This happened occasionally, only three producers reporting such incidents. Their reasons for leaving were similar. One producer described his problems with the network concerning the show he left as follows:

I left it over fights—fights over what I wanted and what other people wanted. I had several changes put into the series. The network and some of the executives of my own company (note: he was one of the few who mentioned problems with his own production company) made cast changes that I thought were major cast changes, which were like falling dominoes, which in turn necessitated changing the shows we were going to start with, which in turn necessitated changing our whole series concept. *I was subjected to what I consider a lot of harrassment and interference, so we mutually agreed that they wanted the series to go a certain way and I another, so they let me out of my contract because I like to do things my way.* I left the show before it went on the air. The show as it appeared on the air was more their way than mine. Now it is going to be the first show canceled, which doesn't make me happy because even though I was right (note: he didn't consider the possibility the show might have failed even if his suggestions were followed), I would rather have been wrong because it means everyone is out of a job.

This is a western you know, but a different kind of western. At least it was in its original conception. The people at the networks say they want something fresh, they want something new, they want something different. You come in with something new, fresh, and different. You work on it a little more and they say, wait a minute—that's a little too different. *They pay lip service to the idea of originality but in actuality the activity takes place along areas that are somewhat familiar to them. They will buy anything they can relate to success.* They don't want it exactly like it was before. If you wanted to do a western that was

□

similar to "Gunsmoke" but not "Gunsmoke," you are in pretty good shape. But if you do something that is totally different or something that is exactly "Gunsmoke," chances are you are dead.

Another producer who left a show over difficulties with the networks experienced a period of unemployment because, according to his report, he had made his grievances public. During the interview he read to me from newspaper accounts of the differences that had developed between himself and the network; he proudly kept these clippings in his desk drawer. The incidents had occurred several years in the past, and he thought that the publicity set his career back several years. His situation is a good example of the type of value conflict that can develop in the industry.

I attacked the show after I had left it. I attacked the show as cheap sensationalism. I have done a number of things in the industry that I am not proud of, but in this case, I felt I had to draw the line somewhere. When I saw this kind of crap, I drew my line. I make a case in point with a script I did not want to shoot. The script was about a bomber pilot in World War II, who was suffering pangs of conscience because he had caused so much damage to other people. The psychiatrist in the script had a five-page speech justifying the killing, and I hardly thought a psychiatrist would talk that way—five pages about what a great and noble deed the pilot performed. I objected to that being seen on a commercial television show. It was one of a series of instances. Another thing I hated was the instant cures. A homicidal maniac visits his friendly psychiatrist and in three weeks you walk out happy. I thought that was an unfortunate thing for the gullible public. What the program said was that anyone with problems can go to their psychiatrist and come out jim-dandy.

I blasted them and caused quite a stink. I have never done it since because it didn't do me much good in the end. It was really biting the hand that feeds. What I should have said is that we have artistic differences. I walked out of a three-year contract over three or four scripts like the one I described. I can tell you I would never do it again.

□

The third producer who resigned a producing job over a conflict with a network was quoted earlier. In order to explain the controversy that developed, the producer said:

On paper it was my obligation to develop the stories, but what they let you do are two different things. The network had an idea what the series should be and I'll admit they told me very early. Their idea was that you never do anything that hasn't been done before successfully. I ignored that completely. I went ahead and developed the material in my own way which appalled them. My whole approach to writing is to develop a character—I know you have to have a heavy in a dramatic western, but to develop a character you have to consider his passions. You say if that were me, I would be this way which means there are shades of gray. I couldn't write him any differently. They want black heavies. As a matter of fact, I wrote a little poem, if I can remember it. The couplet that ended it:
> Ambivalent Heavies are hereby forbid
> Gray is for horses, never the id.

They want a fellow who is totally evil. Your lead will fight him to the death and destroy him. This is not what life is all about. *It is not what I want to write about. That is when the trouble began.* The tragedy of it was that they were supported in the ratings. I had said wait until some of these shows come on. I thought two or three of the shows were magnificent—just beautiful. Whether or not the ratings are accurately representing the public is open to question. But the ratings do tell us what the 1,100 Nielsen families are doing because they are taken every fifteen minutes. You can see what those 1,100 people are doing. The shows I liked, the shows I thought were so valuable, the audience just turned off. But the things they liked I thought were total trash.

The thing I am saying really is that there are two major conflicts—one is creative and one is purely commercial. From the creative point of view they are dead wrong, but from the commercial point of view they are dead right. There is a separation here between those in New York who have to sell the material and those here who have to create the material. There is a vast gap which has never been bridged. There are a few people who can say I see what you are talking about, let me see if I can make it work. But these are a few, very, very few.

□

Producers who are willing to fight the network to the ultimate end of their differences are very unusual. Most producers who have conflicts over specific issues either give in to network pressure or fight in a more limited way. In addition, many producers do not experience pressure or interference from the networks. Table 6–1 shows the number of producers who did or did not experience network interference with story selection and content. These figures apply to the shows in production at the time the producers were interviewed and do not necessarily reflect past experiences.

TABLE 6–1   Pressure from Network

No pressure	23
Occasional	26
Continuous	10
Total	59

When conflicts occur between the producers and the networks, they were often subtle and devious. If a producer is willing to take a strong stand, which will result in either doing the show his way or else, it usually results in his removal from the job. Since producers value their jobs for a variety of reasons (economic considerations are just part of the story), few were willing to confront the networks too directly. Whether producers have direct or indirect conflicts, those who perceive the networks as interfering with the selection process and those who are more willing to fight this interference have outstanding things in common.

Network Pressure and Types of Producers

Why some producers are pressured and others not seems to depend on several factors. The type of show being produced is certainly one factor. As was suggested earlier, the more successful the show, the less likely the network is to interfere; the less political or controversial the show, the less likely the network is to interfere. The type of producer is also important; some producers experience no interference because they carry out the network's suggestions and directives without complaint. Others seem to try to thwart the network directives at every opportunity and therefore are under constant pressure.

The above point can be elaborated by comparing the way the types of producers relate to the networks. While some, regardless of type, do not have any external conflicts with the networks, many producers expressed reservations and apologized during the interviews for not doing shows that were either more political or more creative. It could well be that much of the professing of internal conflict was in response to the producers' belief of what I as an "intellectual" expected. Several producers seemed defensive and expressed the hope that this study would not be another attack on commercial television. What is reported here is a summary of the reactions of several types of producers to network supervision of their day-to-day activities. Much of this comes from answers to direct questions about network interference, but some information was offered in response to questions about how much they like working in television generally and the comparison of television with other media.[24]

The film makers have few expressed conflicts with the network. Because they see their function more as coordinators than as creators, they are less likely to view the network as a constraining influence than are those in the other two groups. They are also less likely to take a stand on story content than the others. It is more important to them to learn all aspects of production, especially direction and editing, so they can go on to make theater films in a more artistic way. They believe in holding their talent in abeyance until the time is right for them to leave series television and become moviemakers. To learn their craft well is the key distinguishing ambition of this group.

□

Because of their craft orientation and comparative youth, they experience little conflict in pleasing network officials by subordinating their own artistic values about film making.

Because they do not think that their function is to be a taste leader or that television's function is to proselytize for political and social change, they see no inconsistency in "giving the public what it wants." Rather, they see television's function as entertainment, not delivering messages. Most claimed to be politically liberal and usually voted for Democratic party candidates, but their personal political views caused few if any conflicts because they had no desire to use the medium as a means of political expression.

While the film makers claimed an interest in politics and considered themselves politically liberal, several were quick to point out that they were not radicals. Just one was active politically, although all had voted Democratic in the last California gubernatorial election. Several commented on Governor Reagan's having been an actor, which made them wary of his qualifications for governor.

Several film makers could not see television as anything but a "day-to-day hack medium because unfortunately the nine-year-olds are in charge of the sets," and none considered television an art form. For them television was a stepping stone. As one of them put it:

I think it is every producer's design to go into motion pictures. Because, for my money, it is the true art form. In television you can make quality only up to a point. There are such things as quality television shows, but it is difficult to do that week after week. I can point at some shows which are really quality shows, some half-hours are good solid commercial television, and sometimes we bomb.

One of my shows which was brilliant was the bottom of the rating. But I am learning, this is what television is all about. You have to get out eventually and hopefully I am on the threshold. But to repeat, this is where you learn. Television is

□

like the B movies of the thirties and forties. It is supposed to provide entertainment. If you want art or messages, you have to leave television.

I have to use television for what it is, and it is not an art form but a business form, and if I can make a name for myself in any way, in moments of artistry or commercialism and artistry combined because one without the other is pointless because we are in business to make money. I would like to use *whatever reputation I make in television to make the transition.*

This same producer, when asked about network interference, was quick to point out that he does not consider it to his advantage to fight the networks. He said that he has little network interference because he knew what the networks would not accept. Occasionally, there was something that the censor's office might object to, but it is usually a minor matter, which is easily corrected. In script selection and in choosing stories, he has had little or no trouble with the networks. He was quite firmly convinced that it is the network's prerogative to control what goes into a show, and he has no difficulty assessing the network's desires. He believes once he leaves television-series production, he would be able to insist on doing what he wants in his own way; but at this time, while he might quarrel over some of the ideas of commercial television, he neither wants to nor feels able to tell the networks what they should do. This particular producer had fairly definite political and social ideas that he would like to put forth either through the films when he could or through serious writing. But for him television series were the wrong time and place for such polemics.

It should be made clear, however, that the film makers occasionally did feel constraints and conflicts in their position. Several openly stated that the medium did not provide freedom, and that in order to produce it was necessary to subordinate their own values, but the rewards (both actual and anticipated) of producing films even under the conditions described were

□

more important than the constraints. They believed that subordinating artistic and political values at that stage of their careers would someday enable them to do as they please, making the kind of films that would express their talent more meaningfully. In brief, although they perceive the basic goals of the bureaucracies as different from their own ultimate or desired goals, the film makers go along with the system as it stands and select content that will meet with network approval.

The writers-producers have the most conflicts with the networks because they are most committed to the ideals of their craft: basically, the writer should have control of what he writes. The writers-producers see themselves more as the chief writers of their series than as film makers. Most became producers to begin with because when they were free-lance writers, the producers they worked for changed or rewrote their scripts, and they prefer to be in a position to control their material. Being involved with both the series concept and the individual scripts and being the most politically committed, they are more likely to incur both network interference and pressure.

Most of their difficulties with the networks are more covert than overt because they know that they must please the network officials to remain in production. For them the story is the most important element in film making. They are also more likely to believe that television should be used to express political views and to change society. Several thought a major qualification for producing is knowing how to fight the network and related numerous incidents describing how social or political messages were put into particular stories over network opposition or deviously. There was much discussion about compromise and the ability to give in when necessary. A "good" producer fights for what he wants but also is able to give in to the networks' authority when necessary. The battle seemed to be continuous, one that was thought to be lost more often than won. A frequently used device is to use cover-up stories to make a point;

135   The Producer and the Network

□

for example, telling a story about Stokely Carmichael as an Indian in a western or historical setting.

Political viewpoints ranged from ultraliberal (several had been socialists in the 1930's) to ultraconservative (supporters of Goldwater for president). Although the stated political viewpoints covered a wide range, most of them had a Liberal or Democratic party designation. In contrast to the film makers they thought television should function as an instrument of social change, and they tended to present programming more racially integrated, more sympathetic to psychiatry and mental health, and more antiwar. It was agreed that the networks are typically apolitical and would support programs successful with audiences regardless of their political content. However, the writer-producer sees the networks as giving in to advertisers and pressure groups because they fear losing their business and support by antagonizing the large mass audience. Therefore, by never presenting controversial stories, they never find out if they could be a success with the public. The networks were seen as apolitical because during long experience in television writing and production, many realized that network norms and beliefs were not rigid but changed from year to year. Indeed, as turned out to be the case, several predicted that more racially integrated programs would be forthcoming. One of their major complaints is that instead of leading public opinion and social change, the networks follow social conditions after they have begun to change.

The writers-producers, more so than the other two groups, see themselves as often manipulated by the system; they definitely express feelings of impotency and constraint. Because they are oriented more toward their craft (script writing) and the content of the script is seen as a force for education and change, they perceive the network's goals as in opposition to their own. They see the network as willing to present anything that would have a high Nielsen rating rather than as civically responsible and willing to offer higher quality shows with a social message.

☐

The old-line producers believe television's function is to sell products by reaching large audiences; they think their role is to provide simple entertainment to large audiences. This group was the most successful of the producers interviewed, with success measured by highest incomes and responsibility for more original series ideas (the writers-producers were next). Because they were successful and were oriented toward the same goals as the network, one would think that they would have few conflicts with the networks. But such was not the case. Since they were responsible for many successful series, they often believe that they are more aware of what would appeal to the viewing audience than the network officials. As already mentioned, the network liaison men are more likely to interfere in story selection for a new series and try to give expert advice to the producer. As the series becomes successful, there is less inter-ference. When an old-line producer becomes involved with a new series, he often battles with the network not so much over political and social ideas but over casting decisions and story ideas, having little to do with social messages. The old-line producers usually have little to do with dramatic television that supposedly would enlighten or inform the public; in fact, one compared the television industry to General Motors because each manufactured a saleable product. Their credo could be expressed by the much-quoted statement: "If you want messages, call Western Union" (attributed to Samuel Goldwyn and Louis B. Mayer, both successful Hollywood producers in the 1930's and 1940's).

Like all the others interviewed, this type of producer would oppose the networks just up to a certain point because they also depend on network approval to continue producing the series. However, because the nature of the conflict is usually apolitical and they have more successes to their credit, the old-line producers are more likely to convince the networks to do things their way than are, for example, the writers-producers. The conflict between the old-line producers and the networks seems to be overt; it is more a contest between equals than between a superior and a subordinate. The political orientation of this group varies from conservative to liberal (most again are Democrats), but this does not influence their roles as television producers because they separate their personal politics from their job performance.

Network as Supervisor (Technical Decisions)

Several producers felt safer taking a stand on innovative techniques or effects than on story content because a recent variety show using sensory effects had been very successful, and because pressure groups usually do not protest film techniques. However, most producers and the networks thought such novel methods had little place in series production; therefore, this caused few, if any, disputes. The producers who did wish to be more creative blamed the older technicians (cameramen, mostly) rather than the networks because they were unable, according to one producer, to handle the newer equipment and were set in their ways—using the same facilities that had been used in Hollywood for over three decades.

Because many of the film makers in the sample were more apt to be educated in departments that stressed filming techniques and the use of cameras, one might expect that, even if relatively uninterested in the message, they would desire to be more innovative technologically. It has been noted that many of the film makers did want to make more "creative" theater films someday, but in television series they saw their major function as show supervision and were more concerned with staying within the budget, maintaining story consistency, and filming in the allotted time.

In the bureaucratic studios where most film makers worked,

□

production duties were divided more among different members of the production team, and the producer had less authority over such matters. How the series was to be filmed was decided before the producer came on the job. In the smaller production companies the filming techniques could (though usually did not) vary from week to week depending on the agreement between the director and the producer.

The Network as Reference Group

The writers-producers in the sample were often more willing to fight network interference and pressures than the film makers were because they are more ideologically committed to certain political and social positions. It is also possible that occupational alternatives are opened to them that are not available to the film makers. Most of the writers-producers had been successful free-lance writers before they became producers, and free-lance writing provides as high or possibly higher income than does producing. Although the film makers are more apt to be trained in film making art or in television techniques and therefore seem more professionally committed, they are also more willing to subordinate their views about what constitutes artful production to network desires as the price necessary to continue to work in the industry. Their goal is to gain the reputation and experience that might give them a chance to do things more independently.

Most of the producers considered themselves liberal politically, but there seemed to be little if any correlation between their expressed political viewpoints and their relations with the network. Most producers, for example, when asked if they favored one publicly supported television channel, said they did not or, if they did, were quick to point out that government controls might limit creativity even more than the networks.[25] There was a great deal of misunderstanding concerning this question although it was worded clearly and clarified several times for them. A few did see merit in having another channel opened, which might give the viewing audience a wider choice of programs, but most were opposed for a variety of reasons, suggesting a misconception of what public television might do or a worry that such a channel might become a propaganda arm for the government. One man opposed such support because he was sure that the programming would be dull. Basically, most agreed that television should be operated as a free enterprise system, although the networks also control creativity and free expression.

The basic difference between those producers who are willing or desire to fight network control and those who are not seems to be their reference-group orientation. The film makers may be directing their communication directly to the networks rather than to the viewing audience or to some internalized group. They are not pressured by the networks because they have learned and accepted the policy for the particular show they are on. Because these men are unlikely to be on a new, untried show, this policy has been standardized in previous seasons. The goals of the network in cases such as these are relatively easy to learn. If such a show should decline in ratings, often the production company will transfer the producer to another show rather than have the network liaison men on the sets. The bureaucratic structure of the production company, therefore, also contributes to the way producers relate to the networks.

The other two groups, the writers-producers and the old-line producers, although otherwise different, both often experience a great deal of network interference. This is not because they are unaware of network policy. If they are unaware in the beginning, they are soon informed by the network officials what is considered acceptable for a particular program. As stated in Chapter 2,

□

the norms and policies of the networks can vary from season to season or even from program to program. Sometimes it depends on the social climate as perceived by network officials, sometimes on the day the show is seen, sometimes on advertiser displeasure. Producers have to relearn policy with each show. Most of the complaints about network interference centered on two reasons: (1) the writers-producers believed that the networks failed to meet their social responsibilities as agents of change and sources of information concerning society, and (2) old-line producers thought they knew what the viewing audience would like to see and the networks did not. In either case the major audience or reference group for these men is not the bureaucracy, although to maintain their position they have to please the networks most of the time. The basic target of their communications is either some internalized standards or the viewing audience as they perceive it. In any case the network is considered both as the controlling agent and as an audience (although not always a primary one) for the content being produced. The policy of the network, however vaguely defined, is important to the producer whether he conforms or overtly or covertly fights control.

NOTES

1   The term "cultural democracy" was used by Bernard Berelson, "The Great Debate on Cultural Democracy," *Studies in Public Communication* 3 (1961): 3–14. Also see Bernard Berelson, "In the Presence of Culture," *Public Opinion Quarterly* 28 (1964): 1–13.

2   See Charles R. Wright, *Mass Communication: A Sociological Perspective* (New York: Random House, 1959), p. 15, for a definition of mass media.

3   See "No Curb on ABC Feature Plans," *Daily Variety*, January 10, 1968, pp. 1 ff., on the American Broadcasting System in movie and telefilm production. This is a relatively new operation for ABC as well as the other two networks. According to a syllabus for the course given by Gordon Stulberg at the University of California at Los Angeles in

September 1963 (course number 803AB), *The Entertainment Industry— Its Structure and Economy,* no mention is made of the networks producing either feature films or telefilms. In 1967 Mr. Stulberg became head of the film-production department for CBS.

4 Sidney W. Head, *Broadcasting in America* (Boston: Houghton Mifflin Co., 1956), pp. 220–222. See also Robert E. Summers and Harrison B. Summers, *Broadcasting and the Public* (Belmont, Calif.: Wadsworth Publishing Co., 1966), pp. 137–174, for a description of the relationship between the networks and the individual stations.

5 Oswald Spilbeck, *ABC of Film and TV Working Terms* (London and New York: Focal Press, 1960), p. 89.

6 Head, *op. cit.,* pp. 228–229.

7 *Ibid.,* pp. 232–233.

8 See Appendix B. *The Television Code,* National Association of Broadcasters, twelfth edition, 1967, pp. 2–10, is reproduced. The Code was revised in 1968 for the thirteenth time but the changes are minor. The twelfth edition of the Code was being used when the interviews took place.

9 Peter M. Blau and W. Richard Scott, *Formal Organization: A Comparative Approach* (San Francisco: Chandler Publishing Co., 1962), pp. 60–66.

10 W. Richard Scott, "Theory of Organizations," in Robert E. L. Faris, ed., *Handbook of Modern Sociology* (Chicago: Rand McNally, 1964), p. 517. Also see W. Richard Scott, "Professional in Bureaucracies—Areas of Conflict" in Howard Vollmer and Donald L. Mills, eds., *Professionalization* (Englewood Cliffs, N. J.: Prentice-Hall, Inc., 1966), pp. 365–374.

11 Walter Gieber, "News Is What Newspapermen Make It," in Lewis A. Dexter and David Manning White, eds., *People, Society, and Mass Communication* (New York: Free Press, 1964), pp. 173–182. Also R. Jones, Vernon Troldahl, and J. Hvistendalh, "News Selection Patterns From a State TTS-Wire," *Journalism Quarterly* 38 (1961): 303–312.

12 Warren Breed, "Social Control in the Newsroom: A Functional Analysis," *Social Forces* 33 (1955): 326–335.

13 Raymond Bauer, "The Communicator and the Audience," *Conflict Resolution* 2 (1958): 66–76.

14 John Riley and Matilda Riley, "Mass Communication and the Social System," in Robert K. Merton, Leonard Broom, L. S. Cottrell, Jr., eds., *Sociology Today* (New York: Basic Books, 1959), pp. 537–578.

15 *Ibid.;* Herbert Gans, "The Creator-Audience Relationship in the Mass Media: An Analysis of Movie Making," in Bernard Rosenberg and David Manning White, eds., *Mass Culture* (New York: Free Press, 1957), pp. 315–324; Breed, *op. cit.*

16 Appendix A, Questions 12, 14, 15, and 23.

17 Charles Winick, "Censor and Sensibility: A Content Analysis of the Television Censor's Comments," reprinted from *Journal of Broadcasting* (Spring, 1961), pp. 117–135, in Otto Larsen, ed., *Violence and the Mass Media* (New York: Harper & Row, 1968), p. 254.

18 "The Johnny Carson Show," which is presented on the East and West Coasts at 11:30 P.M., often has part of the content blipped out.

19 Appendix B. Also see Winick, *op. cit.*, p. 257.

20 *Ibid.*, pp. 258–266.

21 *Ibid.*, p., 267.

22 *Ibid.*, p. 254. Also the producer respondents make the same point.

23 "The Ugliest Girl in Town."

24 Appendix A, Question 23 in particular; also see 12, 14, and 15.

25 Appendix A, Question 30.

The Producer,
Network Control,
and Violence

Following the deaths of Martin Luther King and Robert
Kennedy, violent content in both children's programs and
dramatic shows on television became more of a public issue,[1]
network policy on violence changed between the time of the
first set of interviews in 1967–1968 and the second set in 1970.
The material presented in this chapter was mostly obtained from
the second set of interviews, and it focuses on the producer's
reactions to the change in network policy during the two-year
time period. The issues of violent content and how producers
perceive their role in its presentation provide the best examples of
how network policy about television drama can change and
how network control can operate. Also of interest is the change
in children's programs presented on Saturday morning along
with changes in the western and adventure shows made for the
prime evening hours.

At the time of the first interviews, violence was rarely
mentioned as an issue. The writers-producers were the only ones
who verbally expressed disagreement with the amount of violence
that appeared on television, although they were much more

7

concerned with social policy, messages, and social change. None of the producers of the evening shows showed concern about the effects of content on the viewer. The situation had changed by 1970, and a few producers of Saturday-morning shows were overtly concerned about the harm violent programming might do to young minds.

Of all the issues that generate public and governmental concern about television, the effects of violent content have been most debated. The experimental studies concerning the effects of violence on children have been inconclusive. While an extensive literature on the subject is developing, none of it proves conclusively that television violence is or is not detrimental. There is as much evidence that violence on television does lead to violent or at least aggressive behavior in children as there is alternative evidence that television might provide an outlet for aggressive tendencies.[2]

Of all the controversies about television, this one is most pertinent to the producer of dramatic television. Political themes or stories can be easily deleted because such content is usually obvious. When these themes are subtle or watered down, the producers and the network both seem to believe that their effects are thereby less influential. Racial themes are viewed similarly. In any case, however, such themes are considered to be "messages" rather than entertainment. Sexual references are a somewhat different issue. Here, the rule seems to be "try to get away with as much as possible." If one watches television series over the years (which is possible because of the reruns and syndicated shows), one notes that there is more freedom now about sexual references than five years ago. The reasons for this seem obvious: as the movies and periodicals have adopted a more liberal policy toward sex, other media have changed as well. Whether there is a "sexual revolution" is not the question, although those in charge of producing mass media seem to think there is; this is reflected in the way they present the relationship between the sexes. Because television goes directly into the home, it is not as free as the movies or the stage. Only infrequently has television been accused of contributing to the loosening "moral fabric" of American youth. Generally, only the rock-and-roll teenage dance shows and the late movies made for theater (usually cut to meet censorship requirements) might be considered overtly suggestive. While television producers believe that sexual themes have great audience appeal and are entertaining, most also agree that given the general attitudes of the public and Congress, sex is one area where censorship, both internal and external, is necessary. Admittedly, attitudes and reactions to political, racial, and sexual themes are not consistent; however, it is possible for producers to learn the extent of network policy and public tolerance rather easily.

Violence is another kind of problem. While within certain limits it is possible to tone down or increase violence, it is difficult to define violence or separate it from the dramatic content of the shows. In television a mythology has grown up about the types of stories that draw audiences. Simplistic comedy should be slapstick because action and noise rather than subtle routines attract audiences. In the situation comedy or family comedy show, the plots are minimal, and the interaction among the characters, producers and network officials believe, provides the amusement. In the dramatic series, the western, the mystery and detective story, and the others as well, action over dialogue is not only preferred but is considered a normative part of the dramatic genre. When one thinks of a western or detective story, one immediately thinks of guns, fistfights, broken furniture, and the like. Even in stories that might be considered more "dramatic," producers are often told that a theme is too arty, which usually means too much dialogue, not enough action. In cases where someone protests the lack of action, the common advice is to "put a bear on the beach," meaning that when a script seems slow, action should be added whether or not this fits

□

the dramatic sense of the teleplay. The problem then becomes: when does action become violence? This is an area of continuing controversy.

Throughout the industry the belief persists that mass-media portrayals of violence attract large audiences. The unanswered question is whether or not social behavior is affected by the violence portrayed. Media personnel are prone to declare that because social scientists have failed to establish a link between television violence and violent behavior, none exists. Yet, as Alberta Siegel reports, the television industry "exists and reaps its profits from the conviction that television viewing does affect behavior—buying behavior."[3] Because the medium executives want to attract large audiences and sell products, they contradict themselves by pointing out the lack of effects of television violence, while assuring advertisers of the positive effects of advertising on buying habits.

Even when the networks and producers try to limit violence, the conceptual problem of defining violence remains. Dean George Gerbner and his staff at the Annenberg School of Communication did a content analysis of television entertainment programs;[4] the study was concerned with both the extent and the nature of violence. The study had to be done quickly; in addition, they reported a problem with definitions and conceptualizations. They analyzed network television programs transmitted during prime evening time and on Saturday mornings October 1–7, 1967 and 1968. Although those involved in the study had some misgivings about the haste with which it was done, the findings are particularly valuable for this book, since the content analysis was performed on programs that were being produced when my original interviews took place. Violence as defined by Gerbner and his associates is the overt expression of force intended to hurt and kill, and a violent episode is a scene of any duration between violent parties.[5] By their count during the two weeks of televiewing, 872 violent episodes occurred in a total of 149 plays with 112 plays portraying violence significant to the plot. Out of a total 183 plays analyzed, some violence occurred in eight out of every ten plays. Although violent acts, as defined, did occur in the majority of teleplays made for both children and adults,[6] their study (like this chapter) made no attempt to conclude that the violence had effects on the viewing public.

Not only is it impossible to decide whether violent content affects the audience in an adverse way, it is also impossible through the data-gathering methods used to decide whether violence is as necessary to story plots or to the attraction of audiences as the network officials, the production houses, and the producers themselves seem to believe. It is possible, however, from the data available (from the second set of interviews especially) to shed some light on Bradley Greenberg's suggestion that since the men who write, produce, and direct television films operate under conditions of high tension and aggression, the level of dramatic output is also intense.[7] To the contrary, others believe that Hollywood production people are primarily responsive to the demands of the organizations buying their products, and the interview data I gathered seem to suggest the latter. The children's cartoon shows are the best example of an obvious and overt change from violent to nonviolent content. The western and adventure shows made for early evening viewing provide a second though not as clear-cut example.

Some critics have considered the children's cartoon shows during the last few years to be particularly violent. For example, in 1966 Sam Blum noted in the *New York Times* that television Saturday-morning scheduling was almost "totally a matter of cartoon superheroes beating the brains out of supervillians."[8] Both the television schedules and the respondents in the second set of interviews bear out the claim that the nature of programming for children especially has changed radically since 1966. In the past three years, particularly since the assassination of Robert Kennedy, there has been less violence in space shows, superhero stories, and western adventure series. The networks have been careful not to buy shows for children that have violence as their basic premise.

Because the content had to move away from hitting, punching, and killing, there is more comedy and music than was available several years ago. In addition, the critical success of "Sesame Street" has led to an increasing interest in shows that might have educational value for children.[9] One producer related that a show of his that he could not sell to the networks several years ago (it was considered "too soft") was being reconsidered for network presentation. Another producer who did a syndicated "educational" show for children indicated that he had been approached by one network to make additional episodes for Saturday-morning programming.

To remain in production, a producer must be able to conform to the changing directives of the networks. Those producers who are committed to particular artistic and ethical values have trouble remaining in the commercial field. A well-known producer of a series presently on the air left the field of children's programming because he could not reconcile what he considered the networks' lack of social conscience with his own ideas of good craftsmanship and content. However, he is an exception. Most of those interviewed (not all) seemed willing to go along with network directives, although practically all those producing animation were pleased with the network's new attitude toward violence. One producer, at least, believed that nonviolent cartoon shows were actually more challenging and demanding.

> You get sick doing that crap. We *had* to do it for two years because that is what the network wanted. For a while, from every studio, all programs were the superhero variety. We were glad when this phase ended because it had created a preponderance of violence. It got to the place we were happy the emphasis

shifted away from action because we found we have more fun doing other kinds of shows. We are now using our brains coming up with ways of doing things that do not rely on smashing, hitting, and banging. You go nuts after a while because if you don't enjoy what you do, it is awful, no matter how much money you make. Now we are enjoying our work, have for the last year and a half. Much more than we did the year and half before that.

Producers of Shows Specifically for Children

The reactions to the networks and network control of stories, while not the same for all producers, varied little among those making shows specifically for children. Those making animated films had little trouble conforming to the changing network policy. Since the three large producers of animated films made films for different types of buyers and were engaged in a number of activities each demanding different content, their products were sold on demand. For instance, two of three production houses made animated titles for films and live-action television series. One of these titles actually became a main character in a children's animated series with a very successful run. All three make animated commercials and one makes educational films for the classroom. Two smaller companies make the animated segments of "Sesame Street" as well as their own commercial offerings. As stated earlier, when the network presented them with series ideas, they were able and willing to implement them. In other words, they considered themselves primarily businessmen making films rather than creators of ideas.

The producers who were making shows with live animals also had few problems with the networks because their shows were considered "educational" rather than amusement-oriented. There are only a few of these shows in production. One new show using live animals, which could be considered comic rather

□

than educational, was being produced for the first time when the 1970 interviews took place. Both the shows that have been on the air and the new show are relatively free of network pressure because of the nature of their content. One exception is a show that is a mixture of live-action adventure and has in its cast one live animal. Because its essential ingredient is not necessarily the animal in the cast but the type of stories, it will be discussed later with the westerns.

One of the producers of an animal show is producing a children's series for the first time. His show is unusual in concept; the live animals portray humans. They do "everything people do," to quote the producer, "wash, dress, get into trolley cars, etc." The show is a comedy and, according to the respondent, has "absolutely no violence which is *unnecessary* to the plot." Although the animals in real life are dangerous (I had to sign a release to go on the set), in the show they are "like people." The theme is a bumbling detective and his girl friend who have various adventures each week. When the interview took place, none of the episodes had been on the air. The original show was developed from a theatrical film short that had been made several years before and had been shown around the country to adult audiences as a feature-length film. This film served as a pilot, and the network that bought it decided that the idea would be perfect for a children's Saturday-morning series. The producer and the writers-creators had an adult audience in mind when they presented the idea to the networks, but the network that purchased the show bought seventeen weeks (thirty-four short episodes) to be shown on children's prime time. Because the show was originally planned for adults, there was some concern about the sophistication of the show; the writers and producers had in mind several ideas that though intended to be spoofs could be considered risqué or sexually provocative.

When the interview took place, about one-half of the episodes had been filmed. According to the producer, the

151   The Producer, Network Control, and Violence

□

networks had been very cooperative and supportive in their reactions to the scripts. Their only problems came from the Humane Society, which by law has someone on the set watching the way the animals are handled. When talking about the networks and script control, the producer said:

> The network has the final say in theory but they have never turned down a script we have submitted. We have had no interference from them for approval; there have been only the most minor changes required. Once in a while Broadcasting Standards complain about something. We have to be especially kind to the animals. The Animal Rescue League or whatever it is called is always on the set watching us. But we have one trainer for every animal as you saw.

Producers of Shows for the Family Audience

Those making western adventure-type shows, which are directed to the family audience and broadcast in the evenings, on the other hand, had more problems concerning violence and network interference. Several men in the second sample had also been interviewed in 1967–1968, and their shows had been on the air for a number of seasons. When, at the beginning of the 1969–1970 season, they were informed by the network censorship offices that violence would have to be curtailed in their programs, they thought this would be no problem because their shows were basically nonviolent. The network thought otherwise and those who had had no interference in past seasons found their shows being scrutinized in what they considered a most arbitrary manner.

The producers protested network interferences because they insisted that their content was not violent just for the sake of violence and that the action sequences in the show were there because the drama demanded it. This was a touchy point, because

□

as one put it, "How are you going to have an adventure if nothing is threatening?" All insisted that formerly the networks had been too lenient with others and that now the censorship offices were going overboard in their search for violence. One told a story about one episode he was producing:

> First, I fought with the network over the basic script. The story demanded that several people be killed when a bridge had to be blown up. This was a Revolutionary War story. How can you show war without killings? It would be more dishonest to make war nonviolent than violent. War should be presented as "bad" not "good." . . .
>
> Finally they allowed me two killings—new rule, two killings in an episode. After that was settled and I thought the script was approved, the second day of shooting, I get a phone call from the network. They were upset because my main character was carrying powder to blow up a bridge. Listen, they said, we are upset about him carrying that powder. Could he (the main character) find it when he arrives at the bridge—have it cached there?
>
> The implication is that the story is violent by nature because he is going to blow up something. I told them I had been shooting for a day and a half—I have already established that they are carrying powder—nothing I can do about it now. You know the networks are moral only up to a point. They are not going to spend money reshooting. OK. That settled it.

In refusing to change the scene, the producer indicated his commitment to certain principles of dramatic writing. The mission had to be clearly stated in the first few minutes of the play; the audience had to know what is to be accomplished and how the characters would attempt to accomplish the mission. That, to him, is the essence of the suspense involved in such drama. There can be no suspense if the audience does not know from the beginning what is going on. The producer believed this had nothing to do with violence as such and he appealed to the network vice-president. Seven similar situations had occurred in the 1969–1970 season, compared to only one minor request for

153   The Producer, Network Control, and Violence

□

a change in the amount of violence in a script during the 1967–1968 season. In these similar situations the producer involved sometimes was able to convince the networks to do the script according to the original directions and dialogue but at other times had to yield to the networks to get the show on the air.

During this particular producer's first few years with the show, his situation had been very different. The networks had usually approved his material, and he was able to operate within a framework he could accept. He said that he gave the networks credit for believing that the people they hired to make the show for them were artistically and technically competent to make decisions about content. According to him, nothing had changed; there had been no adverse response from the viewing audience. (This, of course, is not confirmable by the methods I used.) The letters the program received were for the most part complimentary and the ratings were high. However, even though everything indicated that the show was being well received, the network's relationship with the producer changed drastically from the 1967–1968 to the 1969–1970 season. For example, in 1967 this same producer had boasted of his good relations with the networks and of the freedom he had to produce scripts that were rarely changed. To quote him in 1967:

> I haven't found any traditional things that everyone writes about—about sponsor pressure or network pressure. They would like to have the best possible show—and they have never said or done anything with one or two minor exceptions that I felt in any way impeded my creativity. We are doing the best possible show we can do considering the time and money we have to do it with. The network has never turned me down on a script. Sometime they like some scripts better than others but it is always matter of conversation. When they don't like something, I say what can I do to make it better? Sometimes I accept what they say, sometimes I don't. I have inherited a successful show. I have become spoiled. Another show on another network may not be as good. I have no problems.

□

What brought about this drastic change? The network was the same one that received accolades from the producer for being "secure and supportive" in 1967. The producer believed that the Pastore Committee hearings made the networks change policy.

> Now comes the situation where Senator Pastore has put the president of the network on the stand. Presidents of networks are not used to being pushed around. Now everyone is overreacting. Now the networks are telling the producers how to produce, the directors how to direct, the writers how to write.

It cannot be emphasized enough that producers operate in a milieu where the final decisions about stories and content are not theirs. More important, network policy on violence has changed in three years. In order to stay with the show the producer had to redefine his role, and although he fought the networks on specific points, for his purposes he no longer had the autonomy he once had. This is the best example possible to show how the producer's authority is always delegated.

It is impossible for anyone who does not give in to the continuous network pressure to stay on the job. It is possible, of course, for producers to argue and even win occasionally on specific points, but one should recall that all ideas for series depend first on network approval, and all stories, characters, music, and settings must be submitted for network approval before production can begin on an episode.

On the other hand, the networks are dependent to a large extent on the ideas and creativity that come from the studios and production houses. There are just a limited number of people who are able to animate and who are trained in the necessary television and film techniques. This becomes obvious when one realizes that the producers of "Sesame Street" deal with the same studios that already produce the Saturday-morning shows in order to obtain the animation and some of the writing for their educational "commercials." The originators and producers

155　The Producer, Network Control, and Violence

of "Sesame Street" maintain the same kind of control as the networks do over commercial television—final script and art approval—but are dependent for episode ideas for stories on the production-house creative people who write and animate.

The Effects of Violence

When in production the producers rarely consider the effect their shows might have on children, but most (there were exceptions) believed that those considerations were the network's responsibility or maybe the parents, not theirs. It was often stated in the interviews that the networks hire psychologists to study whether shows have negative effects (which, if not true, might be a defensive belief). The newer shows are making a special effort to present educational messages to children in the form of entertainment. These messages stress good manners, racial tolerance, and, especially, the irrelevance of physical differences. Of course, the "good guys" still always win when there is conflict, and since the characters are rarely presented in shades of gray, there is never any sympathy for the "bad guys."

One producer, whose show is on the air for the first time in 1970–1971, stated that he was glad to have the chance to improve television, because television's function should be to entertain rather than inform, a commonly held belief among those producing all types of dramatic programs. This producer thought his shows would uplift children through entertainment.

> Some children's shows have been violent for violence sake, as you probably already know. Here we can be funny, entertain—not hurt anyone. For instance, we have one scene where (the main character—an animal) shaves. The kids love that. We try to show everyday occurrences—wives nagging husbands. We discovered people laugh when they see animals do things people do.
> We really hope that this program will uplift the kids in

certain ways. Certain messages are there. For instance, the main character always brushes his teeth after each meal. And we worry and talk a lot about safety. No one ever goes into a car without fastening his seatbelt. But we don't have any strong messages, nothing controversial. We don't want to antagonize anyone.

Several producers interviewed suggested that even before the Pastore Committee hearings into crime and violence on television, the networks had been developing programs that were nonviolent. The respondents commonly believed that after Robert Kennedy was killed in June 1968, mothers all over America wrote thousands of letters to the networks protesting violent television programs. Producers themselves did not receive these letters, but believe that the networks did. To quote one: "Mothers of America rose in unison to protest." It should be noted that they assume it was the mothers who psychologically opposed the superhero cartoons, not the fathers.

In contradiction, it is also commonly believed that parents never watch the sets on Saturday morning. The producers think the content's noise level might disturb parents, but most parents have no idea about the actual stories or themes used. They see Saturday-morning television, especially among the lower- and middle-class audience, as a babysitter. (Parents, as well as the producers and networks, might want their children mesmerized— but for different reasons: the networks to sell products and the parents to get the children off their hands.) All of this is part of a folklore that has grown up around and influences the production of morning programming. Of course, there is very little evidence for this folklore. Few producers have personally received unfavorable letters about their programs—at least, they did not admit to receiving such letters in quantity. As far as could be discerned from the interviews, the respondents knew of no audience research on parents' uses of and reactions to Saturday-morning programming.

The evening programs and the specials, where a mixed

audience of children and adults is expected, are at a higher level of sophistication. The noise level is also lower for the shows and the commercials. Since the story can be as long as forty-eight minutes, more attention can be given to content. There is also more possibility for audience feedback, because the series might still be in production while episodes are being broadcast. Even so, producers of such shows are more apt to use personal values about entertainment or the reactions of friends and family, rather than a more general feedback from the viewing audience, as their yardstick to determine whether their programs are being well received. As with the Saturday-morning producers, they often use the Nielsen ratings as their best measure of success since the ratings determine in their case whether or not the networks will let them remain on the air.

Even when producers of evening programs receive direct critical feedback in letters, there is a tendency to rationalize or ignore the content, considering such comments idiosyncratic.

One producer received a semicritical letter shortly before the interview took place. A section of that letter follows:

> I am not in the habit of writing to television producers regarding their programs, but in this case I feel I must drop you a line regarding last night. My six-year-old daughter is a viewer for the past couple of years. Needless to say, we have been through many adventures, trials, and tribulations, but I have never seen her as shaken as during last night's program. Not only did she cry her eyes out during the show, I had to keep reminding her during the evening it was only a story and (animal character) in several weeks time would be fine. She also was worried her own pet would suffer a similar mishap.

The producer reacted to the letter by disclaiming responsibility for the emotional health of the children viewing; he argued that the parents should see that their children are not frightened or in any way affected by what is on the air. According to him:

☐

You cannot have it bland—sometimes it has to be upsetting. How can we do it to your kids? What do you mean how can we do it to your kids? We are doing something for *entertainment*, this is our only purpose. If we are not entertaining the kid, we are failing. The entire thing of throwing the burden on us because the kids cry. This is wrong and unfair. If a parent has the child enjoying our program which they do, then it is the parent's responsibility, when it is brought to a point that the parent is worried, then it is the parent's responsibility to see that in an honest and realistic way this is dealt with.

The producer quoted above is representative of most producers of all types of children's programming in his negligible concern about the effects of programming. However, four producers were exceptions and expressed concern in various ways. One producer thought that the networks should spend more money on psychological research. Another would no longer produce for commercial television because of the kinds of programs being produced even though he saw there had been a shift from violence. He thought that the level of the children's shows was still so low that there could be no benefits to the children viewing them. He also protested the lack of freedom to create and was disturbed that he might be forced to work in a medium where the intelligence level required to produce was minimized. Two other producers had publicized their opinions about children's programming. One is an animator who had had limited success in producing. He showed the interviewer several newspaper clippings, which quoted him as saying that the low-level programming, whether or not it was violent, was an improper use of a medium that could be used as a great social force to enhance the intelligence and capabilities of a whole generation of children. He was generally antinetwork television, regardless of the content, because of the commercial aspects of the programs. He believed that when well-known personalities sell products to children, the shows themselves lose their credibility.

159   The Producer, Network Control, and Violence

□

I think children realize when they are being sold even in a
basically good show. This is a universal thing that is wrong
with the industry. The networks can't change. The only hope
is not to change network television, but we must get more
noncommercial TV. "Sesame Street" could not be as successful
on commercial TV because of this. The welfare of children must
come first. Under present conditions this is impossible.

The other producer who had made his views public is
extremely successful in both adult and children's programming,
working primarily with live actors and using animals in many of
his shows. His major concern was the possible effect of television
programs on the minds of children; he thought that the television
industry has definitely not met its responsibilities in several
areas. He felt it was the industry's responsibility to find out what
television does to the minds of children, to use its facilities to
make children more loving rather than more violent. He was so
concerned about television's power to mold the minds of the
young that he actually suggested that no child under six should
be allowed to watch television. He was not only concerned with
content, but also with the hypnotic ability of the medium itself,
regardless of the content. He said that although he "considers
television an entertainment medium and not a charitable
institution, the time had come when all of us, not only the
networks, must remember we live in a world dominated by
television where a child spends more time in front of his set
than in school."

It has been reported elsewhere that producers of children's
programs believe they are "the decision-makers and though they
welcome consultation and endorse research, control is properly
in their. hands."[10] None of the producers interviewed for this
study believed that he had true creative control. In film television,
which may be different from the taped shows made for children,[11]
there is an understanding of and, in most cases, a general
acceptance of network power and control. As pointed out earlier,

□

the network may not choose to exercise this control, but it must always be considered by producers whether they are thinking of story ideas or series concepts. The findings from these interviews, at least, show that producers of animated film series either actively accepted changes in network policy or, more usually, passively accepted them. Reporting no trouble from the network is the most usual response to questions concerning freedom and autonomy (see Appendix A), but it can be clearly seen from the quotations given in this chapter that most producers learn network policy and either give the networks what they want, or they themselves produce without specific directives from the networks because they share the network's ideology concerning what is proper entertainment for children.

In other words, the network sets the policy on violence, not the producers. Violence was the rule in 1968 (at least according to Gerbner's definition and results of his content analysis)[12]; violent content is now considered a taboo to be avoided. The reality of the marketplace today is that a producer who wishes his television shows to be shown on commercial television must first please the buyers of the films. (Eventually, of course, the viewers must be pleased as discussed in Chapter 8.) The evidence also strongly suggests that those who do not cooperate in the commercial milieu cannot become successful producers and writers for major television shows and must leave the medium either by choice or through neglect when their values conflict with those of the organization. Nowhere is this reflected more clearly than in the programming for children. The content for children's shows has changed several times in the last decade, and many of the producers who did sophisticated social criticism in cartoon shows at the beginning of the 1960's then did the superhero shows and space fantasies, and now do rock-and-roll and comedy shows.

Bradley Greenberg's hypothesis that the industry's tense, aggressive working conditions result in intense shows is certainly

□

empirical and cannot be answered by the case-study method.[13] It can be verified whether the working conditions for television's creative people are more highly charged than for other creative people whose products are not as violent in nature, for example, musicians and artists. Some of the evidence in this study is not in agreement with Greenberg's speculation, because, as has been pointed out, the producers are not restricted to merely violent content and can and do make both educational and highly artistic shows when required by commercial television, other media, film, or public television. "Sesame Street," mentioned earlier, is the best example, but the production companies reported on in this study have a variety of films in production, ranging from polar coordinates on a graph to a new nonviolent detective story about a boy detective and his girl Friday. The evidence also indicates that the men who make violent films not only are able to make nonviolent films but prefer to do so.

NOTES

1 Violence in the mass media has been a public issue for some time. For instance, the United Nations published a 491 item bibliography on the subject in 1961. See UNESCO, *The Influence of the Cinema on Children and Adolescents: An Annotated International Bibliography*, Reports and Papers on Mass Communications, (Paris: UNESCO, 1961). See also United States Senate, Committee on the Judiciary, *Television and Juvenile Delinquency*, Report no. 1466 (Washington, D.C.: U.S. Government Printing Office, 1956). Most important for this report, see *Federal Communications Commission Policy Matters and Television Programming*, Hearings before the Subcommittee on Communications of the Committee on Commerce, 91st Cong., 1st sess. (Washington, D.C.: U.S. Government Printing Office, 1969), pts. 1 and 2. These are referred to throughout the chapter as the Pastore Committee Hearings

2 See Richard E. Goranson, "A Review of Recent Literature on Psychological Effects of Media Portrayals of Violence," in David L. Lange, Robert K. Baker, and Sandra J. Ball, eds., *Mass Media and Violence: A*

□

Report to the National Commission on the Causes and Prevention of Violence (Washington, D.C.: U.S. Government Printing Office, 1969), pp. 395–414. See also Richard E. Goranson, "The Catharsis Effect: Two Opposing Views," *ibid.*, pp. 453–460, and Seymour Feshback "The Catharsis Effect: Research and Another View," *ibid.*, pp. 461–472.

3 Alberta E. Siegel, "The Effects of Media Violence on Social Learning," in Lange, Baker, and Ball, *op. cit.*, p. 281.

4 "Television World of Violence," in Lange, Baker, and Ball, *op. cit.*, p. 311.

5 *Ibid.*, p. 314.

6 *Ibid.*, p. 315 and throughout.

7 Bradley Greenberg, "The Content and Context of Violence in the Mass Media," in Lange, Baker, and Ball, *op. cit.*, p. 449.

8 Sam Blum, "Who Decides What Gets on TV and Why," in *Social Profiles: U.S.A. Today* (A New York Times Book) (New York: Van Nostrand Reinhold Co., 1970), p. 215.

9 "Sesame Street" is a television show produced for preschool children, which appears on National Educational Television (Public Broadcasting Corporation) and is financed by the Ford Foundation and other public and private sources. It is not a commercially sponsored show.

10 Robert W. Shayon, "Media Mystification," *Saturday Review*, October 17, 1970, p. 51.

11 Several commercial shows are videotaped for preschool children, but these were not included in the study. They appear on a daily basis, are not made in the Los Angeles area, and have problems that are different from those faced by producers of filmed series.

12 "The Television World of Violence," in Lange, Baker, and Ball, *op. cit.*, pp. 311–340.

13 Greenberg, *op. cit.*, pp. 425–452.

The Producer and
the Viewing Audience

The audience's preference for different types of stories is a major concern to the series producer. Most producers believe that the story ranks second in importance as a means of drawing audience; only the choice of the cast is more important.[1] In television as in many other communication media the story or theme to be communicated is chosen well in advance of its showing, and the ultimate audience it may draw is unknown. The major quantitative feedback available to the television producers is television ratings and surveys taken after the show is on the air; these, as suggested earlier, have methodological limiatations and provide little detailed information about reactions to the qualitative aspects of the production. A novel and a film often build an audience through word-of-mouth approval, and a play can be changed if certain parts of the script do not communicate in the way intended or do not get a desired response. By contrast a particular show on a television series has to make an immediate impact, and often there is no second viewing. Certain series that have started slowly have been known to build an audience, but it is more likely that a series will not be renewed or even that it will be canceled if its Nielsen rating is low in the beginning of a season.[2] By the time the first ratings are available to the production team, a number of episodes have been made. It

□

is too costly and impractical to redo those shows that are completed. The producer is often well into the season before any other kind of audience feedback is available. In any case this direct feedback is always considered as representative of a minor portion of the audience, and almost all of those interviewed (with some exceptions) considered direct communication from the audience through letter writing and personal conversations to be idiosyncratic.

A number of shows are pretested before a direct audience before they are purchased by the network, but producers in this study expressed much skepticism about the value of such procedures. For a variety of reasons shows that were highly praised in the pretests were often failures when they appeared on the air.[3]

Yet several researchers into the problem of audience control and selection of programs have suggested that most broadcasters must have some preconceived ideas of what the audience wants because it is impossible to communicate a message without an audience in mind. In the previous chapters it was suggested that the producers are concerned with the "secondary" audience, the network and the front-office executives of the studio and the writers, actors, and directors. However, no program can remain on the air long if it does not appeal to some part of the viewing audience, and preferably it should appeal to that part of the viewing audience in the Nielsen sample. If a show is purchased by the networks, it can be assumed that they approved at least the pilot film more or less enthusiastically. To stay on the air both the networks and viewing audience must be considered.

This chapter focuses on how the producers perceive their audience. The producers were asked directly if they knew what kind of an audience views the shows they produce and if this audience is similar or different from other audiences for shows with which they were associated.[4] All producers were asked why they thought so many shows fail shortly after they appear on

□

the air. From the responses to these questions it is possible to develop a picture of how the producers perceive their audiences. This chapter also includes some comments on how the producers themselves, as audience, use the media (television, film, and other media).

The Producers' Description of Their Audience

Most producers, when asked if they knew what kind of audience viewed their shows said they did. This information is made available to them by the networks' production companies and by advertisers who engage marketing-research organizations to do telephone surveys during or after the broadcast of the program. These surveys differ from the Nielsen ratings, although producers often confuse them in their conversations. Nielsen ratings are based on information gathered from audiometers attached to television sets and only record whether or not the set is turned on; these ratings give no information about the sex and age of the specific viewers and, in fact, whether anyone is viewing at all. Of course, the Nielsen company has social and economic information on their sample families (known as Nielsen Families) but no information about who in the household views what shows. However, because of the great importance given to the ratings by the networks and the trade papers, producers often confuse "how many" with "what kind" of people watch the show. This will be evident in several of the quotations cited in this chapter.

Much information about the audience obviously can be predicted from the nature of the show. For example, early shows and those on Saturday mornings often have a large children's audience, and most producers of certain types of adventure series prefer the early viewing hours in order to capture the younger

◻

audience. The time between 7:30 P.M. and 8:30 P.M. is seen as the family viewing hour, when the mother has finished the dishes and the whole family, mother, father, and younger children, sit together around the television set. Several producers whose shows were on at that time felt that their particular show would have a better chance at a later hour since their basic theme was not geared to children. A few of them did consider the possibility of "two-set" homes where the parents could be watching one show and the children another, but, in general, they thought television watching at that hour a family affair and a factor to be considered when content was selected.

Those who produced shows that were on during the later hours usually described their audience as between thirty-one and fifty years old. The majority of producers thought their audiences lived in the smaller towns and the country, and there seemed to be a consensus that if your show had a format that appealed to the rural or semirural audience, the show's chance for success was greater than if the show were sophisticated and urbane.

Table 8–1 shows how the producers perceived the audience, as indicated by their free response to the question about the kind of people who watched their shows.[5]

TABLE 8–1   Perception of Actual
Audience

Rural-unsophisticated	25
Urban-sophisticated	12
Combination	14
Not categorized	8

The producer's images of his television audience seem to have little relation to actual survey data about the geographic distribution and character of the audience for his show.

For example, one producer of a show that was successful (on

167   The Producer and the Viewing Audience

the air for three seasons and at the time of the interview renewed for the following season) stated that his show:

Captured immediately half the country, the whole southern half. ———— ———— (the main character) is a southerner and a small town boy. He shows the most strength in the rural areas and the small towns, but he *also has surprisingly high ratings in the cities as well.* But then a lot of small town people have migrated to the cities in recent years.

In talking about regional differences in the audience, many other producers as well showed surprise when their shows had large ratings from the cities. This is often explained by attributing rural features to the urban audience. One show that had been aired regularly for a number of years on Saturday night was moved to a week night, and the producer seem astonished at the audience response after the time change.

Up until this year, and this year the ratings are surprisingly high, we were always lower in the thirty-city Nielsen, Trendex, and Arbitron, which are all urban ratings, than in the National Nielsen. When we got the National Nielsen the rating always went up. Apparently this year has proved that this was due to the fact that Saturday night is a very bad night for city people. They are either having people to dinner, or they are going to the theater or something so they couldn't see it. Now that we have gone to a weekday we thought we would be destroyed, but our ratings have skyrocketed. We are in the top twenty this week and for a show that is — years old this is astonishing. The interesting thing is that we *didn't try to change the format or the story for the new time period so as far as we can tell we have always had this potential audience.*

Of the shows discussed above, one is a western and the other has a country theme. Both are basically aimed at the small-town audience, and both producers seemed to shift their conception of their audience when the ratings showed that they appealed to city people as well as to those in the less populated

□

areas. This did not cause them to shift from a theme that they thought might be basically unappealing to an urbane audience. Instead, they seemed to shift their view of the city audience from more sophisticated to less so. Both producers stated that for their shows to draw large audiences in the cities, all American audiences must be "rural, regardless of where they lived, unsophisticated, and uneducated."

More recently, shows are being produced that seem to be aimed at a more sophisticated audience. The producer of one of these shows, which focuses on a city police force, acknowledged that he is aiming specifically at the city audience and, in fact, the show does have higher ratings in the cities. Not only does the producer choose themes that might have more meaning to those living in large urban areas but, according to him:

> We cut the show a little sharper, and the show has a nervous pace. Because we are a city show and because the city is more violent than the country, we have more action in our shows. We aren't appealing to the bumpkin audience but one which is more sophisticated.

The producers' views of who watched their shows seemed to be quite limited; the picture they give of their audience is drawn broadly and in aggregates of characteristics. Producers rarely discussed the specific composition of the audience in any detail. Their concern is with the mass audience, rather than a segmented one, although an occasional sponsor might specifically request that a certain type of audience be reached. For example, a hair-coloring manufacturer deliberately looked for a format that would appeal to young working women, who normally might not be considered the optimal viewing audience. The rationale was that although such young women might have little time or inclination to watch television, they might watch a show where they could identify with the main character. The program the sponsor selected features an attractive young woman whose

□

adventures, according to the producer of the show, were: "deliberately made zany but escapist and glamorous also so that the office worker and the clerk would be able to identify and emulate her. Even though our star isn't a blond, she obviously has more fun. That was our aim when we got the idea for the show, and the ratings and surveys show we are reaching the group we hoped for."

On the other hand, shows that appear to have a particular audience in mind sometimes capture an unexpected audience as, for instance, the westerns and country shows, which often get a large share of the city audience in addition to the rural audience they were intended for. Several shows that cast men as bachelors were originally considered by their producers to be aimed at women, but surveys showed that they may have appealed to the men in the audience more. It seems that the teen-agers and young adults are not watching as much television as they once did, and shows that are primarily directed at them either have low ratings or capture another audience. In addition, many of the producers think it impossible to predict whether a show will draw an audience with certain demographic characteristics before it goes on the air.

In any case surveys and ratings seemed too impersonal and sterile to many of the producers, especially those who had been performers or playwrights and who missed contact with live audiences. Many of the older producers formed opinions about their audience from the fan mail and the personal contacts they had with people they met who watched the show. Even those producers who are aware that only a tiny part of the audience can be reached through direct contact seemed to put more credibility in the comments of friends, family, and people met casually than in reports from the survey and marketing-research firms available to them. One producer of a show that, by all criteria, is meant for children knows that much of his audience

□

is made up of adults. He was adamant in explaining that he was not making his show just "for kids":[6]

> We are not making it for kids. We don't sit down to make a show for kids. We don't write for kids. We try *not to*. I wouldn't know how to do it. How many people understand teen-agers, let alone little kids. I have grandchildren now. I see them and say "hello there" but I don't know anything about them. And even though you might consider this is a children's program, *I know we get an audience which is made up of adults as well as children.*

(How do you know this?)

> I come in contact with people—traveling around the country making the shows (this show does use locations in various parts of the United States), you get an insight into how many people watch the show. I like to think of myself as a rather sophisticated person. I do sophisticated things. I drink booze and go with girls. I play golf at a very posh club, and I have a friend there; the man is a very sophisticated guy. Drinks more booze than I do. I know he watches my show and did long before he met me.

This quotation raises a question: if an intended audience is not always in the producer's mind, who, if anyone, does the producer think of when he produces or selects stories? The answers varied from producer to producer. Some producers who claimed to think of the viewing audience constantly when making decisions actually used their own taste as the yardstick to measure what might appeal to the viewing audience. This was sometimes formulated rather clearly. For instance, one producer explained that he did not believe in ratings, although his were high, because

> in a comedy series especially you try to keep their interest. I realize, more than most producers, that even if they have their sets on we haven't really captured them. They are watching a show at home with the phone ringing, access to the apples, the bathroom, and other people for conversation. I try to keep a story going with everything in my power to hold them. I try all different devices I can think of so they won't get up and leave me. *I do think of the audience constantly.*

171   The Producer and the Viewing Audience

□

(How do you know what will appeal to them?)

The only answer I have is that if it appeals to me in a broad sense it will appeal to the audience. In other words, I would not try to appeal to half the audience. I would not do a show that was appealing to only the Democratic party because I would lose the Republican party. I try to keep everybody happy without selling my soul.

Other producers also thought of themselves as their reference audience. One producer who had created and produced three series on the air for two or more years attributed his success to his being in tune with the television audience. As he explained:

I think of myself as audience. If it pleases me—I always think it is going to please the audience. I write quite a lot and from what I write I pick that which amuses and interests me the most. I have the ability to have fun. I have a mind of a little boy when I write some of these things. The trouble with a lot of people in this business is that they write down. They try to find the level I've been talking about. I think it always fails to write down to people. For some reason, I enjoy finding the niche down there. Perhaps I am limited in certain ways; whatever it is, I can write a story and have fun doing it. I'm not conveying any great messages. Oh, I try to fight evil, but I don't hammer it. From that point on, it is all fun and games. That is what it is meant to be. If you don't like what you're doing, the audience won't like it. That is a truism.

Potential Audience

Generally, most producers had a low opinion of their audience's intelligence, urbanity, and discrimination. However, they differed in their opinions about the potential audience. Some producers think that those who could watch television and did not kept away because the programming content is at a "low level"; if the

□

networks could present better programming, a more intelligent audience could be reached.

The producer's view of what makes a successful series is in large part derived from his conception of his audience. One group of producers thought shows failed because they were simplistic and nonartistic; another group thought shows failed because they were highbrow.

The common characteristic of those producers who think the audience is potentially more intelligent is their own aspirations. The writers-producers who want to make higher-level television shows usually think an audience would watch such shows. However, most of the men, especially the film makers and the old-line producers, were quick to admit that because television is a commercial enterprise, it is difficult for networks to take chances by being too enterprising. In contrast the writers-producers think that the networks by being too conservative are losing a valuable group of viewers. These two views concerning the audience and success can be summarized by two direct quotations. The first producer quoted does not see intellectuals as part of the audience.

Television shows often fail because they are not directed to the right audience. This is a vague thing but we *try not to do anything controversial. Nor do we try to reach people of high intellect. Because of this we are a success.* When you think this way your chances are better. I don't mean you should exclude them from your conception but these people aren't part of your audience. The appealing things have been proven, they are the successful shows. *The formulas work for television and will continue to work.*

The second producer insisted that the responsibility for success or failure did not lie with producers but with the networks. He ridiculed network officials who live in big houses in Bel Air (an exclusive suburb of Los Angeles) or in fancy apartments in New York and claimed they have a pipeline to the general audience.

□

Every year I persuade the network to do one show which I consider mine. They can be persuaded once if you work hard at it but the fight is tremendous. *The rest of the shows are Mickey Mouse and I do them for the network and Nielsen Families. I know the audience is smarter, more intelligent than they think it is. One of the reasons so many shows fail is that the networks and others underestimate the IQ of the audience.* How many of the same kinds of shows can be on the air? There should be shows with more character and originality that tap the more intelligent audience.

Film makers differ from the old-line producers in one respect. Although both see the actual and potential television audience as unsophisticated and of low intelligence and economic position, the film maker often hopes some day to provide a different kind of entertainment or even "high culture" to the kind of audience who prefers novels, plays, and art films as their source of entertainment. They mentioned several former television writers and producers who were doing this. One young producer left producing because he considered "prostituting himself" an evil necessary to television. According to him, any medium that has as its essential function the merchandising of soap and patent medicine cannot appeal to an audience closer in taste and background to himself.

In views expressed, both the producers who think networks underestimate the intelligence and taste of the audience and those who think the existing audience is the only one possible for the medium agree that they subordinate their own personal values and tastes to produce the filmed series as they are presently conceived. Both see themselves as different, at least at this time, from the creators of "high culture" or polemic material (which many wish they could produce). Those producers who defend the present audience think that to produce a different kind of show would mean having a smaller audience or fewer economic rewards. One producer who did give up producing for writing was aware, he said, that he would be unable to live as he had in the past, but it would be worth it for him to be able to do what he wished. Others looked forward to that time in the future when they would be economically secure or artistically competent. Those who thought that the networks underestimated the intelligence and taste of the audience also seemed to look for ways to convince the networks that they were losing a potential audience. Some who are active in the Writers Guild hope that the Guild will by collective action change the network orientation. Several producers called attention to audience surveys that showed that viewing was generally down in all groups in the population.

It is interesting that the producers themselves expressed the kinds of criticism and praise that are often found in the press and in more scholarly appraisals. Both the criticism and approval concerned television's relationship to society and its function and uses as a medium; however, only a few discussed the effect of television on the audience (see Chapter 7). Whether the kind of entertainment they provided encouraged passivity or violence in their audience did not seem to concern most of the producers interviewed, or, at least, they did not verbalize it. Nor did they seem to think that they were providing a kind of entertainment that "brutalized and narcotized"[7] the audience. Rather, many of them see the series as providing an escapist form of entertainment. Some producers think that this was a good rather than bad result, but those who think the function of television was to present more meaningful kinds of programs with a "message" are not so sure.

Direct Audience Control

The problem whether there is audience control of the medium cannot be resolved by this study. Several people (Herbert Gans in particular) have suggested that because the creation of content in the mass-media industries is a group process, the creators

□

thereby function as self-appointed representatives of conflicting public tastes.[8] Occasionally, such a conflict was reported in the interviews, especially if a producer thinks that a potential audience is not being tapped and argues his point with the network liaison men and the production-company executives.

The only evidence for direct audience control were two programs that had been canceled or not renewed and that, after receiving public support for continuation, were eventually renewed. In one intance, a western, support came not only from letters to the network from the public but from legislators and other public officials as well. The protest was so heavy that station managers of the network affiliates threatened to boycott all of the network's offerings unless the program was renewed. The reaction astonished the show's producer who had thought his audience consisted of lower-class and unsophisticated persons; as a consequence, he had to re-evaluate his conception of his audience.

During the season when the interviews took place, there occurred another example of direct audience control, which received wide coverage in the press and was well documented. The following account was written as part of the complete history of the show, "Star Trek,"[9] and gives the details of the audience response to the failure of the network to renew the series for the year 1968–1969. The Nielsen ratings had not been high, and few around the production office or on the sets were optimistic about the chances for renewal.[10]

Star Trek was renewed for at least the first half of its third season, but not without a fight. As the rumor of impending cancellation spread among fans of the show, a ground swell of protest began to rise. During the months of January and February that ground swell assumed the proportions of a tidal wave. A highly articulate and passionately loyal viewing audience participated in what is probably the most massive anti-network programming campaign in television history.

□

NBC-TV (both New York and Burbank offices) was deluged with letters of protest. Most of these letters were personally addressed to Mort Werner. A sizable number were also addressed to Julian Goodman, president of NBC. All demanded, pleaded or urged that Star Trek be kept on the air.

The furor increased with each passing day. Star Trek's chances for renewal became a topic of discussion in newspaper columns across the country. Student protest movements were organized. Cal Tech students marched, along with other Star Trek supporters, against NBC's Burbank office, carrying a petition urging the renewal of the series. . . .[11]

One could, of course, conjecture whether the networks really wish to carry programs they consider unprofitable. Letter writing, marching, and protesting involve just a small portion of the larger viewing audience, but when programs get this kind of support, the networks usually re-evaluate their original decision in order not to distress any of the audience, if possible. Overt audience response can also work against the interest of the producers as well as in their favor, of course, because pressure groups, which are a form of public opinion, can have a show canceled or its format changed.

As explained earlier, very few programs have been or can be selected by the viewing audience. I know of no instance where a pilot film shown in the summer months gained sufficient popular support to make a network change its mind about buying the show. Once a show is on the air, the audience's desires and opinions become more important than during the time shows are evaluated for purchase. However, from the reports of the producers, it does seem that while more so-called scientific methods are available, most producers rely either on their own tastes or the perceived desires of the network officials as guidelines for the selection of stories, and both producers and network officials rely on established themes apparently already accepted by the audience.

The Producer as Viewing Audience

The television producer's view of the audience and his own relationship to the audience should be reflected in his own tastes and viewing habits. However, the television producers seemed to use both the mass media and more quality media in ways different from other people. Few of them, for example, watch the television series for entertainment. Almost two-thirds of the sample (thirty-six) report that during the year they would occasionally watch series to see what the "competition was doing" or to see what the new series are like. This viewing is usually done at the very beginning of the season or during the middle of the season when the shows that failed are replaced. Most reported that otherwise they only watch news or sporting events. Regardless of how they verbalize their conception of the audience or the functions of television, nearly all of the producers think that series are at too low a level for them. However, eight of the producers report watching one particular series regularly because they claim it was technologically superior to the others. Most also try to watch their own shows with their families when they are broadcast. They want to see how the show appears on the smaller TV screen, because they view it earlier on larger movie-size screens in studio projection rooms. They also want to experience the reactions of their wives and families. Several think that their children are more typical of the general audience than themselves, and several, concerned with reaching teen-agers in the audience, seek critical comments from their own children. Their families also help them evaluate how successful they are in communicating their message or story.

One producer reported that he had once insisted that his teen-age sons watch a particular segment he had produced since he wanted them to see how bad television could be. He thought that the show in question was an example of television at its worst; it had been the effort of a "committee," rather than his own personal accomplishment. The youngsters, contrary to expectation, thought the show had been good entertainment, and this, in turn, caused the producer great concern. He questions both his own critical faculties and his conception of the audience, which he thought to be potentially more highbrow and discriminating.

The producers judge their use of other media as small, due to the time consumed by their occupation. Many claim to have little time to read, attend the theater, or go to movies because their workday is often as long as fourteen hours, and most of their spare time is spent reading scripts and rewriting. However, all producers stated that they read both the local daily paper (the *Los Angeles Times*) and the trade papers (*Daily Variety* and *Hollywood Reporter*). Both the general newspaper and the trades are used as sources for critical comments about their shows and for information concerning the industry. A few claimed they also read a newsmagazine or the Sunday *New York Times*. All are useful to them as sources of ideas and for trends of change in styles. Few, if any, think the comments of critics have any meaning as a measure of success for a series. The few who had received praise from critics were pleased, but several pointed out the lack of relationship between a show's success with the audience and critical acclaim. One went so far as to suggest that critical acclaim could be a kiss of death for a show, since the networks see the critics as representing the smaller intellectual community and not the people en masse.

Most producers read trade papers because they thought it necessary to keep informed of industry events. The trades published weekly lists of shows in production, the names of those cast in the parts, the names of producers and directors, rumors of shows considered failures and likely to be dropped, and the like. Network financial news and reports of Guild activity are also available. All of the producers are skeptical of the gossip columns found in the trade and local papers. Several producers had worked during their careers as publicity men for stars and studios and know how often fictitious items are planted. Reviews of series in the trade and local newspapers are regarded with the same skepticism; several claimed that interpersonal relationships influence the reviews written. Of course, if the reviewer is a friend of the producer, he is more likely to give a better review.

The few who habitually read novels and magazines (one producer said he read everything he could find) said that they did so to get ideas for stories, to find new writers with fresh ideas, and to develop their own writing technique. Those who do read extensively also said they liked to read; it was a form of relaxation from the tensions and pace of the job, which also helped them keep in tune with new trends and ideas.

Most of the producers attended films whenever they could. Many took advantage of the Writers Guild biweekly Sunday-evening showings of new American and European films. Films are also seen as a source of ideas, but mainly they provided an opportunity for seeing firsthand new filming techniques. They also kept them informed on the direction and development of the movie industries throughout the world.

The communication behavior of the producers is tied to their occupations as film makers and writers; they used the media primarily as a source of information and sometimes as a source of advice for their craft. Such use was more specialized than that of the average viewer. Although no measures were built into the study to find out whether producers try to emulate the methods of other television producers or movie directors, several volunteered information that they do. Others also said they would like to try some of the techniques they admired when they make feature films with their greater freedom.

Audience Feedback

The relationship between the television producer and the audience is complex, and very little is explicitly known about the influence of the audience on those creating for the mass media. Herbert Gans argues that "there is active, although indirect, interaction between the audience and the creator, and that both affect the make-up of the final product."[12] Raymond Bauer, too, argues that communication should be viewed as a "transactional process in which both audience and communicator take important initiative."[13] Both men have claimed that their "general feedback hypothesis" is quite different from the theoretical approach that sees the audience as passively receiving what the communicators provide. One problem with this view of the interaction between communicators and audience is that it is difficult to test. It is not known, for instance, whether feedback, as defined by Herbert Gans and John and Matilda Riley, has any effect at all on communicators.[14] They define feedback as "information about the outcome of previous messages."[15] Using that definition, feedback does exist for the television producer. There are a number of devices to measure audience preferences and the number of people viewing shows. The effect of these surveys and other measures, however, are difficult to evaluate. Both Herbert Gans and the Rileys agree that this kind of feedback is indirect but seem to disagree on whether it is "active" as Gans believes, or "obscure and scant" as the Rileys suggest.[16] However, both agree that the impact of information about audience preferences and viewing *on the communicator* rarely has been scrutinized systematically.

The gatekeeper studies by Walter Gieber and others point out that news editors select content according to the way they perceive the values and desires of the audience.[17] Other studies

□

have shown that these perceptions can be quite different from what the audience, in fact, really does desire. Kenneth G. Johnson, for instance, studied editors' selection of science news stories and compared their choices with groups of science writers, scientists, readers, and nonreaders.[18] The editors evaluated stories primarily on the basis of color and excitement, while the readers and others emphasized accuracy and significance. Obviously, the editors who selected the science news were not perceiving the desires of the readers. It should be pointed out, however, that science writers (who write the stories and therefore might be compared to producers) appeared to be better judges of readers' choice than were the editors.

Another recent study also indicates that presentations in the mass media are often based on a misconception of the audience's views. J. C. Nunnally, Jr., points out that mass-media decision-makers have a distorted view of the public's conception of mental illness;[19] mental illness is portrayed in the media according to the reference points of those selecting content and not according to the public's view.

Generally, the findings in this area seem to be consistent. Selection of content by specialized communicators does not reflect the desires of the audiences. The audiences' communication channels to the communicators (feedback) are weak. The problem of trying to ascertain what audiences want to see, read, and hear is complicated by several factors. The methods used to measure preferences provide information about present programming but few inferences about future presentations. In addition, the actual audience for television in particular is so large that some studies have shown it contains many "publics."[20] A specific program may appeal to a combination of these publics, but it is difficult with the techniques used to discover which combinations would be more likely to view a certain program.

The questions raised at the beginning of this chapter are

just partially answered. The producers' image or perception of the audience is not always closely tied to the reports available from surveys and ratings. Whether or not such surveys accurately measure audience preferences is not particularly relevant for this study, but certainly someday it should be systematically researched. It is also possible that the structure of television as entertainment makes the existing rating procedure the most efficient method for measuring general audience appeal.

The audience most producers and the networks try to reach may be, indeed, the audience they succeed in reaching. On the other hand, this may not be the case if the producers who suggest that the networks are losing a potential audience because the series are too simplistic are correct. What might be operating, then, would be self-fulfilling expectation, because the stories are selected to be simplistic, without depth and social significance, to reach a mass audience, "heterogeneous and large." If the goal were to reach segmented "audiences," the television series as well as other television drama would take different forms.

More important for this discussion is the question raised about the tastes of the producers in comparison with their audience. Most producers, regardless of their view of the actual or potential audience, think that their taste is superior and that the television series are both artistically and intellectually too "low level" for them. While several stated that they choose content using their own taste as a guideline, they rarely watch any of the series on television. Personal taste and values have to be subordinated to the realities of commercial television regardless of the conception of the audience. For example, one producer said he never did any television or film to please anyone but himself. He added:

> You must understand, though, I do work within the framework of the medium. Here I please myself least. Because the framework is smaller. I have made a couple of feature films where I pleased myself to the fullest because I took all the chances I wanted

to take. I did what I wanted to do. If nobody liked it, it was my fault—no one else's. I don't know how to please eight million people. I don't know the formula for that. I don't think anyone does. They think they do. Sponsors think they do. I never watch —————— —————— (the show he is producing). I sat down and watched it the day I got the job. *This kind of drama does not appeal to me.*

No other responses in the interviews were as contradictory as those concerning the viewing audience. A basic concept in reference-group theory is that if an individual has multiple reference groups, the result may be serious personal conflict.[21] Each producer adjusts in his own way to the conflicts (if any) among his reference-group orientations. Some conflicts result in either rationalizing or compromising. This is further discussed in Chapter 9. Generally, however, the audience, because of its size and distance, may be the least important of the reference groups considered when content is selected.

NOTES

1 Leo A. Handel, *Hollywood Looks at Its Audience* (Urbana, Ill.: The University of Illinois Press, 1950), p. 118, says that audiences' likes and dislikes of different types of motion-picture stories have been of concern to producers since the beginning of the film industry. Studies of the position of story type relative to other components of a film rank it second to the cast in drawing power. The evidence in this study shows the same results. Almost all the producers said that series will fail if the stories are not "right." As this chapter will point out, however, there is no consensus about what kinds of stories should be shown. All the producers thought the series must have appealing main characters to be a success.

2 Appendix C explains the Nielsen system in detail. For a description of other rating systems, see Robert E. Summers and Harrison B. Summers, *Broadcasting and the Public* (Belmont, Calif.: Wadsworth Publishing Co., 1966), pp. 247–266.

3 In order to get some audience reaction, a pilot film is shown to an

audience in the larger cities (usually New York or Los Angeles) in a theater on a large screen. While a positive reaction by this pretest audience is important to the network and the advertisers, it may not predict the way a general audience throughout the country, viewing alone or with their families, will react to a show. The pilot itself is usually a more polished film than the regular series episodes, and although the testing services claim that the pretest audiences represent the larger viewing audience in demographic characteristics, most producers are aware that this is not possible. (In Los Angeles, for example, where the audiences for the test showings are obtained by handing out tickets in parking lots of various supermarkets throughout the city, the testing service insists that all regions of the country are represented because the tourist population of the city is large!) In addition, several people have suggested that a "professional" audience for pretests has built up owing to the method of obtaining tickets. All these seem to be legitimate criticisms, but no criticism seems more pointed than one concerning pretest viewing conditions.

The audience at a test viewing is seated in an auditorium containing about 200 seats that are equipped with certain electronic devices to record their likes and dislikes. Two different kinds of equipment are used. The audience is asked if any of them has ever attended a viewing of this kind in the past. If a person indicates he has attended such a performance, he is seated in a section of the theater equipped with devices that he attaches to his fingers. The purpose of these devices is to record certain biological changes that are supposed to determine if the wearer becomes excited at certain parts of the show. The remainder of the audience, those who state that this is their first experience at such a showing, are seated in a separate section, which is equipped with seats with arm buzzers. The audience member is to push this buzzer when he finds a particular scene better than the others. In other words, the audience is expected to be able to discriminate immediately between good and bad scenes of the film. There is little chance for a person to become involved in the story. Those who may become so engrossed that they forget to press their buzzers are not recorded in this part of the test.

There is also a short questionnaire for the audience to fill out, reporting on the respondent's occupation, income, residence, buying habits, and other characteristics. After the show a few people are selected for a group discussion, usually lasting one hour, during which the qualitative aspects of the show are dissected and the appeal of the cast, the story line, and the individual sequences are evaluated. Participants in the discussion are not chosen on a random basis. Rather, individuals are asked first whether or not they are regular television viewers: those who say they watch sparingly are excluded from the discussion group. Furthermore, the members of the discussion group are chosen before the show

185   The Producer and the Viewing Audience

□

begins and therefore are aware that they will be questioned extensively about their reactions to the films.

    If a show receives audience approval during such pretests, it has a better chance of being bought by a network. However, because the pretest audience is a captive one, not interrupted by the usual kinds of distractions a home-viewing audience may be subject to, the responses to the pretest may in no way resemble the Nielsen ratings when the show comes on the air. While the advertisers and networks may take the pretest into account, the television producer rarely considers it. Of course, the producer would rather get a favorable response than an unfavorable one, but he does not seem to reformulate his conceptions of the audience because of the pretest.

4 Appendix A, Questions 16 and 17.

5 Appendix A, Question 16.

6 This show had a statement of purpose, which they gave to prospective writers, definitely stating that the show was a "children's show." The writers are directed to write suitable shows for children.

7 Paul F. Lazarsfeld and Robert K. Merton, "Mass Communication, Popular Taste and Organized Social Action," in Bernard Rosenberg and David Manning White, eds., *Mass Culture* (New York: Free Press, 1957), pp. 457–473.

8 Herbert J. Gans, "The Creator-Audience Relationship in the Mass Media: An Analysis of Movie Making," in Rosenberg and White, *op. cit.*, p. 318.

9 Stephen E. Whitfield and Gene Roddenberry, *The Making of Star Trek* (New York: Ballantine Books, 1968).

10 *Ibid.*, p. 391.

11 *Ibid.*, pp. 393–394.

12 Gans, *op. cit.*, p. 315.

13 Raymond Bauer, "The Initiative of the Audience," *Journal of Advertising Research* 3 (1963): 6.

14 Gans, *op. cit.*, p. 315; John Riley and Matilda Riley, "Mass Communication and the Social System," in Robert K. Merton, Leonard Broom, and L. S. Cottrell, Jr., eds., *Sociology Today* (New York: Basic Books, 1959), pp. 537–578.

15 *Ibid.*, p. 566.

16 Gans, *op. cit.*, p. 315; Riley and Riley, *op. cit.*, p. 566. It should be noted that the feedback, according to Gans, can also come from secondary audiences such as networks, studios, and those on the sets.

17 Walter Gieber, "News Is What Newspapermen Make It," Lewis A. Dexter and David Manning White, eds., in *People, Society, and Mass*

Communications (New York: Free Press, 1964), pp. 173–182. See also Percy H. Tannenbaum and Bradley S. Greenberg, "Mass Communication," *Annual Review of Psychology* 19 (1968): 353, for other gatekeeper studies.

18 Kenneth G. Johnson, "Dimensions of Judgment of Science News Stories," *Journalism Quarterly* 40 (1963): 315–322.

19 J. C. Nunnally, Jr., *Popular Conceptions of Mental Health* (New York: Holt, Rinehart and Winston, Inc., 1961), pp. 232–234.

20 Elliot Friedson, "Communications Research and the Concept of the Mass," *American Sociological Review* 18 (1953): 313–317. Also see Gans, *op. cit.*, p. 316.

21 Herbert H. Hyman and Eleanor Singer, *Readings in Reference Group Theory and Research* (New York: Free Press, 1968), p. 11.

Summary and Conclusion

The ways in which the producers resolve the conflict of orientation to the various groups in their environment has been the major topic discussed throughout this study. The conflicts that can emerge when one group perceives that important "others" in the environment have norms and beliefs about mutual endeavors differing from themselves were also of concern, as well as the rewards and support the reference groups provide. The reference groups examined were those associated with the craft aspects of the occupation (writers, directors, and actors, in particular); those groups associated with the bureaucratic structure of the networks (the network censorship office and the liaison men who represent the network programming division); and, lastly, the audience who views the programs on the television screens.

In analyzing the interviews, three types of producers stand out: the film makers, the writers-producers, and the old-line producers. Each of these types relates differently to the reference groups identified in this study. In this conclusion each type is analyzed in terms of the questions asked in the study in order to understand fully the available data and to summarize the findings. However, it should be made clear again that because television series are made by "committee," it is possible (in fact probable) that all three types can be found on the production team and can be represented in the final product. However, the film makers are more apt to be used by the production company on the dramatic shows, westerns, and detective series. The writers-producers are usually connected with the mystery and detective stories, the more sophisticated comedies and westerns. The old-line producers are likely to be associated with simpler situation-comedy shows featuring a well-known star. Most (not all) of the producers of animated Saturday-morning shows closely resemble the old-line producers in orientation.

Film Makers

The film makers are usually younger, although a few of the middle-aged group fit into this category as well. They were trained in the communication media, usually through a formalized educational program in one of the universities in the Los Angeles area. They tend to have middle-class origins and are for the most part college graduates. Most of them stated that they had always wanted to be in the entertainment or communication field, but it was not until they were in college or beyond that they knew they wanted to make films. Most of them had worked in no other communication medium, or if they had, it was for a short time as either a radio announcer (disk jockey) or as a journalist. Often this work experience was in conjunction with their education and was used as a means to help finance it. Most became producers by coming up through the ranks of a major studio in the Southern California area, starting as a mailroom messenger, a publicity man, or a rewrite person. By writing scripts on a free-lance basis or through personal contacts within the organization, they were able to call attention to themselves. Most had worked as assistant producers before they were given producing assignments.

While it is not possible to know if they are manipulated by

□

the system, it is possible to know how they react to the
bureaucratic structure of which they are a part. Since they think
that their main role at this time is to coordinate the various
parts of the film making process, they are satisfied with their
working arrangements for the most part. Of all types of producers,
they have the least control over the material presented, because
they had nothing to do with the original series idea and did not
often rewrite material or stories that they received from the
writers. Most of them state that they are using the system to
enable them to become more independent and to use their
creative talents someday in a more meaningful way. Their main
ambition is to become a film maker of some importance. A few
expressed some concern about whether they would be considered
"sellouts" by their former classmates and professors, who often
express critical views about the medium generally. However, they
rationalize both their high salaries and lack of creative independence in two ways: (1) They are learning to make films
under more practical conditions than the conditions under which
films are made in school. Several pointed to certain well-known
directors (William Wyler, in particular) as examples of good
directors who started in the B movies. (2) Their high salaries
enable them to accumulate part of the working capital necessary
to make an independent film someday.

They expressed few conflicts concerning the network and
the production company. Because they see their function at this
time as a coordinator rather than as a creator, they are less likely
to view the networks as a constraining influence than the other
two groups. They are also less likely to take a stand on the
story content than either of the other two groups, but it did seem
that they are more likely to want to try new techniques.
Occasionally, this does styme them, but it is a minor area of
conflict, since it is more important for them to learn all aspects
of production and especially direction and editing so they can
go on to make the theater films in a more artistic way. They are

holding their talent in abeyance until the time is right for them to leave series television and become moviemakers. Often they look forward to directing a few of the series episodes as a further learning experience. Learning their craft is the key distinguishing ambition of this group. Since they are craft-oriented and young, they see few inconsistencies in pleasing the network officials and the production company while subordinating their own artistic values about film making.

Because they have little desire to rewrite or to change writers' scripts they have few conflicts with the writers, and they do not often have scripts that have to be arbitrated through the Guild Committee. Scripts are only changed when there is an issue involving technological know-how, costs, or the inability to carry out the writer's desires because of an emergency situation. They work with the writers when necessary, but rarely, if ever, do they write a script. Most belong to the Writers Guild, however, but since they do not consider themselves primarily writers, do not concern themselves with Guild politics. They had not, for the most part, been in the industry during the last Writers Guild strike and therefore did not have the problem of allegiance that the other two groups have had. At this time of their lives, they consider themselves to be middle management.

The film makers' view of the audience was consistent with their role and with their other views. For instance, they consider themselves to have artistic tastes that are superior to those of the television audience, whom they usually regard as unsophisticated, rural, and lower class. But since they do not think that their function is to be a taste leader or to proselytize for political or social change, they see no inconsistencies in "giving the public what it wants to see." Rather, they see the function of television to be entertainment, and all seem to think that television does this adequately and well for the audience to whom they are directing the content. Their own entertainment patterns and media usage are quite different from what they

□

imagine to be those of the "ordinary" viewer, who, as one said, "Comes home from the factory or shop, has dinner and a beer and turns on the tube to be 'tuned-out' from the problems at work."

Although several of the film makers hoped someday to make films with a social message, these films would be for a different audience, one with tastes closer to their own. Most said that they are politically liberal and voted usually for Democratic party candidates, but here also their political views cause few if any conflicts because they view the networks as apolitical and personally do not want to use the medium as a means of political expression. Several thought that the movie personalities, both liberal and conservative, who use their popularity with the public for political action are not serving the best interests of the public.

It is not being suggested that the film makers feel no constraints or conflicts in their positions. Several verbalized that the medium does not provide freedom and that in order to produce, it is necessary to subordinate their own values, but the rewards (both actual and anticipated) of producing under the conditions described are more important than the constraints. Whether or not these men will go on to realize their ambitions is quite beside the point. It is quite possible that the "system" or their own talents will limit their future progress. The problem of talent is important but impossible to evaluate in this study. For other groups in the entertainment industry, such as musicians, actors, possibly directors, and to some extent free-lance writers, a consensus seems to exist among people in the industry about who has or has not talent. But for the producer talent may or may not be an important variable; since the role covers so many different activities and since the product is somewhat standardized, talent or creativity may be of negative rather than positive value.

In any case the film makers believe that by subordinating artistic values (seen as either technological and visual skills or as more meaningful stories) at this stage of their careers, they

□

will someday be able to do as they please and make the kind of films that will express their talent more meaningfully. This particular characteristic does seem to determine how they choose writers and how they select stories. Not only are they less apt to rewrite than other producers, but they are more apt to follow directives both from the censorship office and the production company with a minimum of struggle or conflicts. When they select writers, for instance, they seem to look for those with the greatest record of successes and are less often looking for new writers with new ideas.

Most important, although they perceive the goals of the bureaucracies involved as basically different from their ultimate or desired goals, the film makers go along with the system as it is because the rewards at present outweigh the costs.

Writers-Producers

The writers are mostly middle-aged (forty-five and over) but several of the younger men, especially those between thirty-six to forty-five, fit this category. Their training and backgrounds vary more than the film makers', but they were mostly free-lance script writers immediately before going into production. Indeed, free-lance writing brought them into producing. A majority of the writers-producers had some college education, and this education seems generally relevant to their present careers. Several were trained as journalists, others were English majors with emphasis on writing, some had worked in the theater art departments of eastern universities. They had worked in several different communication media, but their most recent experience before the advent of television had been in radio or in the movies. Those who were in radio work had been writers primarily, although several had also been news editors. Those who came to television from the movies had usually been script writers under contract to the large studios. When these studios stopped producing B movies in large quantities, the writers' contracts were not renewed. From movie writing to television free-lance writing and then to producing was not a linear progression, but does represent the major career pattern. For many there were high and low peaks in their careers, and several went from free-lance work to producing and back again with relative ease. Their careers seemed to be a succession of failures and successes, but for most of their working years they enjoyed high incomes and the style of life that went with those incomes. They either came to producing indirectly from free-lance writing to assistant producing, or they became producers directly. Their reasons for deciding to become producers when the opportunity presented itself was that as writers their stories were often changed and rewritten, and they wanted to control their own material.

This group has the most conflicts with the networks and also with their own production company because they are most committed to the ideals of their craft—principally, that the writer should have control of what he writes.[1] The writers-producers tend to see themselves as the chief writers of series rather than as film makers. Because of this they have the most difficulties not only with the bureaucratic structure but also with their fellow writers. However, they also know more writers well and have a cadre of writers on hand who can be depended on to do blocks of episodes for the series. They are also the most interested in new ideas and in the political aspects of story writing. Yet they are also the most likely to rewrite or to change scripts that they think are not consistent with the series concept.

Most of their difficulties with the networks are covert rather than overt, because they know that unless they please the network officials, their chances to remain in production are uncertain. They think the story is the most important element in the making of a film, and they are more likely to feel that television should be used to express political views and to change the social scene. They related numerous incidents about how they were able to get a social message into a particular story. There is much reference to compromise and ideals but, especially, compromise. Many thought a primary qualification for producing was knowing how to fight the network. A good producer is one who not only fights for what he wants but also is able to give in to the authority of the networks when necessary. There is continuous battle, one that they thought was more often lost than won. When the battle is lost, a few give up producing for a time to return when they are offered an opportunity to produce a series "right" for them, or they give up with the hope that someday they would be able to produce a show or series that fits their value system more perfectly.

Their political viewpoints ranged from ultraliberal (several had been socialists in the 1930's) to very conservative (supporters of Senator Goldwater). All agreed that the networks were apolitical and would support programs that were a success with the audiences regardless of the political content. The trouble, as they see it, is that the networks give in to the advertisers and pressure groups because they are afraid of losing their means of support and the large mass audience. While their political viewpoints cover a wide range of opinions and attitudes, most could be typed as liberal Democrats, who were basically in agreement with the free enterprise system now prevailing in the industry. They often want to present more racially integrated programming, more programming sympathetic to psychiatry and mental health, and more antiwar programming. Because of their long experience in television writing and production, they are aware that the norms and beliefs on these problems are not rigid but can change from year to year. Indeed, several suggested, as turned out to be the case, that more racially integrated programs would be forthcoming. Others pointed to the time when several shows on the air were more realistic about social problems and expressed the hope that another such "era" would come soon.[2]

In spite of their verbal assertations about the function of

television, few are in favor of even one publicly operated national television channel. Several said that such a channel could become a propaganda arm for the government; others think that public television in other parts of the world is dull and uninteresting; still others point to the success of the American series in all parts of the world where they are shown as an indication of the universality of the series and of the ability of series' producers to satisfy tastes throughout the world. A few think that a public channel, given the right amount of financing, would be able to meet the needs of a select audience for more programming containing information and "high culture." However, several suggested that if the networks do not present some public-service programming of that type, commercial television would sink to an even lower level than it presently occupies.

Most of the producers in this group believe either that the viewing audience is more intelligent than the networks believe it is, or that the measuring devices now used are inaccurately portraying the audience as less sophisticated and more rural than it actually is. Several show a rather well-informed knowledge about the operation of the Nielsen surveys and are also aware of some of the informed criticisms about its operation—for instance, the possible effects on the Nielsen families of the knowledge that such devices were attached to their sets.

While many of the writers-producers express feelings of impotency and constraint, few seem willing to leave the medium for other livelihoods, although this was always considered a possibility for them. The financial rewards, for one thing, keep them working in the medium, but since most of them can equal or surpass their incomes with free-lance writing, the income is not the important thing that keeps them producing. Most of the writers take a genuine pleasure in their work, enjoying the excitement and the daily decisions and problems that have to be solved. Most preferred the immediacy of television production to the slow pace of moviemaking for the feature films, for instance.

□

However, the writer-producer does think that often he is being manipulated by the system since they are oriented more to the content of the script and since they are well-trained and experienced in their craft, they often perceive the network's goals as in opposition to their own. The network, whom they see willing to show anything as long as it has a high Nielsen rating, is not trying to meet its civic responsibility to show more educational series or series with a message.

The above descriptions of the writer-producer and the film maker are oversimplifications, as is always the case with heuristic types. Men, operating in a complex social setting, often have a number of motives, desires, and abilities that must be considered and that contribute to their performance and actions. However, both types do exist in the industry as does the old-line producer to be described next. The main difference between the writers-producers and film makers, on the one hand, and the old-line producers on the other, is that the former are aware of criticisms of the mass media and television and are self-critical, rationalizing their behavior to fit their self-image. The old-line producers do not.

Old-Line Producers

Most of the old-line producers are the older men in the sample, but several come from the other age groups as well. This name was chosen for them not because they are necessarily old, but because they are closer to the Hollywood producer type described by Powdermaker and others.[3] As a group they have less education than the other groups, but several were educated in relevant fields in college. In addition their origins were often more humble than those described earlier, but this is highly correlated with age rather than work orientation (see Appendix D). Their

□

ambitions varied; several of the older men were looking forward to retirement; others want to make movies or become independent television producers; several are satisfied with their present situation and think they have reached the apex of their careers. This group represents the most successful of the producers interviewed. Their success can be measured in several ways: they have the highest incomes; they are responsible for more original series ideas; they had more pilots produced; and, finally, more of the pilots they produced were made into series. Several are executive producers as well as on-the-line producers.

This group also has problems with the network. Since most of the men in this group have been responsible for so many successful series, they often feel that they are more aware of what will appeal to the audience than the network officials. When a series is new, the network liaison men are more likely to interfere in story selection and try to give expert advice to the producer; if a series is a success, there is less interference. When the old-line producers are involved with new series, there are battles with the networks. The conflicts are not so much value conflicts over political and social ideals, but they are often struggles over casting decisions or story ideas; the character of the hero or the direction of the series concept is often at issue. Like all the others interviewed, this producer type can only battle with the networks so far; essentially, they are also dependent on them for ultimate approval. However, their former successes and the apolitical nature of the conflicts often makes it possible for them to win these battles. The very nature of the conflicts, of course, would make them overt in nature. Based on impressions obtained in the interviews, the conflicts are between equals rather than between those in superordinate and subordinate positions.

Their relationship with the script writers as well is different from that of the other two groups. Many of the shows these men produce are situation comedies, which are more likely than other types of shows to have a permanent writing staff responsible for stories. Even when the show does not have permanent writers, these producers are more likely to use two or three free-lance writers on a regular basis. A writer, for instance, might be hired to do ten out of the twenty-six necessary scripts. Under these circumstances rewriting is unlikely. Occasionally this type of producer will write a few of his own scripts; however, when rewriting is necessary, this task is more often delegated to story editors, assistant producers, and others.

The old-line producer also sees the audience as unsophisticated and especially rural or semirural (small town). Most shows produced by this type are aimed directly at that audience. Producers in this group are quick to point out that while the bulk of the audience may be rural, their shows also appeal to the educated, urban audience as well. They seem to think the simple situation comedies or family-type shows have universal appeal. Mainly, however, they pitch their shows to the "mass" audience, whom they perceive as unsophisticated and rural.

The old-line producers do not think they are subordinating their own values and beliefs by producing television because they share the networks' goals. Their political orientation varies from conservative to liberal, but this has little relevance for their roles since they separate personal politics from their job performance.

Conflict Reconciliation

The three types of producers reconcile their work values and their desire (or lack of desire) for more autonomy with the realities of the work situation. Each type of producer views the controls, constraints, and rewards differently. Of the three types, the film maker might be considered by some to be the most professionalized; his training was in film making and related fields

□

and his work career is directed toward the goal of feature films. However, the means they are using to obtain their goals would seem to place them closer to those with a "local" orientation rather than a "cosmopolitan" one. Alvin Gouldner, for instance, has described academicians as locals if they are high on loyalty to the employing organization, low on commitment to specialized role skills, and likely to use an inner-reference-group orientation. On the other hand, cosmopolitans are those low on loyalty to the employing organization, high on commitment to specialized role skills, and likely to use an outer-reference-group orientation.[4]

According to these definitions, the actions of the film makers are very much in line with the goals of the organization. As pointed out, the film makers rarely have conflicts with the organization. However, the models of possible orientations to the work structure suggested by Gouldner and others seem over-simplified when applied to producers in general. Because of their mobility from studio to studio and network to network, all producers could be considered cosmopolitan; they all may be more likely to be more concerned with their discipline than with their organization. However, it is important to emphasize that the disciplines of the various types of producers are different.

All three types of producers perform the same or similar tasks, that is, select stories for the series; help select supporting actors; have the final say about sets, directors, and related decisions; and supervise the cutting, dubbing, and the other postproduction processes. Yet all three types of producers see their occupational role differently, and consequently each reacts differently to bureaucratic controls and bureaucratic standards.

Film makers, for instance, with their training in Southern California schools and their primary work experience in television, may see film making (especially film making for television) as part of a bureaucratic enterprise, requiring a structure and organization. In any case film makers are more compatible with the system than are the writers-producers. They do not see the system as manipulating them, but view it as providing an

□

opportunity to learn more of their "trade" and to accumulate the funds necessary for further advancement in their chosen field.

The writers-producers are closer to the ideal of the lone creator, more similar to the artist, composer, novelist, and playwright than the other two types. Since they make up the largest group in the sample, they also may be the most important theoretically. Under Alvin Gouldner's definition of a "cosmopolitan," they can be definitely considered cosmopolitan rather than local. They seem to have little loyalty or sense of obligation to the network or even to the production company for which they work, but are more oriented to their discipline (script writing). Television producing is a substitute for script writing primarily because it enables them to gain control of their material.

T. H. Marshall and Lee Taylor have compared the professional to the lone artist in Western society.[5] Marshall says that the artist, like the professional, cannot work in a detached, impersonal atmosphere, "with his eye on the clock and his mind on his cheque," but "must give something that is deeply rooted in his nature, something that cannot be commanded or coerced. . . ."[6] Those who see themselves as lone writers with something important to say must be able to reconcile the values that go with such a self-concept with the controls and commands of the organization for which they work. Their dilemma is that they have less freedom when they free-lance than when they work for an organization. If they were still free-lance writers, their scripts would be subject to more change and revision than is the case when they produce their own show.

Joan Moore describes the full-time television writer as having "little or no control over any aspect of their writing except the invention of dialogue and incident. Their work is often rewritten as a matter of routine. It may be changed without their knowledge or consent by a story editor, producer, director or actor."[7] The evidence in this study bears out Moore's contention. Producers have to worry about changes by the network, but the free-lance writers have to be concerned about continuing script changes.

□

Producers have more control, yet conflict does arise because the organizational structure makes it impossible for the writer-producer to follow his discipline without controls and constraints.

The way the writers-producers operate points out the basic dilemma in their position. They see themselves as writers with a social message to be communicated, and the medium available to them to present their message is film television. If they leave producing, which is an alternative open to them, it is unlikely that any other medium in which they might work would provide as many facilities or have the audience that television does. (In addition, they might have to give up their present style of life.) Therefore, they often feel themselves trapped. They have to give in to the bureaucratic controls, but to satisfy themselves while performing their role, they try to select stories that are "socially significant." They see the inconsistency in their position and verbalize the dilemma. If they satisfy themselves, they are likely to incur the displeasure of the network.

The difference in orientation between the writer-producer and the networks is basically one of standards; the networks' standards are quite different than the ideal standards of work held by the writer-producer. An example of how the networks and one writer-producer differ on what should be produced is the following:

> The network said they will "never" do a college series. No matter how it was done they said that it has to be controversial. If it deals realistically, as I conceived the series, with the happenings on the campuses, you will be attacked for taking sides no matter which side you take or even if you try to be objective and take none. And if you take the other course and duck reality and present a fantasy college world which doesn't exist today— everybody will jump on you for obvious phoniness. The network says we can't win. And the viewing public loses. . . .

The quotation indicates one difference in standards. The networks operate under the assumption that all segments of the

□

public (including the government) must not be aroused, while the writer-producer sees one of his responsibilities as informing the viewing audiences about the social realities of the world in which they live. Since it is impossible to do this overtly, such messages are hidden within other contexts so that the message is not detected by the networks. However, because of this subterfuge, timely messages are often superficial. The writer-producer, therefore, directs the series or episode primarily to the network and uses internalized standards about content, while the audience plays a secondary role.

The old-line producers react to the networks differently from the other two types of producers. They see themselves as businessmen producing entertainment as a product, and this orientation affects their relationship with the network in a special way. Since the old-line producers think they know what will sell, they often quarrel with the networks and even their own production company, but these quarrels are not value conflicts. Their fundamental aspirations are the same as the network executives and the studio heads—to be successful. They therefore have no conflicts with the present system of deciding what will stay on the air or of selecting the kind of stories. They have no desire to produce television films with a social message. The old-line producer directs the series he produces to an audience he sees primarily as simplistic, unsophisticated, and rural in outlook. For them the networks play the secondary role, although the economic realities of the situation make it impossible to ignore the network completely.

Adaptation and Autonomy

With some exceptions the material reported in this study seems to be in line with much of the reports of other occupational groups in entertainment and communication. As those who have

□

studied such occupations in the past point out, "career lines characteristic of an occupation take their shape from the problems peculiar to that occupation."[8] Howard Becker argues that the major problem of musicians, for instance, "revolves around maintaining freedom from control over artistic behavior."[9] He continues, "control is exerted by outsiders for whom the musicians work, who ordinarily judge and react to musicians' performance on the basis of standards quite different from his own."[10]

Producers, like musicians, must make a series of adjustments to the "network of institutions and formal organizations and informal relationships"[11] in which they practice their occupation. For producers to operate in the system as it now exists, there are several modes of adaptation. At the extreme they can conform to network policy and deny conflict or, if they cannot conform at all, quit producing as several have done. The adaptation of those who neither conform completely nor quit seems rather similar (with some differences) to that of the newsmen studied by Breed. The more critical and independent producers (usually the writers-producers) deviate from known policy whenever possible without rebelling or quitting. The film makers seem to repress values for more instrumental ends, while the old-line producers repress conflict when it interferes with income.[12]

A few in the sample did attempt to compensate for their lack of freedom by writing a novel in their spare time, by working on a political film for a candidate, or by taking an active interest in the Writers Guild activities, which were directed toward more script control by the writers.[13]

The typology presented in this study is also similar to the one developed by Mason Griff for commercial artists.[14] Griff also identifies three types of artists. The first, the *traditional-role* artist, works as a commercial artist in order to accumulate enough money to be financially independent. A second type, *compromise-role* artists, conceives of themselves as responsible for improving the public's taste in art and raising the standard of living by creating new and better desires. These may be considered closer to the writers-producers with certain differences—commercial artists do not have the political orientation of the writers-producers. The third type, the *commercial-role* artist, has its counterpart in the typology of producers presented in this study. They think of themselves as the clients' instruments and their ideological commitment is to be pleasing and satisfying to clients;[15] therefore they are closer to the old-line producers.

While there are similarities between Griff's typology and the one developed in this study, there are differences as well. Each artistic occupation (and others also) develops in a unique context, both structurally and historically. The tradition role, as Griff presents it, is not comparable to the film makers. Those individuals in his sample who are identified as fine artists (the tradition role) were most apt to experience conflict, while the writer-producer experienced the most conflict in this study. The important point in Griff's analysis is that most conflict was caused by the identity the individual held when he entered the field of commercial art.[16]

Other studies make similar points. In a study of the role conception of government bureaucrats, Leonard Reissman finds that their conflict and rewards stem from their identity with their professional group and the way they orient themselves to the bureaucracy.[17] Both Simon Marcson and William Kornhauser believe that the conflict experienced by scientists working in industries is caused by the scientist-professional being in an employee role.[18] These two roles, the one to which the scientists were socialized and their present role as an employee, give rise to different and often conflicting positions.

The findings from this study and the others cited specifically lead to a formulation that could be tested with others working as communicators and entertainers for mass media. The formulation is based on the relationship of the socialization process (training and apprenticeship) and occupational identity to attitudes about work in a bureaucratic setting. In this study it was found that the occupational orientation of producers differed, depending on their previous work and training experience and their aspirations. The film makers, for instance, see the function of television producing differently from the other two groups, who, in turn, see it differently from each other. *Occupational identity (defined as a combination of two factors, specialized training and apprenticeship and aspirations) determines role performance (the attitudes, beliefs, and at times actual behavior).* The method of selecting content and the relationship of communicators to the work structure could be predicted from the training and aspirations of those studied. This formulation could have general application to those occupational groups in the communication and entertainment industries that have members of different backgrounds performing the same functions, such as public relations men, advertising copywriters, and newsmen.

In this study it was seen that film makers are more future-oriented and therefore have different reference groups than the other two groups. In addition, their background, both in educational training and apprenticeship, differs from the others. If the criteria were specialized knowledge and training, it could be said that this group is the most professional. On the other hand, the writer-producer seems to depend more on colleagues in his own occupation both for rewards and work appraisal; thus he could be considered more professional in terms of the definition used in this study. His background in free-lance writing seems to have influenced his attitudes and beliefs concerning the work situation. The old-line producer orients himself more toward those who can reward him in his present position. This group had the least formalized training but the longest history of work in television and other related media (especially movies and radio).

Concluding Remarks

Unfortunately a problem that has not been discussed complicates continuing investigations: the communications industries are constantly changing. The organizational model and the producers presented here are based on a particular two-year period.

Even in the two-year period studied, changes occurred in television, which affected the conflict, strain, and stress producers experience in the work setting. The change in network policy on violent content provides one example of such a change. Basically, the structure of the industry remains the same, although production of actual series continues to become less important as part of overall television programming. (Professional sporting events and full length movies have become more important.) Consequently, fewer series are being made in Hollywood. This structural change once more points out the dependency of television film makers on the networks who make programming decisions. This and other evidence highlights how important it is to study network operations to determine who makes the decisions and how and what decisions are made at that higher level. The evidence from this study more than suggests that American commercial television programming is basically determined by the three networks. How the networks make decisions, what publics they try to satisfy, and thereby what publics are denied access to the kinds of shows they might want are still open questions, but questions that could be subjected to research.

As more film students are graduated from colleges and universities and as the industry is able to draw on more experts from production and writing, the industry's organization, as well as the occupational groups in the industry, may change. An important question beyond the scope of this study is whether the product of television will change as well if more professionals become part of the production team. The central task of a mass-communication organization is to formulate content, which is submitted to an audience. How this content is chosen, by whom, and under what social and political conditions remains a complex question; one that should be explored further. Since this study only considered the producers' perceptions and attitudes, much is left unanswered. Whether or not the audience, for instance, would prefer other kinds of entertainment to supplement or in place of the series cannot be answered in a study that does not go directly to the audience for that information. That would be a separate investigation. Self-regulation and governmental controls were also of only peripheral interest here, but should be explored because of their relevance. The interaction of the whole social fabric must necessarily be studied if one is to answer fully some of the questions on the complexity of content selection, audience reactions, and the people who work for communication media.[19] In addition, the social, political, and economic conditions, both within and without the industry, and their interaction to form the content have yet to be investigated.

NOTES

1 See Cole Trapnell, *Teleplay* (San Francisco: Chandler Publishing Co., 1966), pp. 161–162.

2 Most producers were referring to the 1962–1963 season when such shows as "East Side West Side" and "The Defenders" were on the air.

3 Hortense Powdermaker, *Hollywood: The Dream Factory* (Boston: Little, Brown and Co., 1950), pp. 11–130.

4 Alvin Gouldner, "Cosmopolitans and Locals: Toward an Analysis of Latent Social Roles—I," *Administrative Science Quarterly* 2 (1957): 290.

5 T. H. Marshall, *Class, Citizenship and Social Development* (New York: Doubleday and Co., 1964), pp. 163–164; Lee Taylor, *Occupational Sociology* (New York: Oxford University Press, 1968), pp. 425–426.

6 Marshall, *op cit.*, p. 163.

7 Joan Moore, *The Hollywood Writer*, unpublished manuscript draft, p. 92.

8 Howard S. Becker, "Careers in a Deviant Occupational Group," in *Outsiders* (New York: Free Press, 1963), p. 102.

9 *Ibid.*

10 *Ibid.*

11 *Ibid.* Note Becker is quoting from Oswald Hall, "The Stages of a Medical Career," *American Journal of Sociology* 53 (March 1948): 327.

12 Warren Breed, "Social Control in the Newsroom: A Functional Analysis," *Social Forces* 33 (1955): 334.

13 "Writers Guild Prexy Powell Feels Networks Receding in Responsibility to the Public," *Hollywood Reporter*, January 19, 1968. This article is a report of a Writers Guild meeting, which was directed to the quality of television. I attended the meeting, which was held on January 17, 1968 at the Beverly Hilton Hotel, on the invitation of one of the producer respondents who was actively supporting Dick Powell, president of the Guild.

14 Mason Griff, "The Commercial Artist," in Maurice R. Stein, Arthur J. Vidich, and David Manning White, eds., *Identity and Anxiety* (Glencoe, Ill.: Free Press, 1960), pp. 219–240.

15 *Ibid.*, pp. 226–236.

16 *Ibid.*, p. 240.

17 Leonard Reissman, "A Study of Role Conceptions in Bureaucracy," *Social Forces* 27 (1949): 205–210.

18 Simon Marcson, *The Scientist in American Industry: Some Organizational Determinants in Manpower Utilization* (New York: Harper & Brothers, 1960); William Kornhauser with Warren O. Hagstrom, *Scientists in Industry: Conflict and Accommodation* (Berkeley: University of California Press, 1962).

19 Paul Lazarsfeld, "Some Reflections on Past and Future Research in Broadcasting," in Gary E. Steiner, ed., *The People Look at Television* (New York: Knopf, 1963), pp. 410–422; Otto Larsen, "Social Effects of Mass Communications," in R. E. L. Faris, ed., *Handbook of Modern Sociology* (Chicago: Rand McNally, 1964), pp. 349–381; Herbert Gans, "The Shaping of Mass Media Content: A Study of the News." Mimeographed, expanded version of a paper presented at the 1966 meeting of the American Sociological Association.

The Interview Schedule

Topic I: Present Situation

1 What is your present title?
2 What duties go with that title?
3 Do you consider this your major occupation? (If not, what is your major occupation?)
4 Are you a salaried employee?
    If yes, who pays your salary?
    If no, how are you paid?
5 Do you have a contract with the studio or network that employs you?
    If yes, would you mind telling me the length of the contract?
    If no, does this mean you can be fired at any time?
6 Who is your employer?

Topic II: Training and Work Record

7 In what year did you start working in television?
8 What was your first job in television?

☐

9 Have you worked steadily in television since that time?

    If yes, can you list the jobs you have held in the industry?

    If no, how much time have you spent in the industry since you started?

        a. What jobs have you held in the industry since that time?

        b. What jobs outside the industry during that time?

10 How did you get started in the industry?

11 How did you become a producer?

Topic III: Ambitions and Satisfactions or Dissatisfactions

12 All things considered, how do you like working in television generally?

13 Is there another occupation you would like to have other than the one you now have, either in or outside the industry? Why?

        a. To put it another way, what are your ambitions?

        b. Is your present job a step toward those ambitions?

        c. What would you like to be doing five years from now?

Topic IV: Comparison of Television with other Media

14 What are the assets and liabilities of television as compared with other media? For instance:

a. Does television give one as much chance for creativity as other media? By other media, I mean movies, radio, writing novels or articles, the theater, etc.
b. Is there more or less security in television compared with the other media?
c. What advantages does working in television have in comparison with other media?
d. What disadvantages does working in television have in comparison with other media?
e. If not mentioned, do you have more autonomy or freedom in television compared with other media that you have worked in?

15 Do you have any particular gripes with working in television?

Topic V: The Product

16 What kind of an audience views the show you are now on?
17 Does this audience differ from audiences for other shows of which you have been a part?
   a. If yes, how do you know this? In what ways?
   b. If no, how do you know what kind of audience views the show?
18 How do you go about choosing actors for a show other than the permanent cast?
19 How do you choose a director for a show?
20 How is a new series or show chosen for viewing?
21 How about the actors? Who chooses the actors for a series? Are the stars and supporting cast chosen the same way?
22 When choosing a script for this series, how do you go about it? (What is wanted here is their concepts of the process.)

☐

23 From newspaper and magazine accounts of television, there seems to be a concern with network and advertising interference. How much pressure do you get from either source when you are working? Can you give any specific examples?

24 Several people have spoken of television by "committee." What does this mean? Are there better ways (or possibly different ways) of producing television shows? What might they be?

25 Since so many television shows fail shortly after they appear, how do you account for the success or failure of a show?

Topic VI: Politics and Political Behavior

26 Are you active politically?

27 Did you vote in the California gubernatorial election in 1966?

        a. If yes, would you mind telling me whom you voted for?

        b. If no, ask why. If not resident in California, find out if he voted in last gubernatorial race in his home state.

28 What is your party preference? If none, which party do you generally support?

29 Do you consider yourself a liberal, moderate, conservative?

30 What do you think about *one* government sponsored or subsidized TV channel?

Topic VII: Social, Work Relations with Others in the Industry

31 Is there one particular person or several persons with whom you discuss "business" more often than with others in social situations? If yes, who? Do you admire this man's work?

32 Hypothetically, if you could work with any director in the business, whom would you choose? Why? What is there about him or his work that you like? Would this vary according to the program you are doing?

33 What are the key positions in television production? Why?

34 What is the most creative job in making a film for television? Does this vary for the feature film?

35 From what you have read or possibly seen, how does American television production differ from production in Europe? Movie production? Which system do you think is the most creative?

Topic VIII: Communication Behavior

36 What newspapers do you read regularly? List:
Any others?

37 If not mentioned: Do you ever read *Variety* or *Hollywood Reporter*? Yes—How often? No—Why?

38 What magazines do you read regularly? If not mentioned: Do you read such magazines as *TV Guide*, the movie magazines?

39 Is there a special columnist or critic that you read regularly either in the magazines or newspapers? If yes, why?

□

40 In an average week how many hours do you spend listening to the radio?

41 What kind of programs do you listen to? Do you have a favorite station?

42 In an average week how many hours do you spend watching TV?

43 What kinds of programs do you watch? Do you favor one network over another?

44 Is there a particular time of the year you may watch more TV? Why?

45 Do you often attend the legitimate theater? How often? What kind of theater do you prefer?

46 How often do you go to the films? What kind of films do you prefer?

47 Do you have a favorite moviemaker?

Topic IX: Organizations

48 To which guilds or related organizations do you belong?

49 Do you attend meetings of the organization? How often? If yes or no, why or why not?

50 Have you ever held an office in any of the above organizations? Which one? What office? How long?

51 If not, would you like to hold an office? Why?

52 If yes (presently an officeholder), why are you holding that office? Why did you take the office?

Topic X: Social Background

53 What is or was your father's usual occupation? (Or that of the person by whom respondent was raised.) Please describe his main work activities.

□

54 What was the last grade he completed in school?

Grammar School	Jr. & Sr. High School	College	Grad School
1 2 3 4 5 6	7 8 9 10 11 12	Fr So Jr Sr	1 2 3 4 5

Trade School?   Business School?   Other (specify)?

55 What was the last grade you completed in school?

Grammar School	Jr. & Sr. High School	College	Grad School
1 2 3 4 5 6	7 8 9 10 11 12	Fr So Jr Sr	1 2 3 4 5

Trade School?   Business School?   College major?
Other (specify)?

56 What was the last grade your wife completed in school?

Grammar School	Jr. & Sr. High School	College	Grad School
1 2 3 4 5 6	7 8 9 10 11 12	Fr So Jr Sr	1 2 3 4 5

Trade School?   Business School?   Other (specify)?

57 Do you have a religious preference? No? Yes? May I ask what it is? (Get denomination if possible.)

58 May I ask your approximate age?

59 Are you single? Married? Separated? Widowed? Divorced?

60 Income: Approximately ———.

61 Does your income vary much from year to year?

62 What neighborhood do you live in in Los Angeles?

63 Where were you born (city or town, state, country)?

64 How long have you lived in Los Angeles?

65 Spouse's occupation, if any?

66 Was wife (husband) ever connected with the industry (or a related one)?

67 Do you ever discuss business problems with your spouse?

□

68 Are there any comments about working in television that you'd like to add to what we've covered?

Sex:

Race:

Date:

Name of Show:

The Television Code

Preamble

Television is seen and heard in every type of American home. These homes include children and adults of all ages, embrace all races and all varieties of religious faith, and reach those of every educational background. It is the responsibility of television to bear constantly in mind that the audience is primarily a home audience, and consequently that television's relationship to the viewers is that between guest and host.

The revenues from advertising support the free, competitive American system of telecasting and make available to the eyes and ears of the American people the finest programs of information, education, culture, and entertainment. By law the television broadcaster is responsible for the programming of his station. He, however, is obligated to bring his positive responsibility for excellence and good taste in programming to bear upon all who have a hand in the production of programs, including networks, sponsors, producers of film and of live programs, advertising agencies, and talent agencies.

The American businesses which utilize television for conveying their advertising messages to the home by pictures with

SOURCE: Reprinted by permission of the National Association of Broadcasters, 12th edition, 1967 sections I–IV, pp. 2–10.

sound, seen free-of-charge on the home screen, are reminded that their responsibilities are not limited to the sale of goods and the creation of a favorable attitude toward the sponsor by the presentation of entertainment. They include, as well, responsibility for utilizing television to bring the best programs, regardless of kind, into American homes.

Television and all who participate in it are jointly accountable to the American public for respect for the special needs of children, for community responsibility, for the advancement of education and culture, for the acceptability of the program materials chosen, for decency and decorum in production, and for propriety in advertising. This responsibility cannot be discharged by any given group of programs, but can be discharged only through the highest standards of respect for the American home, applied to every moment of every program presented by television.

In order that television programming may best serve the public interest, viewers should be encouraged to make their criticisms and positive suggestions known to the television broadcasters. Parents in particular should be urged to see to it that out of the richness of television fare, the best programs are brought to the attention of their children.

I   Advancement of Education and Culture

1   Commercial television provides a valuable means of augmenting the educational and cultural influence of schools, institutions of higher learning, the home, the church, museums, foundations, and other institutions devoted to education and culture.
2   It is the responsibility of a television broadcaster to call upon such institutions for counsel and cooperation and to

work with them on the best methods of presenting educational and cultural materials by television. It is further the responsibility of stations, networks, advertising agencies, and sponsors consciously to seek opportunities for introducing into telecasts factual materials which will aid in the enlightenment of the American public.

3 Education via television may be taken to mean that process by which the individual is brought toward informed adjustment to his society. Television is also responsible for the presentation of overtly instructional and cultural programs, scheduled so as to reach the viewers who are naturally drawn to such programs, and produced so as to attract the largest possible audience.

4 The television broadcaster should be thoroughly conversant with the educational and cultural needs and desires of the community served.

5 He should affirmatively seek out responsible and accountable educational and cultural institutions of the community with a view toward providing opportunities for the instruction and enlightenment of the viewers.

6 He should provide for reasonable experimentation in the development of programs specifically directed to the advancement of the community's culture and education.

7 It is in the interest of television as a vital medium to encourage and promote the broadcast of programs presenting genuine artistic or literary material, valid moral and social issues, significant controversial and challenging concepts, and other subject matter involving adult themes. Accordingly, none of the provisions of this Code, including those relating to the responsibility toward children, should be construed to prevent or impede their broadcast. All such programs, however, should be broadcast with due regard to the composition of the audience. The highest degree of care should be exercised to preserve the integrity of such

programs and to ensure that the selection of themes, their treatment and presentation are made in good faith upon the basis of true instructional and entertainment values, and not for the purposes of sensationalism, to shock or exploit the audience, or to appeal to prurient interests or morbid curiosity.

II Responsibility toward Children

1 The education of children involves giving them a sense of the world at large. It is not enough that only those programs which are intended for viewing by children shall be suitable to the young and immature. In addition, those programs which might be reasonably expected to hold the attention of children and which are broadcast during times of the day when children may be normally expected to constitute a substantial part of the audience should be presented with due regard for their effect on children.

2 Such subjects as violence and sex shall be presented without undue emphasis and only as required by plot development or character delineation. Crime should not be presented as attractive or as a solution to human problems, and the inevitable retribution should be made clear.

3 The broadcaster should afford opportunities for cultural growth as well as for wholesome entertainment.

4 He should develop programs to foster and promote the commonly accepted moral, social, and ethical ideals characteristic of American life.

5 Programs should reflect respect for parents, for honorable behavior, and for the constituted authorities of the American community.

6 Exceptional care should be exercised with reference to

□

kidnapping or threats of kidnapping of children in order to avoid terrorizing them.

7 Material which is excessively violent or would create morbid suspense, or other undesirable reactions in children, should be avoided.

8 Particular restraint and care in crime or mystery episodes involving children or minors should be exercised.

III Community Responsibility

1 A television broadcaster and his staff occupy a position of responsibility in the community and should conscientiously endeavor to be acquainted fully with its needs and characteristics in order better to serve the welfare of its citizens.

2 Requests for time for the placement of public service announcements or programs should be carefully reviewed with respect to the character and reputation of the group, campaign, or organization involved, the public interest content of the message, and the manner of its presentation.

IV General Program Standards

1 Program materials should enlarge the horizons of the viewer, provide him with wholesome entertainment, afford helpful stimulation, and remind him of the responsibilities which the citizen has toward his society. The intimacy and confidence placed in television demand of the broadcaster, the network, and other program sources that they be vigilant in protecting the audience from deceptive program practices.

□

2 Profanity, obscenity, smut, and vulgarity are forbidden, even when likely to be understood only by part of the audience. From time to time, words which have been acceptable acquire undesirable meanings, and telecasters should be alert to eliminate such words.

3 Words (especially slang) derisive of any race, color, creed, nationality or national derivation, except wherein such usage would be for the specific purpose of effective dramatization such as combating prejudice, are forbidden, even when likely to be understood only by part of the audience. From time to time, words which have been acceptable acquire undesirable meanings, and telecasters should be alert to eliminate such words.

4 Racial or nationality types shall not be shown on television in such a manner as to ridicule the race or nationality.

5 Attacks on religion and religious faiths are not allowed. Reverence is to mark any mention of the name of God, His attributes and powers. When religious rites are included in other than religious programs the rites shall be accurately presented. The office of minister, priest, or rabbi shall not be presented in such a manner as to ridicule or impair its dignity.

6 Respect is maintained for the sanctity of marriage and the value of the home. Divorce is not treated casually as a solution for marital problems.

7 In reference to physical or mental afflictions and deformities, special precautions must be taken to avoid ridiculing sufferers from similar ailments and offending them or members of their families.

8 Excessive or unfair exploitation of others or of their physical or mental afflictions shall not be presented as praiseworthy. The presentation of cruelty, greed, and selfishness as worthy motivations is to be avoided.

9 Law enforcement shall be upheld and, except where essential

□

to the program plot, officers of the law portrayed with respect and dignity.

10 Legal, medical, and other professional advice, diagnosis, and treatment will be permitted only in conformity with law and recognized ethical and professional standards.

11 The use of animals, both in the production of television programs and as part of television program content, shall at all times be in conformity with accepted standards of humane treatment.

12 Care should be exercised so that cigarette smoking will not be depicted in a manner to impress the youth of our country as a desirable habit worthy of imitation.

13 Criminality shall be presented as undesirable and un- sympathetic. The condoning of crime and the treatment of the commission of crime in a frivolous, cynical, or callous manner is unacceptable. The presentation of techniques of crime in such detail as to invite imitation shall be avoided.

14 The presentation of murder or revenge as a motive for murder shall not be presented as justifiable.

15 Suicide as an acceptable solution for human problems is prohibited.

16 Illicit sex relations are not treated as commendable. Sex crimes and abnormalities are generally unacceptable as program material. The use of locations closely associated with sexual life or with sexual sin must be governed by good taste and delicacy.

17 Drunkenness should never be presented as desirable or prevalent. The use of liquor in program content shall be de-emphasized. The consumption of liquor in American life, when not required by the plot or for proper characterization, shall not be shown.

18 Narcotic addiction shall not be presented except as a vicious habit. The administration of illegal drugs will not be

□

displayed. The use of hallucinogenic drugs shall not be shown or encouraged as desirable or socially acceptable.

19 The use of gambling devices or scenes necessary to the development of plot or as appropriate background is acceptable only when presented with discretion and in moderation, and in a manner which would not excite interest in, or foster, betting nor be instructional in nature.

20 Telecasts of actual sports programs at which on-the-scene betting is permitted by law should be presented in a manner in keeping with federal, state, and local laws, and should concentrate on the subject as a public sporting event.

21 Program material pertaining to fortune-telling, occultism, astrology, phrenology, palm-reading, numerology, mind-reading, or character-reading is unacceptable when presented for the purpose of fostering belief in these subjects.

22 Quiz and similar programs that are presented as contests of knowledge, information, skill, or luck must, in fact, be genuine contests and the results must not be controlled by collusion with or between contestants, or any other action which will favor one contestant against any other.

23 No program shall be presented in a manner which through artifice or simulation would mislead the audience as to any material fact. Each broadcaster must exercise reasonable judgment to determine whether a particular method of presentation would constitute a material deception or would be accepted by the audience as normal theatrical illusion.

24 The appearances or dramatization of persons featured in actual crime news will be permitted only in such light as to aid law enforcement or to report the news event.

25 The use of horror for its own sake will be eliminated; the use of visual or aural effects which would shock or alarm the viewer, and the detailed presentation of brutality or physical agony by sight or by sound, are not permissible.

26 Contests may not constitute a lottery.

□

27 Any telecasting designed to "buy" the television audience, by requiring it to listen and/or view in hope of reward rather than for the quality of the program, should be avoided.

28 The costuming of all performers shall be within the bounds of propriety and shall avoid such exposure or such emphasis on anatomical detail as would embarrass or offend home viewers.

29 The movements of dancers, actors, or other performers shall be kept within the bounds of decency, and lewdness and impropriety shall not be suggested in the positions assumed by performers.

30 Camera angles shall avoid such views of performers as to emphasize anatomical details indecently.

31 The use of the television medium to transmit information of any kind by the use of the process called "subliminal perception," or by the use of any similar technique whereby an attempt is made to convey information to the viewer by transmitting messages below the threshold of normal awareness, is not permitted.

32 The broadcaster shall be constantly alert to prevent activities that may lead to such practices as the use of scenic properties, the choice and identification of prizes, the selection of music and other creative program elements and inclusion of any identification of commercial products or services, their trade names or advertising slogans, within a program dictated by factors other than the requirements of the program itself. The acceptance of cash payments or other considerations in return for including any of the above within the program is prohibited except in accordance with Sections 317 and 508 of the Communications Act.

33 A television broadcaster should not present fictional events or other nonnews material as authentic news telecasts or announcements, nor should he permit dramatizations in any program which would give the false impression that the

227   The Television Code

□

dramatized material constitutes news. Expletives (presented aurally or pictorially) such as "flash" or "bulletin" and statements such as "we interrupt this program to bring you . . ." should be reserved specifically for newsroom use. However, a television broadcaster may properly exercise discretion in the use in nonnews programs of words or phrases which do not necessarily imply that the material following is a news release.

34 Program content should be confined to those elements which entertain or inform the viewer and to the extent that titles, teasers, and credits do not meet these criteria, they should be restricted or eliminated.

35 The creation of a state of hypnosis by act or demonstration on the air is prohibited, and hypnosis as an aspect of "parlor game" antics to create humorous situations within a comedy setting cannot be used.

The Nielsen Ratings

Ratings are estimates, mostly projections, obtained from sampling techniques, and expressed most often in terms of the percentage of a portion of the population that is viewing a particular TV program, the percentage of sets in use or homes watching television in the area being sampled at a given time, and the share of audience a particular program is drawing in comparison with those programs being televised at the same time. Over 200 broadcast-rating services or audience-research firms exist in the United States, of which the largest and most powerful is the A. C. Nielsen Company.[1]

The Nielsen research organization was founded in Chicago in 1923 by Arthur C. Nielsen, Sr.; by 1933 it was established in the market-measurement business. It is now a worldwide operation with a 1962 gross income of over $40 million, servicing over 1,000 U. S. clients annually. About 80 percent of Nielsen's business comes from food, drug, and other market surveys; 18 percent comes from the broadcasting division—Media Research Division—which produces the ratings reports. Advertisers and ad agencies rely on Nielsen ratings in buying more than $900 million worth of network TV time and programs each year. Along with the national television networks, they have invested over $20 million annually in Nielsen contracts. Each of the major networks (NBC, CBS, and ABC) alone spends over $300,000 for

□

various audience-research reports, and rely on Nielsen for 90 percent of their information.[2]

The basic component of the Nielsen broadcast-research operation is an automatic recording device called an audimeter, which was purchased in 1936 from the Massachusetts Institute of Technology, patented, developed, and tested over the course of seven years at a cost of $12 million, and manufactured for $300 each. The audimeter was the basis of computing the Nielsen Radio Index and was easily adapted for use in the television industry with the establishment of the Nielsen Television Index Service in 1949. The device is wired, out of sight, to the television set in each of some 1,160 participating sample homes, which comprise Nielsen's fixed panel. When the set is in operation, the audimeter records minute-to-minute set tuning on 16mm film in a cartridge that is changed every two weeks by the set owner. At that time the cartridge ejects two quarters in payment. The film is mailed to the company, computer inspected for accuracy, decoded, converted to IBM cards, sorted, tabulated, computed, and printed. The completed data are then analyzed by the staff and reports are drawn up.

The Nielsen Company gathers and computes both local and national data for the television industry and issues information to subscribers through a variety of reports released at various intervals. Local audience measurements are reported through the Nielsen Station Index, whose reports are issued (on a four-week survey period of local samples varying in size from 220 to 880 homes, depending on market size and the total reach of individual stations) anywhere from once every two months to once a year, relative to the size of the market. National data are presented in several different reports. The Nielsen Television Index is a consecutive two-week survey issued twice a month, containing a variety of information. The bimonthly Complete Reports contain more detailed information, including cumulative audiences, audience flows, demographic reports, and cost (of

□

time and talent) per thousand (persons in household audiences) figures. The weekly Multi-Network Area Ratings contain figures for about thirty metropolitan areas under conditions of multi-network competition.

Of all the reports the Nielsen Television Index is perhaps the most influential in the television industry. It includes estimates of the number of U. S. television households and the number of persons in them; the average viewing audience composition; the number of U. S. television households using TV at various times; average audience (homes viewing during an average minute of a program) and total audience (homes viewing the program in excess of five minutes), according to the percent of U. S. television households and the projected number of households reached; the share of the audience, during the average program minute, according to the number of sets actually in use at the time; the average audience by program time segments; and the number of stations and programs covered.[3] Also included are sponsor and program indexes, audience estimates by sponsorship, program-type audiences, television audience trends, and a national ranking of top programs.

The complex and influential Nielsen rating service has drawn criticism—both positive and negative—directed chiefly toward the Nielsen sampling technique and the audimeter.[4] Some advantages to the Nielsen system include the facilities for rating programs every week of the year (except four), the highly comparable nature of data over time due to the continuity of the sample, and the possibilities of tracing audience flow from minute to minute and program to program, and the opportunity to measure the accumulation and duplication of audiences over time.[5] These factors make possible a detailed analysis of program strengths and weaknesses. Some limitations to Nielsen's system include the sample size itself (0.0002 of the nation's 56 million TV households), and the representativeness of a predesignated sample of which 33 percent refused to cooperate;

231   The Nielsen Ratings

□

the reduction in usable data due to human and mechanical fault (estimated at 10 percent); the possibility of bias because of aberration from normal viewing habits in some sample homes through the psychological effect of the monitor; the simple fact of expense in operation and subscription; and the weighty fact that the audimeter method is purely quantitative by sets in use— it provides no data on viewers per set, actual audience composition, or audience reaction.[6]

NOTES

1 Nielsen is dominant over six major contenders. See "Standing On the Status Quo," *Television*, 19 (April 1962), pp. 73–75.

2 *Ibid.*

3 Laurence Meyers, "On The Reliability of The Ratings," *Television Quarterly* 1 (February 1962), 50–63.

4 Leo Bogart, *The Age of Television* (New York: Frederick Ungar Publishing Co., 1956), p. 330.

5 *Ibid.*

6 Also see *The Madow Report*, 87th Congress, 1st Session, House Report No. 193 (Washington: U.S. Government Printing Office, 1961), House Committee on Interstate and Foreign Commerce investigation of 7 major radio and TV rating services including Nielsen. Report made twelve specific recommendations for improvement of services but generally approved.

☐ Appendix D

Background
Characteristics
of Producers

In all seventy-nine men and one woman were interviewed. There were actually eighty-three interviews collected because, as mentioned earlier, three producers were interviewed both in late 1967 and again in early 1970. The age range of the total sample was thirty to sixty-five years old. Only fifteen people were under thirty-six years; thirty-six were between thirty-seven and forty-five, and the remaining twenty-nine were forty-six and over.

In general it is questionable whether certain characteristics such as religious background and place and family of origin are particularly relevant to the general context of the inquiry. However, these things are often of general interest and have definite meaning and importance to those who are interested in stratification and mobility in the United States. Other sociological studies have pointed out that entertainers in general are likely to come from those religions considered to be socially disadvantaged.[1] Leo Rosten does not consider religion when he discusses the social characteristics of moviemakers,[2] but he does point out, that many of the important people in the movie industry, at the time he did his study, were thought to be Jewish, when in reality they were not. Even so, considering that both the Jewish and Catholic population of the United States is relatively small (3 percent Jewish and 20 percent Catholic approximately), both groups (the Jewish group especially) have been overrepresented in the entertainment and other mass-culture industries as a rule.[3]

In this study approximately one-half were Jewish, one-quarter Catholic, and the remainder past or present members of various Protestant sects (see Table D–1). These proportions

TABLE D–1   Religious Characteristics of Producers N = 59

Age	N	Jewish	Catholic	Protestant
30–36	N = 15	6	4	5
37–45	N = 36	17	9	10
46–62	N = 29	13	7	9
	Totals 80	36	20	24

refer to the producers who had Jewish, Catholic, and Protestant backgrounds and not to the number who are presently actively church members. Both the broadcasting and movie industries of the United States have been considered Jewish businesses because the founder of the networks and several (not all as Rosten points out) of the prewar movie-studio czars were frequently of Jewish background. Religious prejudice has not existed in these industries, and they have provided routes of mobility and opportunity for Jews and Catholics. Often those who have come from these traditionally disadvantaged groups have been children of immigrant parents as well. This is especially true of the older men in the sample. Fifty percent of those over thirty-five years old, regardless of religion, were likely to have had one or more parents who migrated from Europe. Several of those interviewed themselves had been born in Europe.

While the movie and broadcasting industry seems to provide a mobility route for some, it is not entirely without prejudices nor does it provide a mobility route for all disadvantaged groups in society. Notably lacking from the sample were women and Negroes, for example. Only two women were interviewed: one was a producer of animated children's programs; the other was not included in the sample since she was part of the six-person pretest. Although she is active in film production, she produces fashion documentaries rather than series or dramatic shows. Several women were in fairly high positions in the studios as assistant producers or executive secretaries with authority and high salaries. However, the men who were interviewed insisted that production positions were open to women and that many women were successful free-lance writers. It is possible that women have avoided production because it is too time-consuming for those who want to raise families and lead "normal" home lives. A producer's secretary, for instance, said she had been an assistant producer but gave up the job because it meant spending fourteen hours a day at the studio. The usual route to producing is working first as an assistant producer, and in this case, at least, one woman was not willing to sacrifice her time for a "career" in production.

There were no blacks among the producers interviewed, nor were there blacks other than prop men in the production crews of the sets visited. However, the one apprentice met on the sets was a black from a southern school who had made several films as a student. Of course, this could be a misreporting of what might be a changing situation. More black actors and actresses have been used in recent years, and it can be assumed that blacks will increasingly be assigned to all phases of production. It was observed that several of the secretaries to the more important producers were black women; they held very demanding jobs, requiring considerable skill in handling situations and people. (The secretary is the gatekeeper who prevents the many aspiring actors, writers, and their agents from harassing the producer. She also is in contact with production sets and must be able to judge whether a so-called emergency is actually one or not.)

Most of the first sample came from large cities in the United States. In fact, practically all grew up either in Los Angeles or New York (or their vicinities). Among the exceptions six were from the Midwest and three grew up in Europe. Those who were raised in Europe also spent most of their childhood in large, urban centers, and the midwesterners were from places like Chicago and Kansas City. Several producers from the West and Midwest did, however, spend parts of their childhood on farms. Only one of those interviewed came from the South (Texas) and one grew up in South America, both of these again living in cities rather than in the country. The older men who had been born in Europe but were brought here as young children or babies mainly grew up in New York City or in other urban centers.

The second sample of children's producers was somewhat different: of the twenty-four people interviewed, about one-half were from the Midwest and the South and only six were from New York City. One grew up in Europe and one came from Europe as a child. When one examines religious background and place of origin, it is obvious that a real difference exists between those who are animators and those who make live-action drama. Those making live-action series are more likely to be Jewish and to come from large urban areas; animators seem more likely to be Protestant native-born (their parents as well), and to come from smaller towns. However, there are so few animators and artists in the sample that a real comparison is inappropriate.

Another background characteristic studied was fathers' occupations and incomes (see Table D–2). Studies of inter-generational mobility use father's occupation as the main comparative variable to judge whether or not the status of one generation is higher than another.[4] Considering the high income of this group of men and the general aura and prestige that

□

TABLE D-2 Father's Major Occupation

Occupation	Age Group		
	30–36	37–45	46–62
Professional, technical, and kindred workers[a]	8	12	9
Managers, officials, and proprietors[b]	2	8	7
Clerical and kindred workers	0	4	0
Farmers	2	3	4
Sales workers	2	5	5
Craftsmen, foremen, and kindred workers	1	4	4
Totals	15	36	29

[a] Includes those whose parents were in entertainment.
[b] Many, as previously stated, had fathers who owned small businesses, and they are included in this category. This is a difficulty with the Edwards classification.

seems to be part of the Hollywood legend, one could safely consider these men working on the line as high status. The North-Hatt scale does not consider producers of television shows or other kinds of producers.[5] In reality there are no empirical data that give clues to the prestige ranking of officials, supervisors, and craftsmen in the movie and television industry. Other measures of status, however, such as income and neighborhood where people live, rank producers high. Their average income of the first group interviewed was between $50,000 and $65,000. The highest income reported (including residuals) was $150,000; the lowest income reported was $25,000. However, there is reason to suspect this low-income report because the producer wondered whether I was a "spy" for his ex-wife who was trying to get her alimony increased (see Table D-3). Several reported incomes above $100,000 (including residuals).

This is a successful group, and reported incomes are much higher than the national average. Their incomes are also higher

237 Background Characteristics of Producers

□

Salaried Income (not including royalties, residuals, and profit)

Age	Below $30,000	$30–50,000	$50–65,000	$65,000 and over
30–36	2	9	4	0
37–45	1 [a]	10	16	9
46–62	0	3	13	11 [b]
Totals	3	22	33	20

[a] One man reported an income of $25,000. I am not sure if this is correct because he was worried that I was a "spy" for his ex-wife who was trying to get her alimony increased (see Text.)

[b] Two not reporting. One was a very successful producer whose income probably was above $100,000 a year. The other had the interview interrupted at this point because he was called away for an "emergency."

than what would be usual for middle management in other industries where the responsibilities and duties might be of equal importance. Most, of course, were far better off financially than they had been when growing up. Although two respondents would not divulge either present income or income range for the last five years, it can be assumed from what is known about the industry generally and from the reports of the others that they were making at least $30,000 a year and most likely more. When a respondent refused to divulge income, he was asked what a producer would usually make. Several times this was enough to give the respondent a chance to tell his own income. It is interesting that the two who would not answer directly stated the average income to be at least $65,000 a year.

Because of this high status and high income and because so many were children of religiously disadvantaged and immigrant parents, you might predict that the entire group was of higher status, both occupationally (from impressionistic data) and in relation to income measures, than their parents. In the majority of cases this is true. However, the comparison is not easy to make since in so many instances the fathers were more mobile than the sons being interviewed. Of the fifty-nine men in the original sample, twenty-three of them had fathers who would be considered in the lower-status ranks by any occupational scale used (Edwards, NORC, and the like).[6] Six were farmers (usually on the outskirts of Los Angeles), nine were sales workers and seven were either craftsmen (carpenters, plumbers, and so forth) or laborers (usually factory workers). One was a bookkeeper. The remaining thirty-six were, on the other hand, mostly of high or upper-middle status originally. Several of the fathers owned successful manufacturing business (usually clothing). Several were professional men; there were physicians, a lawyer, and a dentist, plus one rabbi, among this group. Several of the producers came from successful movie families; six of those interviewed had at least one parent who had been a successful screen writer, producer, director, or second-generation moviemaker. The final group were children of small shopowners and because I am using the Edwards classification scale, it is difficult to know whether the nonretail sales occupations and the operation of candy and small grocery stores really do differ very much in actual status. In any case those whose fathers were salesmen and proprietors can be considered to have more money and probably more status than their fathers, while one cannot be sure of those whose fathers had professional and movie backgrounds (Table D–2).

More important for the whole study, and for the question of mobility and status as well, is the education of the men interviewed (see Table D–4). This is a vital question to the general study because, theoretically, education can help determine the reference-group orientation and certainly is germane to the entire socialization process. Because of its importance education was considered in more detail in Chapter 5, but here it should be noted that since many of the men interviewed come from backgrounds that are usually associated with a college education

□

TABLE D-4 Educational Background

Age	High School or less[a]	Some College Not Related Field	Some College in Related Field[b]
30–36	1	5	9
37–45	7	13	16
46–55	8	15	6
Total	16	33	31

[a] One-half of this group had graduated from high school.
[b] This, of course, can be broken down further into those with degrees and those without. In addition, it can be broken down into which related field their educational training had taken place. See the body of this appendix for more detail.

in our society, it is not surprising that in all ages more than half went to college and among the younger men (under forty-five) only four did not attend college at all. This is only mentioned briefly here because it is necessary to have a general picture of the people and their background. In order to be able to talk about how content is selected, it is important to know something about who is doing the selecting. As noted in Chapter 5, the characteristics mentioned above do vary for age group as one might expect. Certainly history is a factor in who and what kinds of people are recruited into various occupational groups.

NOTES

1 Sidney Willhelm and Gideon Sjoberg, "The Social Characteristics of Entertainers," *Social Forces* 37 (1958): 71–76.

2 Leo C. Rosten, *Hollywood: The Movie Colony, the Movie Makers* (New York: Harcourt, Brace and Co., 1941).

3 See Suzanne Keller, *Beyond the Ruling Class: Strategic Elites in Modern Society* (New York: Random House, 1963), p. 304 and Willhelm and Sjoberg, *op. cit.*

4   For instance, Peter Blau and Otis Dudley Duncan, *The American Occupational Structure* (New York: John Wiley & Sons, Inc., 1947).

5   North-Hatt Scale, a measure of occupational prestige. National Opinion Research Center, "Jobs and Occupations: A Popular Evaluation," *Opinion News* 9 (1947): 3–13. The National Opinion Research Center conducted the surveys (first in 1947) designed to measure the relative prestige of an occupation. Findings from these surveys have become a major scale of occupational prestige known as the North-Hatt scale.

6   Alba Edwards, 1870–1940 *Comparative Occupational Structure of the United States* (Washington, D.C.: U.S. Government Printing Office, 1943).

□ References Cited

ARENDT, HANNAH. "Society and Culture." In *Culture for the Millions*. Edited by Norman Jacobs. Boston: Beacon Press, 1959. Pp. 43–52.

BARBER, BERNARD. "Some Problems in the Sociology of the Profession." *Daedalus* 92 (1963): 669–688.

BAUER, RAYMOND. "The Communicator and the Audience." *Conflict Resolution* 2 (1958): 66–76.

———. "The Initiative of the Audience." *Journal of Advertising Research* 3 (1963): 2–7.

BECKER, HOWARD S. "Careers in a Deviant Occupational Group," *The Outsiders*. New York: The Free Press, 1963.

BERELSON, BERNARD. "In the Presence of Culture." *Public Opinion Quarterly* 28 (1964): 1–13.

———. "The Great Debate on Cultural Democracy." *Study in Public Communication* 3 (1961): 3–14.

BLAU, PETER and OTIS DUDLEY DUNCAN. *The American Occupational Structure*. New York: John Wiley & Sons, Inc., 1967.

BLAU, PETER and RICHARD SCOTT. *Formal Organizations: A Comparative Approach*. San Francisco: Chandler Publishing Co., 1962.

BLUM, SAM. "Who Decides What Gets on T.V. and Why." *Social Profiles: U.S.A. Today*. New York: Van Nostrand Reinhold Co., New York Times Book, 1970: 215–216.

BLUMLER, JAY G. "Producers Attitudes towards Television Coverage of an Election Campaign: A Case Study." *The Sociological Review Monograph: Sociology of Mass Communications* 13 (1969): 85–115.

BOGART, LEO. *The Age of Television*. New York: Frederick Ungar Publishing Co., 1956.

BREED, WARREN. "The Newspaperman, News and Society." Ph.D. Dissertation, Columbia University, 1952.

———. "Social Control in the Newsroom: A Functional Analysis." *Social Forces* 33 (1955): 326–335.

BROWN, ROGER L. "Approaches to the Historical Development of Mass Media Studies." In *Media Sociology: A Reader*. Edited by Jeremy Turnstall. Urbana, Illinois: University of Illinois Press, 1970. Pp. 41–57.

CANTOR, MURIEL G. "The Sociology of The Television Producers: A Sociological Analysis." Ph.D. Dissertation, University of California, Los Angeles, 1969.

———. "The Role of the Producer in Choosing Children's Television Content." Vol. I in *Television and Social Behavior: A Report to the Surgeon General's Scientific Advisory Committee*. Washington, D.C.: U.S. Government Printing Office.

CAPLOW, THEODORE. *The Sociology of Work*. New York: McGraw-Hill Book Co., 1964.

CAPLOW, THEODORE and R. J. MCGEE. *The Academic Marketplace*. New York: Basic Books, 1958.

COMPTON, NEIL. "T.V. Specials." *Commentary*, June 1968, p. 69.

Daily Variety (Western Edition). "Hyphenates Hop Over to PGA." 12 October 1967.

———. "No Curb on ABC Feature Plans." 10 January 1968.

———. "T.V. Shows in Production." 14 July 1967.

———. "T.V. Shows in Production." 5 December 1969.

———. "Who Lowers Boom on Web Nabos? Lee Rich, That's Who." 11 October 1967.

DEMINOR, JOHN. "Universal: The New Hollywood." *Life*, 20 December (1963) 46–50.

Dictionary of Occupational Titles. U.S. Department of Labor, Bureau of Employment Security. Washington: U.S. Government Printing Office, 1965.

DIZARD, WILLIAM P. *Television: A World View*. Syracuse, New York: Syracuse University Press, 1966.

EDWARDS, ALBA. *1870–1940 Comparative Occupational Structure of the United States*. Washington: U.S. Government Printing Office, 1943.

FAULKNER, ROBERT. *Hollywood Studio Musicians: Their Work and Careers in the Recording Industry*. Chicago: Aldine Atherton, 1971.

———. "Hollywood Studio Musicians: Their Work and Contingencies in the Film Industry." Ph.D. Dissertation, University of California, 1968.

Federal Communications Commission Policy Matters and Television Programming. Hearings before the Subcommittee on Communications of the Committee on Commerce, 91st Congress, First Session. Washington: U.S. Government Printing Office, 1969.

FESHBACK, SEYMOUR. "The Catharsis Effect: Research and Another View." In *Mass Media and Violence: A Report to the National Commission on the Causes of Violence*. Edited by D. L. Lange, R. K. Baker, and Sandra J. Ball. Washington: U.S Government Printing Office, 1969. Pp. 461–472.

FOOTE, NELSON N. "The Professionalization of Labor in Detroit." *The American Journal of Sociology* 58 (1953): 371–380.

FRIEDSON, ELLIOT. "Communications Research and the Concept of the Mass." *American Sociological Review* 18 (1953): 313–317.

FRIENDLY, FRED. *Due to Circumstances beyond Our Control.* New York: Random House, 1967.

GANS, HERBERT J. "The Creator-Audience Relationship in the Mass Media: An Analysis of Movie Making." In *Mass Culture.* Edited by Bernard Rosenberg and David Manning White. New York: Free Press, 1967. Pp. 315–324.

———. "How Well Does T.V. Present the News?" *New York Times Magazine,* 11 January 1970, pp. 30–35, 38.

———. "Popular Culture in America: Social Problem in a Mass Society or Social Asset in a Pluralist Society?" In *Social Problems: A Modern Approach.* Edited by Howard S. Becker. New York: John Wiley and Sons, Inc., 1966. Pp. 549–620.

———. "The Shaping of Mass Media Content: A Study of the News." Presented at Miami Beach, Florida, American Sociological Association Meeting, 1966.

GIEBER, WALTER. "Across the Desk: A Study of Sixteen Telegraph Editors." *Journalism Quarterly* 33 (1956): 423–432.

———. "News Is What Newspapermen Make It." In *People, Society and Mass Communications.* Edited by Lewis A. Dexter and David Manning White. New York: The Free Press, 1964. Pp. 173–182.

GORANSON, RICHARD E. "The Catharsis Effect: Two Opposing Views." In *Mass Media and Violence: A Report to the National Commission on the Causes and Prevention of Violence.* Edited by D. L. Lange, R. K. Baker, and Sandra J. Ball. Washington: U.S. Government Printing Office, 1969. Pp. 453–460.

———. "A Review of Recent Literature on Psychological Effects of Media Portrayals of Violence." In *Mass Media and Violence: A Report to the National Commission on the Causes and Prevention of Violence.* Edited by D. L. Lange, R. K. Baker, and Sandra J. Ball. Washington: U.S. Government Printing Office, 1969. Pp. 395–414.

GOULDNER, ALVIN W. "Cosmopolitans and Locals: Towards An Analysis of Latent Social Roles—I." *Administrative Science Quarterly* 2 (1957): 281–306.

GREENBERG, BRADLEY. "The Content and Context of Violence in the Mass Media." In *Mass Media and Violence: A Report to the National Commission on the Causes of Violence.* Edited by D. L. Lange, R. K. Baker, and Sandra J. Ball. Washington: U.S. Government Printing Office, 1969. Pp. 423–452.

GRIFF, MASON. "The Commercial Artist." In *Identity and Anxiety*. Edited by Maurice R. Stein, Arthur J. Vidich, and David M. White. Glencoe, Illinois: The Free Press, 1960. Pp. 219–240.

HALL, OSWALD. "The Stages of a Medical Career." *American Journal of Sociology* 53 (March, 1948): 327–336.

HALL, RICHARD H. *Occupations and the Social Structure*. Englewood Cliffs, New Jersey: Prentice-Hall, Inc., 1969.

HALL, STUART and PADDY WHANNEL. *The Popular Arts: A Critical Guide to the Mass Media*. Boston: Beacon Press, 1964.

HANDEL, LEO A. *Hollywood Looks at Its Audience*. Urbana, Illinois: The University of Illinois Press, 1950.

HEAD, SIDNEY W. *Broadcasting in America*. Boston: Houghton Mifflin Co., 1956.

"Hollywood and Television." *London Times*. 12 January 1962.

Hollywood Reporter "Writers Guild Prexy Powell Feels Network Receding in Responsibility to Public" 19 January 1968.

Home Testing Institute TVG. "A Study of New Programs." 1965–1966.

HYMAN, HERBERT H. and ELEANOR SINGER. *Readings in Reference Group Theory and Research*. New York: The Free Press, 1968.

"Jobs and Occupations: A Popular Evaluation." *Opinion News* 9 (1947): 3–13.

JOHNSON, KENNETH G. "Dimensions of Judgment of Science News Stories." *Journalism Quarterly* 40 (1963): 315–322.

JONES, R., VERNON TROLDAHL, and J. HVISTENDALH. "New Selection Patterns from a State TTS-Wire." *Journalism Quarterly* 38 (1961): 303–312.

KAPLAN, NORMAN. "Essay Review: Professional Scientists in Industry." *Social Problems* 13 (1965): 88–97.

KELLER, SUZANNE. *Beyond the Ruling Class: Strategic Elites in Modern Society*. New York: Random House, 1963.

KNIGHT, ARTHUR. *The Liveliest Art: A Panoramic History of the Movies*. New York: The Macmillan Co., 1957.

KORNHAUSER, WILLIAM (with the assistance of WARREN O. HEGSTROM). *Scientists in Industry: Conflict and Accommodation*. Berkeley: University of California Press, 1962.

LANG, KURT and GLADYS ENGEL LANG. *Politics and Television*. Chicago: Quadrangle Books, 1968.

LANGE, DAVID L., ROBERT K. BAKER, and SANDRA BALL, eds. *Mass Media and Violence: A Report to the National Commission on the Causes and Prevention of Violence*. Washington: U.S. Government Printing Office, 1969.

LARSEN, OTTO N. "Social Effects of Mass Communications." In *Handbook of Modern Sociology*. Edited by Robert E. L. Faris. Chicago: Rand-McNally, 1964. Pp. 349–381.

————, ed. *Violence and the Mass Media*. New York: Harper and Row, 1968.

LAZARSFELD, PAUL F. "Some Reflections on Past and Future Research in Broadcasting." In *The People Look at Television*. Edited by Gary E. Steiner. New York: Knopf, 1963. Pp. 410–422.

LAZARSFELD, PAUL F. and ROBERT K. MERTON. "Mass Communication, Popular Taste and Organized Social Action." In *Mass Culture*. Edited by B. Rosenberg and D. W. White. New York: The Free Press, 1957. Pp. 457–473.

LIPPMANN, WALTER. "The Problem of Television." *New York Herald Tribune*. 27 October 1959. Reprinted in Harry J. Skornia, *Television and Society: An Inquest and Agenda for Improvement*. New York: McGraw-Hill Book Company, 1965. P. 247.

MCGINNISS, JOE. *The Selling of the President: 1968*. New York: Simon & Schuster, Pocket Books edition, 1970.

MACGOWAN, KENNETH. *Behind the Screen: The History and Techniques of the Motion Picture*. New York: Dell Publishing Co., 1967.

MCQUAIL, DENIS. *Towards a Sociology of Mass Communications*. London: Collier-Macmillan Ltd., 1969.

The Madow Report, House Report No. 193, 87th Congress, 1st Sess., House Committee on Interstate and Foreign Commerce. Washington: U.S. Government Printing Office, 1961.

MARCSON, SIMON. *The Scientist in American Industry: Some Organizational Determinants in Manpower Utilization*. New York: Harper and Brothers, 1960.

MARSHALL, T. H. *Class, Citizenship and Social Development*. New York: Doubleday and Company, 1964.

MERTON, ROBERT K. *Social Theory and Social Structure*. Rev. ed. Glencoe, Illinois: Free Press, 1957.

MEYERS, LAURENCE. "On the Reliability of the Ratings." *Television Quarterly* 1 (February 1962): 50–63.

MILLER, MERLE and RHODES EVANS. *Only You, Dick Daring!* New York: William Sloane Associates, 1964.

MILLS, C. WRIGHT. *White Collar*. New York: Oxford University Press, 1953.

MOORE, JOAN. *The Hollywood Writer*. In progress.

————. "Occupational Anomie and Irresponsibility." *Social Problems* 8 (1961): 293–299.

NUNNALLY, J. C., JR. *Popular Conceptions of Mental Health*. New York: Holt, Rinehart and Winston, Inc., 1961.

PARSONS, TALCOTT and EDWARD A. SHILS, eds. *Toward a General Theory of Action*. New York: Harper and Row, 1951.

PETERS, ANNE. "Acting and Aspiring Actresses in Hollywood: A Sociological Analysis." Ph.D. Dissertation, University of California, Los Angeles, 1971.

POOL, ITHIEL DE SOLA and IRWIN SHULMAN. "Newsmen's Fantasies, Audience, and Newswriting." In *People, Society and Mass Communication*. Edited by Lewis A. Dexter and David Manning White. New York: The Free Press, 1964. Pp. 141–159.

POWDERMAKER, HORTENSE. *Hollywood: The Dream Factory*. Boston: Little, Brown and Co., 1950.

Public Television: A Program for Action, The Report of the Carnegie Commission of Educational Television. New York: Bantam Books, Inc., 1967.

REISSMAN, LEONARD. "A Study of Role Conceptions in Bureaucracy." *Social Forces* 27 (1949): pp. 205–210.

RILEY, JOHN and MATILDA RILEY. "Mass Communication and the Social System." In *Sociology Today*. Edited by R. K. Merton, L. Broom, and L. S. Cottrell, Jr. New York: Basic Books, 1959. Pp. 537–578.

ROSTEN, LEO C. *Hollywood: The Movie Colony, The Movie Makers*. New York: Harcourt, Brace and Company, 1941.

————. "The Intellectual and the Mass Media: Some Rigorously Random Remarks." In *Culture for the Millions*. Edited by Norman Jacobs. Boston: Beacon Press, 1959. Pp. 71–84.

SCOTT, W. RICHARD. "Professionals in Bureaucracies—Areas of Conflict." In *Professionalization*. Edited by H. Vollmer and D. L. Mills. Englewood Cliffs, New Jersey: Prentice-Hall, Inc., 1966. Pp. 365–374.

————. "Theory of Organizations." In *Handbook of Modern Sociology*. Edited by Robert E. L. Faris. Chicago: Rand McNally and Company, 1964. Pp. 485–529.

SELDES, GILBERT. *The Public Arts*. New York: Simon and Schuster, Paperback, 1964.

SHAYON, ROBERT W. "Media Mystification." *Saturday Review*. 17 October 1970, p. 51.

SHERLOCK, BASIL J. and RICHARD T. MORRIS. "The Evolution of a Professional: A Paradigm." *Sociological Inquiry* 37 (1967): 32–37.

SIEGEL, ALBERTA. "The Effects of Media Violence on Social Learning." In *Mass Media and Violence: A Report to the National Commission. on the Causes of Violence*. Edited by D. L. Lange, R. K. Baker and Sandra J. Ball. Washington: U.S. Government Printing Office, 1969. Pp. 261–283.

SKORNIA, HARRY J. *Public Television: A Program for Action, The Report of*

□

the Carnegie Commission of Educational Television. New York: Bantam Books, Inc., 1967.

SPILBECK, OSWALD. *ABC of Film and T.V. Working Terms.* London and New York: Focal Press, 1960.

STINCHCOMBE, ARTHUR L. "Bureaucratic and Craft Administration of Production: A Comparative Study." *Administrative Science Quarterly* 4 (1959): 168–187.

STULBERG, GORDON. "The Entertainment Industry: Its Structure Economy." Syllabus for Course No. 803AB, University of California, Los Angeles, 1963.

SUMMERS, ROBERT E. and HARRISON B. SUMMERS. *Broadcasting and the Public.* Belmont, California: Wadsworth Publishing Co., 1966.

TANNENBAUM, PERCY H. and BRADLEY S. GREENBERG. "Mass Communications." *Annual Review of Psychology* 19 (1968): 351–386.

TAYLOR, LEE. *Occupational Sociology.* New York: Oxford University Press, 1968.

Television. "Hollywood and Television." 20 (September 1963), entire issue.

———. "Standing on the Status Quo." 19 (April 1962): 73–75.

———. "They're Off as Often as Not." 24 (March 1967): 23–25.

———. "Where Do Shows Come From? Where Do They Go?" 24 (September 1967): 46–47.

The Television Code. National Association of Broadcasters, 12th edition, 1967. Pp. 2–10.

Television and Juvenile Delinquency. United States Senate Report of the Committee on the Judiciary, Report No. 1466. Washington: U.S. Government Printing Office, 1956.

TRAPNELL, COLE. *Teleplay.* San Francisco: Chandler Publishing Co., 1966.

TUNSTALL, JEREMY, ed. *Media Sociology: A Reader.* Urbana, Illinois: University of Illinois Press, 1970.

UNESCO. *Reports and Papers on Mass Communications, The Influence of the Cinema on Children and Adolescents: An Annotated International Bibliography.* Paris: UNESCO, 1961.

VAN DER HAAG, ERNEST. "A Dissent for the Consensual Society." In *Culture for the Millions.* Edited by Norman Jacobs. Boston: Beacon Press, 1959. Pp. 53–62.

VOLLMER, HOWARD and DONALD MILLS. "Industrial Technology." In *Professionalization.* Edited by Vollmer and Mills. Englewood Cliffs, New Jersey: Prentice-Hall, Inc., 1966. Pp. 21–27.

WHITEFIELD, STEPHEN E. and GENE RODDENBERRY. *The Making of Star Trek.* New York, Ballantine Books, 1968.

□

WILENSKY, HAROLD L. *Intellectuals in Labor Unions.* Glencoe, Illinois: Free Press, 1956.

WILLHELM, SIDNEY and GIDEON SJOBERG. "The Social Characteristics of Entertainers." *Social Forces* 37 (1958): 71–76.

WINICK, CHARLES. "Censor and Sensibility: A Content Analysis of the Television Censor's Comments." *Journal of Broadcasting* (1961), pp. 117–135. Reprinted in Otto Larsen, ed., *Violence of Mass Media.* New York: Harper and Row, 1968. Pp. 252–272.

WRIGHT, CHARLES R. *Mass Communication: A Sociological Perspective.* New York: Random House, 1959.

WYLIE, MAX. *Clear Channels.* New York: Funk and Wagnalls Company, 1955.

☐ Index